JONATHAN CLEMENTS, is the a
Moon in the Pines and *Confuci*
time between Jyväskylä and
www.muramasaindustries.com

Other titles in this series

A BRIEF HISTORY OF

THE VIKINGS

THE LAST PAGANS OR THE
FIRST MODERN EUROPEANS?

JONATHAN CLEMENTS

RUNNING PRESS
PHILADELPHIA · LONDON

In Memory of
Thorkill Clements
born in Reykjavik, died in London

Constable & Robinson Ltd
3 The Lanchesters
162 Fulham Palace Road
London W6 9ER
www.constablerobinson.com
This edition published in the UK by Robinson,
an imprint of Constable & Robinson, 2005

A copy of the British Library Cataloguing in
Publication Data is available from the British Library

UK ISBN 978-1-84529-076-4

5 7 9 10 8 6

First published in the United States in 2005
by Carroll & Graf Publishers
This edition published in 2008 by Running Press Book Publishers

9 8 7 6 5 4 3
Digit on the right indicates the number of this printing

Library of Congress Cataloging-in-Publication Data is available on file

US ISBN 978-0-7867-1599-2

Running Press Book Publishers
2300 Chestnut Street
Philadelphia, PA 19103-4371

Visit us on the web!
www.runningpress.com

Printed and bound in the EU

CONTENTS

ILLUSTRATIONS

Wooden post with carved animal head. From the Oseberg grave. Norway, ninth century AD.
Photo: akg-images, London

Trelleborg Fortress.
C M Dixon/Ancient Art & Architecture Collection Ltd

Reconstruction of the Viking barracks at the fortress of Trelleborg. It is considered to have been built by Harald Bluetooth. Slagelse, Denmark, AD 980–981.
Werner Forman Archive

Interior reconstruction of the Viking barracks at Trelleborg, built following the pattern of the original foundation post holes. Trelleborg, Denmark, AD 910–1020.
Werner Forman Archive

St Olaf, patron saint of Norway (Olaf Haraldsson), Norway, 13th century, found in Gotland.
Werner Forman Archive/ Statens Historiska Museet, Stockholm

Smith's mould for casting both Christian crosses and Thor's hammers.
Werner Forman Archive/ National Museum, Copenhagen

L'Anse aux Meadows National Historic Park (Newfoundland, Canada), Viking settlement, c.AD 1000: (oldest known European settlement in North America).
Photo: *akg-images, London/Jürgen Sorges*

A berserker, chewing on his shield, amid the piece of the Lewis chess set.
C M Dixon/Ancient Art & Architecture Collection Ltd

The Lindisfarne stone, depicting a raiding party of Vikings.
C M Dixon/Ancient Art & Architecture Collection Ltd

PREFACE AND ACKNOWLEDGEMENTS

There are already several excellent books on the Viking Age, such as the works of Magnusson, Brønsted, Sawyer and Roesdahl, and my personal favourite for all-round factual information, Gwyn Jones' revised *History of the Vikings*. Accordingly, I have tried to steer a course between the other available authorities, concentrating on the personalities of the Viking era, who made up that remarkably small handful of families and interlocking dynasties who were the prime movers of the Viking expansion. In order to accomplish this, I have included several family trees to aid the reader in appreciating the Viking Age not as the clash of armies but as a series of family dramas, complete with feuds and reunions, as descendants of local leaders in Scandinavia entwine with the kings and queens of medieval Europe. In a small way, I hope to achieve something of the sense of the sagas that preserve so much of Viking culture for us, showing the people of Scandinavia through their personal lives, or at least, as romanticized and distorted by their later descendants in Iceland. When saga claims veer far from the evidence of archaeology or other orthodox sources, I have endeavoured to strike a balance.

I have stayed clear of some of the more famous passages that can be found in the works of others. Ibn Fadlan's infamous treatment of Rus funeral rites, human sacrifice, gang rape and all, features largely in the works of Brønsted and Jones, and need not be repeated here. Instead, I have concentrated on a passage in Ibn Fadlan that I find far more evocative of the Viking experience in the East – an account of declining trade and the desperation that can ensue. Similarly, nothing encapsulates the Vikings' relationship with the Native Americans better than Gudrid's heart-rending conversation with a Skraeling in her tent, which I have chosen to quote in place of the more usual tales of Vinland. With such an approach, I hope this book will provide a new perspective even for those who already familiar with other studies.

I have used some names that are anachronistic to aid ease of recognition. I refer to the great bay in southern Norway as 'the Vik', as the Vikings did themselves, but also make reference to its northern shores as 'Oslo', a town not founded until the time of Harald the Ruthless. I use the term Trondheim to describe the area that the Vikings called Nitharos or Hlaðir, preferring to use the term applied to it from the time of Olaf 'Crowbone' Tryggvason and only widely used long after the Viking age was over. It is easier, sometimes, to refer to 'Estonia' for example, than it is to refer to 'the region of the Aesti, part of which would at some future date be known as Estonia'. It is only where the medieval distinctions were of crucial importance, such as in the separate states that made up what we now refer to as 'Great Britain', that I have clung to the terms as used by the people at the time.

Regarding Norse names, the available texts are a confusion of Swedish, Norwegian, Danish and Icelandic renderings of the originals, many with contradictory ways of romanizing elements of the *futhark* runic alphabet. In most cases I have dropped the diacritic marks that distinguish vowel forms for Norse speakers, and followed the editorial policy of the 1997 *Complete Sagas of Icelanders* for transliterating the 'thorn' rune and other unusual phonemes.

I have done my best to differentiate the many similar names; it is easier, both editorially and narratively, to refer to Harald Greycloak as 'Greycloak', and so avoid confusion with the numerous other Haralds in the text, even though he only gained the 'Greycloak' sobriquet relatively late in his life. In most cases, I have dropped patronymics, although I do occasionally use them in place of surnames when no nickname is readily available. In some cases where two figures share the same name, I have deliberately employed acceptable variants to differentiate them, as in the case of Olaf Crowbone and Olof (*sic*) Skötkonung. Norse writers rarely distinguished between the *Sámi* people of Lapland and the *Suomi* people of Finland, calling them all *Finns* – I have endeavoured to use the correct terminology where possible. In the case of Harald Bluetooth (*Blátönn*), it is now widely agreed that the colour intended was closer to 'black' in medieval Norse, but I have retained the more popular usage. This is not only because he is referred to as Bluetooth in other English sources, but in recognition of his newfound fame in the twenty-first century. When looking for a name for a wireless technology allowing disparate Scandinavian computers to communicate with each other, someone decided that the name of Denmark's first kingly unifier would be nicely appropriate. It seems churlish now to change his name to the more semantically correct Blacktooth.

References to Icelandic sagas are mainly to the excellent Leif Eríkssonur five-volume *Complete Sagas* (CSI + volume number in my notes), or to the landmark University of Texas translation of *Heimskringla* by Lee Hollander. The over 200 endnotes are there for any reader who wishes to expand this necessarily 'brief' history into an examination of my sources.

The family trees are heavily simplified, and often show only partial counts of offspring. Vikings both pagan and Christian had many wives and concubines, and it is impossible to fully match their dynasties with the claims of the saga authors. The trees are just detailed enough to demonstrate the interconnections of the Viking Age from a Scandinavian point of view – there are even more links on the English side, but they belong in a different book.

Much about the Viking world is best understood by experiencing it first-hand. I am fortunate to have travelled from south-west Norway to the icy wastes of Lapland. Members of the Mäki-Kuutti family have been my guides and companions for wanderings in Finland and Sweden, and their support has been invaluable. Back in England, University College London's School of Slavonic and East European Studies proved particularly useful for its collection of rare nineteenth-century and Finno-Ugric sources on the Vikings' interactions with their eastern neighbours. I am indebted to the SSEES, its superb Language Unit, and my long-suffering teacher Elina Rautasalo. I was also able to gain access to rare Native American, Inuit and Muslim materials, thanks to the holdings of the nearby School of Oriental and African Studies.

This book was commissioned by Nicola Chalton, who was always supportive and ready to champion my unorthodox approach with her colleagues, while my agent, Chelsey Fox of Fox and Howard, was able to channel the spirit of Freydis whenever work needed to be done with an axe. Becky Hardie of Constable & Robinson was a patient and flexible editor, who diligently made this book better than it should have been, while Roger Hudson was benignly ruthless in excising my unnecessary *kennings*. Edward James made many helpful comments on the manuscript, and pulled me up on several important issues of nomenclature and classification. However, I did not take his advice on every occasion, and made several decisions which may indeed turn out to be my own mistakes, certainly not his. Although this book manages to incorporate some research material published while it was still being written, this might also be a good point to mention that many of the relevant books in my collection are over 25 years old – notably a Magnusson and a Brønsted given to me as a child by Penny Clements and Stephen Jones. So they are at least partly to blame for my obsessions.

This book would not have happened at all were it not for Kati, whom I met on Saint Olaf's day in a place called Harald's, and who will claim endlessly not to be an inheritor of any sort of Viking tradition, despite combining all the very best traits of Aud the Deep-Minded, Gunnhild Kingsmother and Thorbjorg Shipbreast.

My grateful acknowledgement goes to Penguin Books for permission to quote from *The Vinland Sagas*, translated by Magnus Magnusson and Hermann Palsson, from *The Vikings* by Johannes Brønsted, and *Byzantium: The Apogee* by John Julius Norwich; and to Weidenfeld & Nicolson, a division of the Orion Publishing Group, for permission to quote from *The Anglo-Saxon Chronicles*, translated by Michael Swanton. Quotation from *Orkneyinga Saga*, translated by Hermann Palsson and Paul Edwards, published by Hogarth Press, has been granted by permission of The Random House Group Ltd.

The University of Wisconsin Press acknowledges that my quotation from *The Kensington Stone: A Mystery Solved* by Erik Wahlgren is within the bounds of fair dealing, for which I am also grateful.

INTRODUCTION: BRITANNIA DESERTA

THE DARK AGES

Sometime in the fifth century AD, a group of soldiers had a farewell party. We have no record of precisely where it was held or what the menu may have been. There is no evidence of any remarkable after-dinner speeches or entertainment. But we still know the party took place, because they clubbed together and bought a token of their appreciation for their leader, Aurelius Cervianus. A local British craftsman was hired to engrave a bronze dish, its lower half showing a collection of exotic beasts, including a pair of peacocks and a somewhat boss-eyed lion.[1] The upper half has a number of troops under Cervianus's command, with their legion insignia and designations – XX Valeria Victrix, and II Augusta. Between them lies Cervianus's name, and a message from the boys: *Utere Felix*, 'Use this Happily'.

Valeria Victrix and II Augusta had long histories, but both

had spent much of their operational lives in Britannia. Originally a frontier legion on the banks of the Danube and Rhine, the men of Valeria Victrix had garrisoned the British island for centuries. They had gained their title, 'Valiant and Victorious', after serving the empire well in the suppression of the revolt of Queen Boudicca.[2] II Augusta was even older, with a regimental history that may have even stretched back into the days when Rome was still a republic. Both legions had formed part of the original Roman invasion force, and had made Britannia their home for many generations of service. Now they were leaving.

The Romans were deserting their farthest outposts. The soldiers were required closer to a 'home' which some of them had never even seen. We do not know what happened to Cervianus, but his hardwearing dish eventually turned up, intact, in what is now France.

Most books about the Vikings begin long after this time. The 'Viking Age', such as it was, is taken by most authorities to span the period from the infamous raid on Lindisfarne in AD 793, to the death of Harald Hardraada in 1066. But the dates were not quite so clear-cut as that. The Vikings did not spring fully formed on to the international stage; they were the inheritors of a long tradition.

There is much to be gained from ignoring such arbitrary barriers as the end of the Classical period, or the start of the 'Dark Ages' – students of the Vikings can learn much from what happened both before and after this historical watershed.

Scandinavia was one of the last places in Europe to be settled. The Ice Age lingered longer in its mountainous, northern regions, and much of its atavistic power can still be felt in a Scandinavian winter. In times of great plenty, when the climate was warm, a few hardy souls ventured further northwards. But when the weather took a turn for the worse, many of those northern explorers were forced back to their ancestral homes.

Hardened by their harsh northern existence, they were often more than a match for their southern kinsmen – population overspill is a common factor in Scandinavian history. The first members of the society to head elsewhere were usually those with little investment in the place of their birth – the young men, deprived of land, wives and wealth, coalescing into gangs that sought new opportunities. If they had the means of mobility, horses perhaps, or boats, then their adventures would take them substantially further than the next settlement.

In the early Middle Ages, such periodic growths of population may have led to the Viking invasions that are the main subject of this book, and are dealt with in detail in subsequent chapters. But there were also many signs of earlier, less well-recorded incursions of Scandinavian settlers before the Middle Ages.

As early as a hundred years before the birth of Christ, the Roman Republic was threatened by an onrushing tide of northern attackers. The Cimbri, originating on the Danish peninsula, and their Teuton allies from the far north of Germany, threw the republic into a state of emergency and were only defeated a generation after their migration began, in a series of battles in what is now southern France. Roman navies also had to deal with tribes that travelled by sea and preyed upon imperial shipping. In 12 BC, a Roman fleet advanced along the northern coast of Europe, and reported a series of skirmishes with the seaborne Bructeri tribe. The earliest recorded circumnavigation of the British Isles was conducted not by the Romans, but by a group of the Usipi in AD 83. Deserting from their posting as Roman mercenaries in Britain, this group stole three galleys which were eventually wrecked on the coast of Denmark.[3]

Denmark was also the place of origin of the Chauci, who soon spread along the coast of northern Europe as far as the

Rhine. Led by Gannascus, a tribesman of the Canninefates who had learned Roman tricks by serving in a Rhine legion before deserting, the Chauci preyed upon the coast of what is now known as Belgium in AD 41, before advancing in force up the river Rhine itself in 47.[4] The Chauci were defeated by the Roman fleet which sailed up the Rhine to meet them in battle. But even this imperial navy seems to have relied heavily on barbarian sailors and seamen. A generation after the incursions of the Chauci, barbarian oarsmen in the same Roman fleet staged a revolt, stole 24 galleys, and fought their way down the Rhine towards the sea. The oarsmen, men of the Batavii, joined with river pirates from other tribes and attacked a Roman troop convoy in the English Channel.

The Romans were able to contain such marine assaults, but only barely. While records of Roman Britain are all but silent about the dangers, the archaeological evidence speaks for itself. During the second and third centuries AD, Roman legions built forts along the eastern coast of Britannia, designed to watch and warn against a mystery threat from the sea. Tribes from the north and east, making greater use of sails over oars, had begun periodic attacks on the British coastline.

By the third and fourth centuries AD, the coast of the Black Sea was ravaged by ships of the Goths and Heruls, originating from Scandinavia. Meanwhile, the northern shore of the European mainland was attacked by a confederation of many tribes, now combined as the Franks. The Franks had been pushed out of their homeland by the fiercer Angles and Saxons, themselves pressured by the Jutes to the north in Denmark. Taking advantage of a local revolt within the Roman Empire, the Franks plundered northern Gaul, also preying for a while on Spain. When order was eventually restored, the Romans consolidated their coastal defences – both sides of the Channel came under the same military command, and a series of fortifications attempted to deal with the problem of pirates and raiders approaching from the North Sea. These defences came to be known as the Saxon Shore-forts, and for a while, they kept the enemy at bay.[5]

Aurelius Cervianus's farewell party and the evacuation it signified did not merely deprive the former colony of Britannia of its military occupiers. It also left the coasts wide open to invasion. Moreover, the pirate problem of the North Sea, once contained at Dover by the Roman fleet, could now spread all along the northern coast of Europe.

The tribes had an additional reason for their movements. The centuries after the fall of the Roman Empire saw a rise in temperature all over the globe, known as the 'Little Climatic Optimum'. During this period, Europe was roughly one degree centigrade warmer than it is today. The warmer climate made it possible to have vineyards as far north as the River Tyne, and ensured rich harvests that helped the population of Scandinavia increase to levels that required resettlement. More ominously, it also caused more polar ice to melt than before. Sea levels rose, only by a little, but it was enough to cause floods throughout the homelands of many north European tribes. In the area now known as the Low Countries, numerous tribes struggled against the rising waters, clustering on high ground and building their homes on artificial mounds. After a few generations, they too gave up, and went in search of less flood-prone lands to settle.[6] Saxon ships began appearing off the coast of Britannia in twos and threes; when they met with no resistance from the deserted forts, they returned in much larger numbers.

Little distinguishes the upheaval caused by the Saxons from that caused by the Vikings several hundred years later – the only real difference is the lack of contemporary reportage. Place names and archaeological evidence offer the only real clues to what happened at the end of the fifth century AD. A great wave of Saxon settlers, we assume, broke upon the eastern coast of Britannia. With the Roman defences unmanned, there was nothing to stop them. They took the land as their own and pushed the locals out.

Eventually, the locals rallied under a heroic leader, and fought the Saxons to a standstill.[7] Accounts written decades after the event refer to him as Ambrosius Aurelianus, a name of suitably Roman origin to imply that his family, education, or background had something to do with the recently departed legions. It is not impossible that some legionaries remained behind in their adopted homeland – spending several centuries in the same place was likely to cause many families to develop local ties that they were reluctant to sever. Centuries later, this resistance was codified into a tale of twelve great battles against the invaders. The last was the one that really counted – Ambrosius, or someone like him, supposedly dealt a crushing blow to the Saxons at the unknown location of Mons Badonicus ('Badon Hill'). The Saxon advance ground to a temporary halt, and the raiders slowly became part of the landscape. The original British, far from united among themselves, held on in Cumbria, south-west Scotland and the reaches of Wales and the West Country, telling tales about a mythical leader who held off the invaders – eventually, the twelve battles would somehow transform into a series of legends about a man called Arthur.[8]

With the passing of the Roman Empire, the map of Europe was redrawn once more. Gaul now bore a name derived from the tribe that had conquered it, Francia, later France. The island once called Britannia was now a patchwork of petty kingdoms – the 'West Saxons' in Wessex, the 'East Saxons' of Essex and the Angles of East Anglia, the Mercians of the Midlands and the Northumbrians 'North of the Humber'. The eastern part of Britannia, home to the Anglo-Saxon settlers, came to be known as Angle-land, or England. Some Britons fled the Saxon advance by sailing for the area in north France that now bears their name, Brittany. The word *Saxon* became synonymous with foreigners and enemies throughout the Celtic realms: the Scottish *Sassenach*, the Welsh *Saesneg* and the Cornish *Sowsnek*.

The Saxons, once described by the emperor Julian as '. . . the fiercest of the tribes who lived beyond the Rhine,'[9] largely developed into Christian farmers, traders and artisans.

Then, in the late eighth century AD, sporadic raids on the coast turned out to be the precursors of another forceful incursion from Scandinavia. The *Anglo-Saxon Chronicles* reported the arrival of these new enemies with utmost horror, loaded with tales of pillage and slaughter. To inhabitants of what had once been Britannia, their enemies were 'Danes'; to the French, they were 'Normans', men from the North; the Irish called them *Gall* ('Strangers'); the Germans named them *Ascomanni* ('Ash-men') after the wood of the ships that carried them. On the eastern edge of Europe, they were called *Rus, Rootsi* or *Ruotsi*, thought to derive from a Norse word for rowers. In Constantinople, they were called *Vaerings* or *Varangians*, 'pledgers' who swore an oath of service to the empire. In Baghdad, they were the *Waranke* or *ar-Rus*, and when they plundered Spain, the Muslim inhabitants called them *Majus* – 'heathen wizards'.[10]

The term 'Viking' is thought to originate with the Scandinavians themselves, in the Old Norse nouns *víking* (a pirate raid) and *víkingr* (a pirate). But how those terms came to mean what they did remains a mystery – scholars still disagree over whether they have their origin in the verb *víkja* (to move swiftly), or the noun *vík* (an inlet or bay). In the latter case it may refer specifically to one bay in particular, the Vik, that leads to the site of modern Oslo. Or, the word may have a different root, leading back through the Anglo-Saxon *wic* to the Latin *vicus*, a place of trade.

Whatever its origins, the term itself was unknown in English until the nineteenth century – the *Oxford English Dictionary* does not record an appearance until 1807 – and remained little used for several decades thereafter.[11] However, by the latter half of the Victorian era, we see a veritable explosion of Viking-related books resting heavily for their inspiration on translations of the sagas of Iceland, particularly Samuel Laing's landmark *Heimskringla*, an account of the early kings of Norway, published in 1844, and reprinted with substantially greater success in 1889.

These Viking tales were publishing gold to the Victorians – lurid and violent, yet also somehow worthy and educational, they rode the waves of the emergent mass publishing industry, finding enthusiastic readers and rewriters in fields ranging from science fiction to music – it is a paper found inside a copy of *Heimskringla* that inspires Jules Verne's *Journey to the Centre of the Earth* (1864), and *Heimskringla* itself that informs Edward Elgar's *Scenes from the Life of King Olaf* (1896).

However, *Heimskringla* was not as accurate as Laing first purported it to be. Tellingly, his first edition was called the **Chronicle** of the Kings of Norway, while the 1889 reprint preferred the title **Sagas** of the Norse Kings – a shift in emphasis from the historically sound to overtones of the largely fictional. It was not Laing's translation that was at fault, but his source material, that often revealed more about the thoughts and beliefs of thirteenth-century Icelanders than the ancestors they claimed to be discussing.

The century since this late Victorian Viking-mania has seen a slow but steady erosion of its vision, using evidence more compelling than tall tales from an Icelandic fireside. In recent decades, Viking studies have been characterized by the growth of archaeological evidence, and the steady dismissal of numerous accounts once taken as gospel. We now recognize that sagas are not necessarily true, and not all chroniclers are even-handed – that written documents need to be weighed against the evidence of archaeology, numismatics and, in more recent times, the findings from new disciplines such as dendrochronology.

What, then, was a Viking? As a schoolboy, I was led to believe that these fierce marauders had suddenly appeared out of nowhere, landing like flying saucers on the coast of England after perilous journeys across the North Sea – the shock-and-awe of the *Anglo-Saxon Chronicles*, imparted to a new generation. In fact, the earliest Vikings were very similar to their Saxon precursors, clinging to the coastlines of northern Europe, so that the only time spent significantly far from land was during the relatively short crossing of the English Channel, or from Norway to the Shetlands. And they did not magically appear, but were brought there by other forces.

The most significant contributions to the arrival of the Vikings had less to do with the rich pickings of undefended English monasteries, and more to do with the strengthening of sea defences elsewhere, and with earlier contacts formed through trade. When the Vikings attacked their victims, it seems that it was rare that they stumbled across a target by accident – they knew what they were looking for because they had been there before. They knew whom they were robbing, because perhaps only months earlier, they or their associates had been trading with them.

Between the eighth and the eleventh centuries, around 200,000 people left Scandinavia to settle elsewhere.[12] These voyagers were primarily men with nothing to lose. The waterways of the Baltic and the inlets of Norway turned them into fishermen and merchants, and the first of their ventures were undoubtedly trading ones.

In some parts of the world, this is how they stayed – their behaviour towards foreigners largely dictated by comparative strengths. Where a land was mainly deserted, such as Iceland or the Faeroes, the new arrivals simply settled and stayed. The dispossessed sons of Scandinavia found some land, bought some wives and slaves and, more often than not, fell back into the farming routine from which they had sprung. Such conditions prevented them, at least, from turning into *bona fide* 'Vikings', although there was no guarantee their descendants might not go in search of plunder elsewhere – even the relatively peaceful Icelanders occasionally exported their criminal element back to Europe.

Where voyagers encountered local inhabitants, their behaviour depended on what they could get away with. While Viking marauders feature in the local histories of England, Ireland and France, such tales are not so well known elsewhere. Encounters with the unquenchable menace of Greek fire, for example, put paid to most Viking attacks on the Byzantine world. In Constantinople, the Byzantine Empire enjoyed generally positive relations with the men from the northern lands, and relied heavily on them as mercenaries. The Islamic community's dealings with the Norsemen were also largely peaceful after a major conflict in the late tenth century. Viking ships were treated to a lesson they would never forget when they ran into a Muslim navy on the Caspian Sea in 943, while no less than 25 rune stones in eastern Sweden commemorate an ill-fated expedition to the Caucasus by one Ingvar the Widefarer, that ended very badly for many of its participants in 1041.[13]

Suitably cowed, the Vikings left the Muslim world alone,

preferring instead to serve as mercenaries in its armies, or trade with it in valuable commodities such as slaves – they may have been raiders at the European end of the trade route, but at the Middle Eastern end they were merchants. Indeed, many of the spoils of Viking predations in Europe, including slaves, ended up traded to the Arab world, while the treasure hoards of many a Viking leader are rich in silver from Baghdad, obtained not on raids, but on trading missions.[14] Similarly, the kidnap victims of the Vikings, peasants snatched from British or Baltic coasts, often ended their days in foreign climes they could never have imagined. When black slaves fell out of fashion in the Arab world in the late ninth century, traders increasingly turned north for alternatives, and the Vikings eagerly met the new demand for white slaves – Viking consignments were less troublesome for the Muslims to obtain than captives from wars with Byzantium on the caliphate's frontier. One Eastern European girl, known only by her Muslim name of Mukhâriq, was plucked from her homeland by Viking raiders, found herself in an Abbasid harem and eventually became the mother of a caliph.[15] The Muslim diarist Ibn Battúta, while staying in the remote Chinese port of Fuzhou after the Viking Age, reported that a friend of his was doing well for himself, with a household that boasted 'fifty white slaves and as many slave-girls.' Such was the eventual fate of many of the Vikings' victims and their descendants.[16]

The Vikings, in their explorations and conquests, undoubt-edly achieved much. However it must be admitted that the leading edge of their expansion chiefly comprised thugs, brigands and outlaws. Latter-day apologists have attempted to soften the image but, by definition, the word Viking refers to pirates. A Viking is categorically *not* a flaxen-haired maiden making attractive jewellery by the side of a picturesque fjord, no matter what some museum curators may imply. The

Vikings were the rejects of Scandinavian society – forced to travel further afield to make their fortune. Some, of course, returned to claim their homeland as their own, applying their experience of foreign wars to internecine struggles.

It was a Viking who kept his retarded son chained like a beast outside his house, a Viking who attempted to skin a horse alive, a Viking who hacked off a live pig's snout to prove a point.[17] But equally, numerous claims made about Viking 'atrocities' need to be regarded in context. Almost *everyone* was atrocious back then – it was a Christian, Saxon king who ordered the ethnic cleansing of all the Danes in England. The Angles, Saxons, Irish and Scots were just as bloodthirsty with each other, and with their Scandinavian foes.

The Vikings were often defined by what they were not. They were, to the contemporary chroniclers that hated and feared them, *not* civilized, *not* local, and most importantly *not* Christian. The so-called Viking Age petered out when these negative traits were annulled. Scandinavia was eventually Christianized, ironically in part through the experiences of its sons abroad, forcing the Vikings to rethink who constituted friend and foe. By the twelfth century, when Scandinavian crusaders converted Estonia to Christianity at the point of a sword, they were now not only raiding somewhere sufficiently out of the way of Western European consciousness, but doing so in the name of the Lord.

The Vikings were a group created by circumstance, not blood – they were not a 'race', nor did they have any patriotism, any sense of 'Viking-ness'. Although they were predominantly men from the areas now known as Norway, Sweden and Denmark, there are mentions in the sagas of Finns, Sámi and Estonians among them. A Welshman supposedly sailed with the Jomsvikings; Scottish scouts accompanied Leif the Lucky in his explorations, and the man who discovered the 'vines' of Vinland was German. When the Vikings prospered abroad, they were swift to throw off their ties to their homeland. Perhaps because of the settlers' reliance on finding local brides, they were notoriously quick to adopt the language and customs of their new lands, so that the legendary Viking vigour was not so much reduced as rebranded.[18] In only a couple of generations, the conquerors of Kiev had taken local wives, and bestowed Slavic names upon their children. Now calling themselves Russians, they would jockey for a thousand years with their Swedish cousins over who ruled the area now known as Finland. Similarly the Norsemen who occupied north France were transformed in mere decades into the 'Normans' who claimed it as their natural home. Meanwhile, hundreds of square miles of the England that the Normans conquered had already been settled by Danes.

Why, then, do the Vikings continue to exert such fascination for us? During the the Viking Age, Western Europe was a backwater. The most powerful and cultured civilizations on Earth were China, Byzantium and Islam. As Christianity struggled amidst the ruins of the Roman Empire, yet another group of rough barbarians stole and murdered on the margins. Why do we still care?

For some, the tale of Viking expansion is one of incredible bravery and dynamism as, after centuries of timidly hugging the coastline, men in fragile wooden ships sail into a watery void, eventually discovering a New World. Then again, almost three *million* Scandinavians emigrated between 1815 and 1939.[19] Such settlers are why Minnesota's football team is called the Vikings, and why the Viking Age continues to interest a large proportion of the American populace – not all white Protestants are Anglo-Saxon. But although the Vikings' landings in America are no longer disputed, the extent of their sailing skills still is. Were the Vikings pioneers of maritime navigation, or is it fairer to describe them as foolhardy blunderers, who made the majority of their 'discoveries' by getting lost and crashing into previously unknown coastlines?

For others, the Viking Age is a tale of supreme victory, not for the Vikings, but for the Christian world they sought to plunder. Within a few generations, the savage marauders were brought into the fold of Christianity, turned into respectable Europeans, vanquished in the war of the soul, even as they bragged of their physical conquests. Modern scholarship finds much to debate here, since the nature of famous conversions is still open to question. Were the Vikings savage beasts tamed by the love of God, or opportunists who paid lip-service to convenient local customs, while still keeping several concubines, owning slaves and killing their enemies?

As supposed rule-breakers, explorers and anarchists, they have injected a barbaric frisson on the cultures of the Europe their attacks helped create. Their martial prowess has become legendary, although their most humiliating defeats were at the hand of Finnish archers and Inuit fishermen. The Vikings have become symbols of all that is dangerous and exciting in the European soul – an attitude that gains even more credence in modern times as DNA tests establish exactly where they went. In many cases and many countries, our enemies did not go away. They stayed, and prospered, and eventually became part of us.

I

SONGS OF THE VALKYRIES

MYTHS AND LEGENDS OF SCANDINAVIA

The Vikings appear in the accounts of their enemies as fearsome invaders, devoid of culture or conscience, prepared to commit the outrageous sin of killing Christian monks. They were the savage heathens that Christianity sought to convert, symbols of the Other and the Devil. Such accounts may present a realistic vision of the terror the Vikings could instil, but reveal little about them personally. Of the Vikings' own literature, we have a rich inheritance of saga narratives, but most date from the later Middle Ages, when the distant descendants of the original Vikings huddled around a fireplace in an Icelandic winter, and told and retold tales of the glory days.

Before the modern age, the most important man in the transmission of Viking culture was arguably Snorri Sturluson (1179–1241), a wealthy Icelandic politician who committed many such oral traditions to paper for the first time, accompanied by remarkably astute editorial observations and criticisms. Snorri's work preserves the mythical *Edda*, and the *Heimskringla*, a long cycle of biographies of Norwegian kings. Both works are crucial to any study of the Vikings, although they present many methodological problems of their own, since even the original material was 'spun' in a way designed to please crowds. Snorri collated kingly biographies sung by *skalds*, the court entertainers of the Vikings – to draw modern parallels, one might imagine Hollywood film-makers, commissioned by modern dictators to tell the story of their lives, supposedly without fear or favour but in reality with an armed focus group who had recently set fire to a church in the vicinity. Snorri himself was able to present a mitigating argument, that since the recitations were often before crowds that comprised the people mentioned and their colleagues, this would itself serve as some form of editorial rein on hyperbole. That, however, cannot save us from the *kenning*, the Viking habit of replacing solid terms with poetic metaphors in the purplest of vocabulary.

If there is a 'solid' form of evidence for our studies of the Vikings, it lies in archaeology. But even then, we are hostages to chance – a single find can transform our previous understanding of Viking culture and deeds, and even scientists cannot agree on all of the evidence presented. Accordingly, there are several parts of this book that deal in some detail with the history of *our* history of the Vikings, outlining some of the controversies that continue to this day. One of them concerns the subject of this chapter – what the Vikings *believed*.

During the twentieth century, the Jungian tradition encouraged attempts at universality, with its sense that human beings share common traumas and psychological experiences, relived through their gods and beliefs. However, linguistic evidence from other cultures, and confusions within Scandinavian mythology itself, present a very different picture of the Norse world. The Norse myths are trying to tell us something, and much of it may be astronomical. The priceless missing piece of the Viking puzzle is a quantifiable knowledge of their astronomy. They did not use the Babylonian constellations common to western European culture, but certainly still paid attention to the stars. To the proto-Vikings, they might have been of relatively small consequence, but as the population spread out across the western hemisphere, on long voyages with few means of reliable navigation, the stars above must have gained vital importance. Vikings from Vinland to Baghdad would have looked up and seen the same stars in the sky, the same five visible planets, the same recurring phenomena, and some of this must have rubbed off on to their mythology. All that we have today are occasional mentions in myths of entities 'thrown into the sky', and a few contradictory stories associated with the evening star. Other sources, particularly the *Grimnismal* in Snorri's *Poetic Edda*, are strange enough to be garbled references to cycles of the heavens, but until such time as a physical representation can be matched with a poetic one, we are left with little but conjecture.

If only we knew the constellations of the Vikings, or which of their rock carvings might not be mere pictures, but star maps, then we should understand much more about their myths, many of which may be mnemonic devices designed to fix the patterns in the sky. Some names may have changed over time, such as which gods were great enough to be identified with a planet, but others may have remained constant throughout the Viking Age. Somewhere in the night sky, the Vikings saw a World Tree, three sisters, a one-armed god, a god with one bright eye, perhaps in a chariot, perhaps hanging from a tree, a hound, twin brothers, a pair of goats, a squirrel, an eagle, a small snake, a much bigger serpent and many other figures familiar from the sagas. If any researcher can crack this code, then it could become the Rosetta Stone of the Viking mind.[1] The answer lies somewhere on an obscure rune stone, or drawn on the shamanic drumskin of a Sámi sorcerer. Until the day it is found, we are left with confusions, dead ends and folklore, retold chiefly by non-believers. Snorri, a leading source for many of the tales of Viking mythology, seemed keen to force some order on the chaotic world of his fore-fathers, introducing quaint notions of a family of twelve gods and goddesses, seemingly modelled on the pantheons of an-cient Greece and Rome. Such a council of twelve may have been inspired by Indo-European religion, or perhaps its ulti-mate root, the houses of the zodiac. Snorri may, however, have simply superimposed Iceland's traditional assembly-quorum of twelve on to his ancestors' beliefs.

Snorri was also a Christian author. *Heimskringla* reports the deeds of those who worship the Norse gods, but Snorri has no time for their supposed divine status. Instead, he is ready to suggest that Odin, the leader of the Viking gods, was once a great chieftain, who arrived in the Scandinavian region and carved out a kingdom for himself. His tribe, if he ever existed, was the Aesir, a name that gives itself to the chief family of Norse gods. The Aesir, a name that Snorri equates with an *Asian* origin, supplanted the Vanir, a weaker tribe whose origin Snorri placed at the Vana Fork, close to the place where the River Don meets the Black Sea.[2] The elders of the Aesir, and a smattering of Vanir survivors, formed the ancestors of the Scandinavians, and, so Snorri concluded, the models for their gods.

Odin is presented as the leader of the gods, his wife Frigg at his side. As in other cultures, lesser deities have their domains and responsibilities – Thor, the god of thunder; Frey and Freya, the twin gods of fertility; Heimdall the Watchman; Aegir, the ruler of the sea; Njord, another god of the sea; Bragi, god of poetry; Loki the god of fire and Hel, his daughter, the queen of the underworld; Tyr the god of war, and Ull, the god of archery. This list is not exhaustive, but covers the main bases – writers on Norse religion have often tried to herd the disparate elements into a unified whole deserving of the term 'religion', itself an invention of later times. As to how much of Snorri's late medieval depiction would have made sense to a Viking audience, that would rather depend on where the audience was from. Study of place names tells us that ancient peoples in what is now Denmark were more likely to worship Tyr. Worshippers of Ull, the archer, were once paramount in southern and central Sweden. Thor-worship became common all over Scandinavia, with the notable exception of the Trond-heim region, whereas place names in honour of Odin are far more widespread in Denmark and Sweden than in Norway or Iceland.

The relative ranks and powers of the Norse 'pantheon', as defined by Snorri, were based on legends swapped by the descendants of only a couple of these contending strains of belief. However, since the ancestors of Snorri's informants presumably comprised a large number of people with access to ships rather than farmers left behind in the old country, it is likely that in his compendium of myths there are many tales that would have been recognized by the Vikings of old. There is also a possibility that, as a higher-class god, Odin attracted the attention of social climbers – would-be rulers and their warrior cronies.[3]

We get a sense of the savagery and bleakness of the life of the proto-Vikings from Snorri's myth of creation. For them, the nascent universe had but two elements, the searing heat of the south and the bitter cold of the north, separated by *Ginnun-gagap*, the great void. Life began in the middle, where these two elements met, thawing Ymir, a titan from whom sprang the first of gods, men and giants. Ymir is fed by suckling on a cow, Audhumla, which has somehow also appeared out of the ice. The cow licks nearby ice for its salt content, and thereby releases another man, Buri, whose grandchildren (he somehow reproduces) are Odin, Vili and Ve. The myth is confused, certainly, but in the sense that it appears to combine several origins – quite possibly the origin-stories of several tribes, some of whose descendants would eventually become the Vikings. In a primal tragedy, Odin, Vili and Ve killed Ymir, his body forming the earth and his skull the dome of the sky above it. The realm of men, Midgard, is shielded from the realm of the giants by a wall or mountain range, made of one of Ymir's eyebrows. The world of men is inhabited by the descendants of two trees on the shore (not descendants of the men already created from Ymir, another possible remnant of ancient rivalries?). The gods, suddenly invested with the power to create things, go on to make the Sun (a female) and the Moon (a male), who pelt across the sky in chariots pursued by wolves.

In accordance with a world-view informed by fjords and islands, separated by seas and mountains, the Viking universe is a series of self-contained domains, reachable only by prolonged effort. At the centre of everything is the giant ash tree Yggdrasill. A tree, of course, forms the centre of the Garden of Eden in Christianity, but Yggdrasill owes its origin to something much earlier, perhaps a prehistoric religion of sky worship, in which heaven was held up by a giant column. If this is the case, then it may have a symbolic cousin in Irminsul, a pillar in ancient Saxony, held to keep the sky from falling, and the Sampo of Finno-Ugric myth, thought originally to be a pillar that held up heaven.[4] Snorri did know of the myths of the Finns and Saxons when he wrote his work.

The tree has three main roots, one in the world of the dead, one in the realm of the frost-giants, and the third in the land of the Aesir, the Norse gods themselves. Near the base of this third root is the Well of Fate, and Fate herself, *Urd*, dwells nearby with her two sisters *Verdandi* (Being) and *Skuld* (Necessity). These traditional translations of their names are misleading, as they represent three Norse concepts of tense, that which should happen, that which has happened, and that which ought to happen – the goddesses, in linguistic terms, of the Subjunctive, Indicative and Optative. These three sisters are the Norns, who weave a tapestry of the world's fate, presumably with Urd and Skuld providing the possible warp and weft, and Verdandi embroidering the way things actually come about. Their knowledge of where things have been, and sense of where things are going, makes them powerful prophetesses and they are consulted often by the gods. Eastern traditions of the Finno-Ugric peoples also posit a World Tree but dispense with the Norns, instead using the tree as an analogy of life itself, with the souls of children stored in its seeds, and the fate of men engraved on its leaves. The fall of each leaf equates with the death of someone in our world.

The Norns thus appear to be a later European addition to an Asian concept. As divine oracles and repositories of knowledge, the Norns bear some resemblance to other European triple goddesses, most notably the Graiae of ancient Greece, although the Graiae were depicted as old women, far less easy on the eye than the maidenly Norns. The Norns, like other women of the Vikings, we may assume, are kept busy. They must water the tree, and cake it in rich mud to keep it young, and also shoo away the animals that feed on its leaves and bark. They may be seen as an allegory of the daily round for many early Scandinavian women – limited animal husbandry and tending of plants, and occasional encounters with forest animals – the most impressive of which are the eagle in the branches of the tree and the snake at its roots, who constantly jostle for position, and trade insults via a squirrel messenger who scurries up and down the trunk.

The myths of the Vikings are those of a people who have travelled far. They begin with wanderings in snow and ice, and end with forestry, goat-herding on mountainsides and simple farm life. They present a view of several different bloodlines and traditions, coming together sometimes in friendship but also in bloodshed. At the end of it all, one god is paramount, but his fellow deities are fractious and argumentative, forced to meet each day at the base of the World Tree to argue out the issues at hand in council. There is talk among the gods of affairs and intrigue, there is jealousy among the goddesses when their husbands take lovers from other races, which they do with great regularity.

What can we gather from the legends Snorri recorded? The Nordic region was untouched territory, almost endless tracts of virgin forests and lakes, which first attracted wandering nomads. In the beginning, there was plenty of space to go round, and the inhabitants were mobile. We may look upon the Sámi in Lapland, who migrate alongside the reindeer herds that are their main resource, as a living example of this lifestyle. There are two routes into Scandinavia proper – one from Asia, through Finland and around the top of the Baltic Sea. The other is from Europe, up through Germany and across the islands that link Denmark to southern Sweden. In earlier times, southern Sweden was itself an island, and then barely a peninsula, connected to Scandinavia by bogs and marshes amid perilous forests. But this region is also the most habitable area – the bulk of the arable land in Scandinavia is clustered in Denmark and southern Sweden. Here arose a people who found the land to be worthy of settlement, transforming from wanderers to farmers, worshipping a fertility god they called Frey or Yngvie – his sons, the Ynglings, were the ancestors of the kings of Sweden.

Frey might have been a harvest god, but he was also savage. He bestowed a mandate on the early Swedish kings that entitled them to rule so long as he was kept appeased. When crops failed or winters grew too long, Frey required additional encouragement, with animal sacrifice. The horse, in particular, was sacred to him, and there are several saga mentions of *Freyfaxi*, a horse named for a particular kind or colour of mane (we don't actually know), that destined it for the god's altar. From clues and hints in Viking sources, it would seem that in particularly lean times, the king would be expected to sacrifice *himself*, submitting to a ceremonial blood-letting that may, in the earliest times, not have been all that ceremonial.[5] Frey's cult was also associated with the worship of the boar, which may link the Swedes back to Eastern Europe, since a similar cult existed among the Aesti (proto-Estonians), and may also have existed among the Cimbri in north Germany.

Somewhere during the sixth century AD, the Swedish region of Uppland gained a ruler called Angantyr (to the English, Ongentheow) – it also had an increase in population. The Iron Age had given the locals sturdier axes, suddenly making it possible to clear far wider areas for farmland and settlement. But large parts of Scandinavia are mountainous, and space in Sweden may have already been tight. It was, notably, not Angantyr himself, but instead his unruly 'sons' who, the legends tell us, preyed upon the neighbouring Goths, inviting retaliation and tit-for-tat raids that escalated into a war. The Goths were put to flight, and their leader Hygelac perished somewhere in an undetermined place called Ravenwood. But strife continued among the Swedes, with the sons of Angantyr fighting over their birthright. Despite being only a legend, elements of the story ring true from what we know of the

Vikings' later *modus operandi*. In a pattern that would be repeated throughout the Viking Age to come, disaffected claimants sought aid overseas, leading to further wars between Swedes and Swedish pretenders with foreign backing.[6]

Uppsala, the region just north of modern Stockholm, is a nexus of ancient Scandinavian culture, surrounded by burial mounds of ancient kings and their successors. Between the sixth and the ninth centuries, the Swedes buried their kings with horses, dogs and other animals, weaponry, grave-goods including everyday objects and rare treasures such as glass goblets. The pattern of exploration and conquest repeats itself to the south and east, where Dan, a son of a king of Uppsala, is supposed to have travelled in search of new lands. He found the islands of Zealand, Lolland and Funen, and from there the peninsula itself, all of which would eventually come to take his name, as Dan's Land – *Danemark*. His brother Angul ventured even further south into the European mainland in an attempt to establish an Angul's Land, thereby foreshadowing links between historical Danes and the Angles. This, at least, is how the story is framed in the *History of the Danes*, a work by the late-medieval author Saxo Grammaticus, who was determined to give Denmark a national origin myth to match those of other countries. Much of Saxo's own source material came from writers in Iceland, and this calls into question many of his assumptions.[7]

Archaeology confirms at least the general thrust of Saxo's claims, although it also tells us that Denmark was already occupied by the time it was supposedly 'discovered'. By the sixth century, Denmark had become almost as strong a kingdom as the Swedish Uppland that supposedly spawned it. The largest Danish island of Zealand is littered with burial sites, some dating back to the Stone Age. The most impressive are around the town of Roskilde (*Hrors-kilde* – the sacred springs

of Hror), a few miles west of modern Copenhagen, where
Dark-Age peoples once dwelt on the banks of the river Lejre,
long since dried up. This, perhaps, is the Heorot of legend, the
gabled hall of King Hrothgar, who features in the old English
poem *Beowulf*. And here, according to the tenth century
Saxon chronicler Thietmar, the ruler of Heorot would maintain his power by sacrificial rights. Every nine years, 99 cocks,
99 dogs, 99 horses and 99 men would be slain to preserve the
king's power. When Beowulf saves Heorot from the regular
attacks by Grendel, we may perhaps be seeing a mangled
account of an attempt to put an end to the human sacrifice.

The Gotlanders, particularly the Gotlanders who travelled
beyond the island of their birth to trade around the Baltic
coasts, favoured a different god to the Swedes' Frey. 'Trade' is
a misnomer – much of their activities probably involved
something closer to extortion, as they accepted tribute in pelts,
eiderdown, amber and other goods. Before the Viking Age had
begun, men were already taking what did not belong to them,
and some did so in the name of a god of battle. Odin to the
Scandinavians, Woden or Wotan further to the south, was the
paramount god to the group of men whose predations are the
main subject of this book. Other peoples in Scandinavia may
have had their own deities of preference, but Odin was beloved
of the raiders, with his only real rival in their affections being
Thor. He also came to be particularly revered in Gotland and
Hordaland, two regions of Scandinavia that were important
centres of seaborne trade, and entrepôts for many of the
traders who would become raiders in lean times.[8] Odin was
a god of battle, but also of poetry, so was regularly cited in the
verses of skalds hoping to impress their kings. As the king of
the gods, he may have also enjoyed more mentions in the royal
verses that have survived down the ages, simply by way of
association with the lords and earls at whose dinners his

exploits were recounted – praise of the chief god was also a backhanded means of praising one's host.

Odin has at least 177 names and kennings,[9] which allow us to see those areas where he was thought to exercise his power. As a leader of the gods, he is known as the Father of Men or All-Father, the Mighty God or simply the Chief. Later saga writers even refer to him as one-of-three, perhaps in analogy to the Christian trinity. He is also renowned for his wisdom – he did, after all, give his eye for it, sacrificing half his vision in order to take one sip from a spring of knowledge. He is called the Mighty Poet and Mighty Speaker (a 'speaker' being the chief councillor at an Icelandic assembly – and therefore perhaps an anachronism from Snorri's time, not a term from the Viking Age).

Odin's wisdom was of secondary concern to his worshippers. He was far more popular with the Vikings for his main stock-in-trade, which was battle. For Odin, on his eight-legged horse Sleipnir, was the Charging Rider, the Spear Lord, the Army Father, the Battle Blind or the Author of Victory. Odin was also the patron of the war-band's fearsome elite – or rather, the brawlers who could be persuaded that standing at the front was a good idea. In Viking tradition they were shape-changers, men with the ability to take on animalistic characteristics. In recognition of their shaman-like animal-pelt costumes, they were often known as 'wolf-skins' and 'bear-shirts' – *ulfhednar* and, more famously, *berserkir*. One is tempted to suggest that such men, dangerous and unpredictable as they were, were liable to attract cautious flattery from any skald who wanted to stay on their good side – they may have been glorified because when those songs were first sung they were standing right next to the singer. Later sagas, written by no-nonsense Icelanders without wars to fight, regard berserkers as dim, oafish nuisances.[10]

Death in battle in the name of Odin was not a bad thing, at least in the eyes of the devout follower. For Odin was also the Chooser of the Slain, the *valkojósandi*. He had female assistants who bore the same name in the feminine form, *valkyrjur*, or valkyries, the terrifying furies of the Viking world. On several occasions in the sagas, there are comedic moments when Viking men seem meekly accepting of a situation, only to have a woman goad them into action – a woman's worth was heavily reliant on that of her man, and the Viking wives could be fierce in their attempts to preserve it. The last bastion of Viking machismo, it often seems, lay not with themselves, but in their wish to appease their women. The Valkyries were this furious nature personified, betraying a surprising terror and reification of female power. Their names are a catalogue of the things prized most by the belligerent Vikings, the famous *Brynhildr* is Bright Battle, but there are 51 others in extant sources.[11] As with the Inuit and their apocryphal twenty words for snow, the Vikings had many terms for discussing conflict. There was a Valkyrie of drunken brawling, Ale-Rune, and another of Taunts. To the Viking mind Battle herself was a woman, as were War, Tumult, Chaos, Devastation and Clash. The names of other Valkyries invoke images of war-goddesses to be appeased, or moments of belligerence personified: Extreme Cruelty, Sword-Time, or simply Killer. The most ominous is the Valkyrie that invokes that moment just before all hell breaks loose, Silence. Even *Skuld*, the Norn of Necessity, is numbered among the Valkyries on three occasions, her name perhaps better translated there as Blame. More prosaic misogyny may be found in others: Unstable, and the minor but still influential figure of Bossy.

Odin and his Valkyries would lead wild hunts across the sky, seen from the ground as the haunting silent light displays of the *aurora borealis*. They would observe the bravest war-

riors in battle in the quotidian world, and bear the noblest
warriors back to Odin's domain, *Valholl* or Valhalla, the Hall
of the Slain. There, deceased Vikings would hunt, drink and
fornicate (the Valkyries having a dual purpose) until the end of
the world, when they would go into battle at the final conflict
between the Viking gods and their enemies. The appeal of this
to a war-band is obvious, but Odin is also presented as the
ultimate host; to those who praised him at banquets and
celebrations, he was the leader to end all leaders, and an
example for the kings and earls to follow. The lifestyle of
Valhalla seems to be an idealized representation of the way the
Vikings saw their lives – an endless round of feasting and
fighting, topped, they hoped, by a glorious death in battle. It
contains elements of the terrorist who expects luxurious
debauchery in paradise, but also of impoverished men with
nothing more to lose.

The attitude of Odinic followers coloured many aspects of
Viking life. Female corpses from the period are generally found
with grave-goods increasing in direct relation to their age; the
older a woman at death, the richer the goods sent with her into
the afterlife by her family. But it was quite the opposite with
the male followers of Odin – as if it was *expected* of a man that
he die relatively young in the midst of battle. The graves of
young Viking men are often cluttered with wealth of objects
and finery, whereas older men are found with little, if anything. Dying of old age was, among the most fanatical of the
Vikings, regarded as something of a failure. It was believed by
Odin's followers that men were welcomed at Valhalla with the
goods placed in their graves – a death in battle required
outfitting for the long haul, but death from old age required
no such honours.[12]

Odin himself could be an old man, ravaged by time. He is
depicted with a spear, or sometimes a staff, one-eyed or

occasionally blind. He is *Jolnir*, the Yule-Figure invited into pagan homes at winter as a form of sympathetic magic, as if making friends with the spirit of winter offers some protection from its cold and deprivation. Through many centuries of confusion and alteration, Odin may even be a precursor to the Christian Santa Claus.[13]

Like many divine figures, Odin is a symbol of knowledge and wealth. In the legends, he bestows weapons upon his loyal followers, and their acceptance of the sword implies service to the death – in an age when metalwork was an expensive operation often likened to magic, weaponry did not come cheap. Many Vikings were limited to axes and spears, which used less iron. A sword, such as that bestowed upon Sigmund the Volsung by Odin, was a valuable item.[14]

Odin appears in sagas offering advice and protection, and even makes his way into supposed histories – Saxo's *History of the Danes* mentions an Odinic vision by the legendary King Harald Wartooth, in which Odin appears as an old man of imposing height, and offers Harald invulnerability in the battle to come. Harald, in return, offers Odin the souls of all the enemies he kills with his sword, a somewhat Faustian pact that must have chilled the blood of Saxo's Christian readership.[15]

Odin's love of battle included a desire to remember. It was not enough that the Vikings fight; they wanted people to talk about it. Whether this is a natural human desire, or an attempt by skalds to increase their own relative importance it is difficult to say, but Odin, as already mentioned, was the god of battle and poetry. Mastery of words made him a master of knowledge, and this in itself had implications of sorcerous capabilities. Singing Odin's songs kept the rowers in time and brought them extra strength (singing any song would have done that, but Odin took the credit), and it is Odin who introduces new concepts of battle to his followers. By knowing words and poetry, or even the art of writing, since Odin was also the master of the runes, warriors were able to preserve new ideas instead of letting them die. Perhaps, in the Scandinavia the Vikings left behind them as they sailed off to plunder, Odin was originally more peaceful, a god whose runes preserved knowledge of blacksmithing, crop rotation or animal husbandry, but such things were of no use to the Vikings. The Odin exported into European consciousness by the Vikings was a lord of conflict. Strategy and tactics, the concepts of battle formation and signals on the field, were couched for the Vikings in terms of Odin's battle religion. Symbols of Odin had practical advantages in battle, functioning as modern signals and codes do today, allowing armies to act as one, while their enemies remained in confusion.

But Odin's religion also demanded secrecy. We may only guess at the meaning implicit in the tale of Harald Wartooth's demise. Odin took his secrets of battle and gave them instead to Harald's rival, Hring. As their armies prepared for battle, Hring's took up a wedge formation – ideal to force its way through the chaotic opposing forces. Harald charged nonetheless, only then realizing that his regular charioteer was absent. Instead, Odin himself drove Harald's horses ever onward, and as Harald begged him for one last victory, he was instead plunged into the midst of enemy forces, fell from his chariot, and was killed.

Poetic licence, of course, must be taken into account, as nobody was around to see Harald's final conversation with his supernatural patron. Perhaps, in the death of Harald Wartooth, there is a warning against telling too much about the secrets Odin imparted. The war-band was to remain close-knit. The leader's service to Odin was to be mirrored in the services of his men. He was to keep them in plunder and resources, and they were to fight on until the end of the world.

Reading between the lines of Norse religion, we may see several distinct strands. One aims to explain natural phenomena – thunder in the distance, sounding like the rumbling of Thor's giant chariot wheels; the mysterious appearance of a rainbow in the sky; the reason for the turn of the seasons or the eclipses of the sun. Tales about such occurrences become conflated with others, fragments of myth about half-remembered battles, disasters or events. As with legends and folktales all around the world, chance puns or misunderstandings contribute to the sources. As early as the twelfth century, armed with a modicum of critical distance, Snorri Sturluson was able to consider the possibility that the mythical god Odin was a genuine figure from prehistory, whose tribe enjoyed a considerable degree of success in the real world. Odin, the grandfather, entered local mythology as Odin the father-god.

But whose locality was this? Scandinavia is not a unified whole. Borders are fluid – the Norwegians of the Trondheim region have a long tradition of ignoring the supposed rule of the Norwegians of the Vik. The land and people of southern Sweden have more in common with the arable regions of northern Denmark, and indeed, were sometimes part of that kingdom until 1657. Other regions and peoples are now assumed not to be part of Scandinavia at all, and yet have formed parts of the area's sphere of influence for centuries. The name *Keel*, which describes the central mountain range dividing Norway and Sweden, does not refer to the 'ship's keel' as a modern English speaker might guess. It literally means 'waste'. Early maps of Scandinavia put Vikings on the coastline and mark as 'waste ground' the mountains of the hinterland, but the land was not empty at all. Throughout the Viking era, the Vikings were in constant contact and uneasy miscegenation with a very different people from a different linguistic and genetic group, not in distant lands but on their very doorstep.

The natives of Lapland, the Sámi, occupy all of arctic Scandinavia, and also dwelt far to the south in Viking times, along the spine of Scandinavia's central mountains. Linguistic archaeology, in place names for example, tells us that much of the inland regions of Norway and Sweden were Sámi territory. There are 3,000 Norse loanwords in the Sámi language, and 200 of them pre-date the beginning of the Viking Age, implying continuous and prolonged contact.[16] Similarly, the Suomi, Karelians and Kainuans of Finland had so much contact with Vikings that they would later spend several hundred years as a province of Sweden, while the Baltic states have often had periods of Norse rule. Viking gods were once worshipped in what is now modern Russia.

Throughout the period under discussion, there was no central religious authority. The old Viking religions held no conclaves like the Christian councils of Ephesus, Whitby or Nicaea, to argue over points of doctrine and establish articles of faith and belief. There was no Viking pope or organized Viking clergy. Sacred spaces were established following the usual animist procedures, accidentally, haphazardly, in places of natural beauty or in prominent sites. Temples came later, after a deity was presumed to have offered aid to the people in return for worship. It seems possible to have picked ten different places in Scandinavia and to receive a different answer each time to the same question: 'Who is your god?'

Odin, alleged chief of the gods in Viking times, may not have been as powerful in earlier times. Roman accounts of 'German' tribes detailed sacrificial rituals to Odin (or his German equivalent Woden/Wotan), but tellingly compared him to Mercury, a lesser god in the classical pantheon.[17] Several centuries before the Viking Age, the most powerful Norse deity appears to have been a sky-god or sun-god, Tiwaz. Tiwaz was equated with Mars, the Roman god of war. He survived in later times as Tyr or Tiw, a one-handed deity of battle some-how subordinate to Odin. As Odin has lost an eye, Tyr has lost a hand, bitten off by a savage hound when he was the only god brave enough to bind it. Tyr may have been successful, but he was also wounded; perhaps it was this vague reference to diminished powers that allowed the followers of another god to seize control.

If Tyr was once the Sun, then perhaps Heimdall was once the Moon. This guardian god, possibly another remnant of the supplanted Vanir, was said to never need sleep, and to function as well during the day as others did at night. His job, according to Snorri, was to keep constant watch over the rainbow bridge Bifrost, bearing a horn to blow in case of attack. Heimdall's senses were greatly heightened – he was able to hear smaller sounds farther away than might be expected. He could hear grass growing, and even the noise made by follicles extruding hair. As a lunar deity, he may also have been associated with childbirth and menstruation; he was said by Snorri to be the 'son of nine mothers.'[18]

Heimdall is also associated with the ram, *heimdali* – a head-butt in Viking days might be described as the 'sword of Heimdall'. We have no way of telling whether the god took his name from the ram, or vice versa, or even if the names are a chance pun in differing dialects, given added colour by later skalds. But if Heimdall is a ram-god, then his time, at least in eastern Scandinavia and Finland, is the end of the year. To this day, in Baltic countries, some villages maintain the tradition of a ram effigy in fir or wicker, the *kekripukki*, assembled in the autumn months and dragged in a parade, before its destruction in a spectacular November conflagration. Santa Claus in Finland is still *joulupukki* – the Yule-goat.

Whichever of these gods may have been the most powerful, they survive in the names of the days of the week in many

European countries. The week as we know it contains reference to the seven heavenly bodies (i.e. Roman gods) most easily visible from Earth: the Sun and Moon, Mars, Mercury, Jupiter, Venus and Saturn. In northern European countries the names have retained their pagan equivalents, Sun and the Moon remain so, but so, too, do Tyr (Tuesday), Woden (Wednesday), Thor (Thursday) and either Frey or Frigg (Friday).

The Roman author Tacitus recorded twin fertility gods among the Germans, the Alcis, a pair of heavenly brothers whose priests dressed as women.[19] Myths of such twin deities can be found in as many northern European religions as in the south, and seem to have extended into many Baltic areas. There are references in Norse sagas to the mother of Thor, Fjorgynn, whose name also exists in an unexplained male variant, Fjorgyn. In the far north where Norway meets Finland, they were twin girls, Thorgerda and Irpa, or male and female skiers, Ull and Ullin. In farming regions (particularly in Sweden) they are a brother and sister, Frey and Freya, occasionally incestuous but always associated with fertility. South in Germany there are references to a Voll and Volla, possibly cognate. A different kind of fertility god could be found closer to the coast, where Tacitus recorded a German fertility goddess called Nerthus, possibly cognate with the Viking sea-god Njord, and if so, originally worshipped on Zealand, Denmark's largest island and the location of modern Copenhagen.

Njord and Nerthus, Frey and Freya are known collectively as the Vanir, a race of gods that was supplanted and largely replaced by a stronger, more warlike family of deities – perhaps earth-worshipping farmers overrun by sky-worshipping nomads, not once, but several times. Such an assumption may also help to explain the number of ungodlike enemies with which the Viking deities found themselves in conflict. A major group of rivals, for example, are the *Jotnar*, or Giants, a race whose names often contain elements of shifty duplicity, cunning and braggadocio. If the Jotnar were a race supplanted by proto-Scandinavians, then we might even guess at their original home, Jotunheim, in south central Norway.[20] The Jotnar are despicable to Norse eyes, violent and uncontrollable, creatures of the mountains, formidable foes, yet whose females are often regarded as desirable brides – a conqueror's view of the conquered. A leading adversary of the Jotnar is Thor himself, whose legends contain many hints that associate him as an unwelcome guest in the Jotunheim region. His mother, for a start, is a giantess herself, Fjorgynn, a mistress of Odin. In an area where goat-herding is a paramount local industry, we find that Thor quarrels with his neighbours over deaths of his flock. He rides in a chariot pulled by goats, and is sometimes referred to as *Oku-thorr*, the Charioteer – in both Old Norse and Sámi, the words for thunder and a wheeled vehicle are punningly similar.[21]

In Lapland, some shamanic drums show a male figure bearing a hammer in one hand and a swastika (thunderbolt) in the other, said to be *Horagalles*, the Norse *Thor-Karl*, or 'old man Thor'.[22] One of the most famous stories of Thor tells of his fight with a giant who leaves a piece of stone permanently embedded in his head. This may be a reference to a ritual at sacred sites of Thor, involving the striking of flint. In other words, with his red hair and beard, and his mastery of lightning, Thor may have been a fire-god, whose trials in myth are allegories of the kindling of sacred fires, and the smiting of foes.

Other races in the Viking mythos can be seen as similarly conquered peoples, associated in the Viking mind with a native mastery of the local woodlands and hills. Such peoples are the *huldufólk*, the 'hidden folk' identified in different parts of

Scandinavia by different names, and ultimately combined by later writers to form a menagerie of supernatural creatures.[23] The *álfar* or elves, for example, and their dark cousins the *dvergar*, or dwarves. Both are occasional allies of the gods, the dwarves renowned for their skills in metalwork, the elves as occasional bedmates and tormentors. At no point during the Viking Age was there any implication of diminutive size in either of these races – their role as the 'little people' of later centuries is thought to have been a function of the suppression of old religions with the onset of Christianity.

Bad dreams were brought by *mara*, a creature often associated with the image of the horse, and surviving today in our 'nightmare'. Other creatures seem to have been personifications of nature, bogeymen like the *thyrs* (ogre) or *troll*. Places of note gained their own guardian spirits, the *landvoettir*, while the ether was thought to crawl with other beings: nymph-like *dísir*, and the ghostly *gandir* and *verdir*. Verdir were often described as the spirits of the dead, able to communicate with the living or cause difficulties from beyond the grave. Other spirits said to interact with humans (or at least with their shamans) included the *fylgjur* ('fetches'), shadows or familiars of a human who watch over entire bloodlines, and *hamingjur*, guardian totem-spirits. Many sub-categories of the supernatural seem to have two names, possibly implying two traditions, that of the Aesir and Vanir, married together in an uneasy and often confused meeting of cultures.

Whatever the origins of these categories and distinctions, many only known to us through asides in sagas or other accounts, the basic belief structure of the Viking world is not too different from that of other pagan religions. It asks the same questions about life and death – what is the difference between a dead body and a living one? If there is a difference, and let us call it the absence of breath or a soul, then what happens to that soul when the body dies? Where did it come from? Can souls survive outside the body? Do animals have souls? Do trees and rocks have souls? If such souls have power, can we communicate with them? Can we appease them? Can we make them angry? In all such cases, who is it among us who can best communicate with them? Such questions are common to the origins of all religions, and Viking beliefs share, at their basic level, assumptions about the natural and supernatural world cognate with beliefs all across Eurasia, as far afield as Japan. It is only in the last decade that scholarly opinion has truly begun to accept the implications of this – that Asian shamanism may have as much to teach us about Viking religion as European paganism. This is particularly notable in the case of the Vikings, when we appreciate that many of the Vikings' shamans were not Indo-Europeans at all, but Finno-Ugric tribespeople of Lapland.[24]

Here, again, is a sign of opposing traditions struggling together in some way, with each enjoying greater prominence in different places. Norse sagas are riddled with reference to Lappish sorcery, and particularly to the mysterious spell-casting abilities of Finnish women. Old Norse even has a verb, *finnvitka*, which means 'to practise magic in a distinctly Finnish manner.'[25]

It would appear, from Norse sources, that when the Vikings wanted magic, they would 'pay a visit to the Finns', a term that survives in modern Swedish as a euphemism for visiting a fortune-teller. Hints of such sorcerous capabilities survive in several sections of Snorri's sagas, a Christian writing much later who wished to disassociate his true religion from the witchcraft of another race. Gunnhild Kingsmother, later to become the wife of Erik Bloodaxe, was supposedly sent among the Sámi to learn the ways of sorcery. As a mark of how she was hated by certain skalds, she was accused of seducing her teachers, using sexual favours to gain additional, secret magical knowledge from them. Much like witches or gipsies in other European traditions, Sámi women are rolled out by poets and skalds as the prophetic instigators of quests and missions. There are references in two sagas to a fateful party in Norway, visited by a sorceress who predicts that the host will soon leave his fatherland to settle in Iceland. Unwilling to leave his old life behind, the protagonist Ingjaldr instead hires three more Finnish seers to undertake a spirit-journey and verify the witch's prophecy. This they do, voyaging from their bodies in a locked house (a drug-induced trance, perhaps?), waking after three days to give a detailed account of the area that would become known as Vatnsdale in Iceland. Another settler in Iceland, so say the sagas, refused to leave Norway until he had sent a Finnish sorcerer to scout the coast, transformed into a whale to make the journey easier.[26]

Perhaps the greatest transformer of all is another of the Norse gods, all the more mysterious for not having any particular area of influence. Loki is a divine trickster, an unwelcome interloper in the hall of the gods, the instigator of childlike mischief that may have endeared him to younger audience members, even if his comedic misdeeds were later punished by the gods *in loco parentis*. Unlike other gods, Loki does not live on in place names in Scandinavia or Iceland. He is as unpredictable as fire (an element with which he is sometimes associated), and like Thor is the offspring of a union between an Aesir (one of Us) and a Jotnar (one of Them); his mother Fárbauti was a giantess. He may also be cognate with Louhi, the Finno-Ugric goddess of the underworld, whose sacred island lay at the south-westernmost tip of Finland, on the Viking trade route with Russia.

By the time Snorri compiled his sources, Loki had perhaps been influenced by several centuries of Christian lore, and was now seen as a far more devilish figure than he may originally have been. But even in his original tales, he appears to have been cunning. Loki works his way into many of the stories of the Vikings, appearing in cameo roles in tales of Odin, Thor and many other gods. But ultimately, it is he who is the cause of many of the gods' troubles. If something goes missing or is stolen in Asgard, it is Loki who gets the blame, and usually with justification. Loki is the jester of Odin's court, a figure of chaos in opposition to Odin's law, constantly taunting the other gods and meddling in their schemes with schemes of his own.

Loki was a great shape-shifter, although his transformations often brought him even more strife. When he wished to interfere with the building of the halls of Asgard, he transformed himself into a mare in order to distract the builder's stallion. The offspring of that union was Sleipnir, Odin's eight-legged steed. It is Loki who can transform into a fly to distract dwarven smiths, or a flea in an attempt to divest the goddess Freya of her precious necklace. He evades pursuit by transforming into a salmon, and even 'borrows' a bird-form from Freya (the sagas report this as if he is simply taking her car for a spin). Loki is the progenitor of all disasters, and the father of both the fearsome Fenris wolf, and Hel, the ruler of the underworld.

There are two disasters for which Loki is most famed. One is better known to Western civilization through its modern re-tellings. While wandering with Odin by a riverbank, Loki sees an otter eating a salmon, and flings a rock at it, hoping thereby to obtain two kills with one stone. Later, they discover that the otter was the shape-shifted form of their host's son, and that Loki has accidentally instigated a blood feud between the gods and the otter's brothers, Fafnir and Regin. There are elements here, perhaps, of ownership and hunting rituals – an animist need to somehow gain permission from a higher authority before hunting in the forests. Viking culture recognized that feuds and vendettas might arise, but also that the injured parties might be bought off with ransom or *manngjöld* – 'man-gold' or blood money. Hreidmar, father of the deceased, determines that the otter skin should be filled with gold, and then piled with further gold, until it is completely covered. Already in this tale we see history shining through the cracks – how might a skin be filled with gold? For the tale to make logistic sense, the gold would need to be in a readily usable form, anachronistic coins perhaps.

True to Viking form, Loki agrees to pay the *manngjöld*, and then sets off to steal it. Why? Surely he is a god, can't he do what he likes? Not if he is a 'god' in a story by an Icelander who would expect social retribution for misdeeds. Just as Loki seems peculiarly shifty for a divinity, he is also suspiciously poor. It would seem that the Viking gods might be able to transform themselves into animal figures, but lack any alchemical abilities to make wealth. As gods they seem rather impoverished, but this again may be a feature of the late telling of the tale. By the time of Snorri's compilation, the Norse gods had already been relegated to secondary status in the eyes of Christians. Although they may have been mighty in the eyes of their surviving followers, to the majority of the Icelandic audience their powers were in doubt.[27]

Loki realizes that the only way to gain that much gold is to steal it from the dwarf Andvari. Here, perhaps, we see a shaky justification for the persecution of a nearby rival tribe – necessity dictates that the gods, Our people, must appropriate resources from the dwarves, Their people. Andvari himself is able to change shape, and almost manages to hide from Loki by transforming himself into a fish. But Loki finally catches him, and pries every last piece of gold from him, including a golden ring to which Andvari clings desperately. The ring, says Andvari is the most precious artefact of all, for with it comes the power to gain a new hoard of treasure. Loki will hear none of it, which is fortunate, for when the skin of the otter is filled and covered as Hreidmar dictates, a single whisker can be seen poking through the top of the pile. Andvari's ring is vital to plug the final gap, and the ransom is paid.

The ring, however, is cursed, and Hreidmar's family eventually squabble over the hoard. Hreidmar is killed by his sons, and Fafnir transforms into a dragon to guard the gold. In what may be another reference to sibling rivalries over power in the Scandinavian region, Fafnir's brother Regin enlists the help of the young hero Sigurd, who kills the dragon, but steals the cursed ring for himself, ushering in another cycle of betrayal and revenge.

Thanks to the operas of Richard Wagner, the story of Andvari's ring is the most familiar to contemporary audiences, albeit in altered form. At the time of Snorri, however, greater resonance would have been felt among his audience for another tale of Loki – that of his greatest misdeed. As with many Viking myths, the story of Loki's betrayal of the god Balder presents an intriguing mess. There are elements of the story of Christ, and of Achilles, both tales that would have been known to the Icelandic audience, that would have muddied the original tale, whatever it may have been. It may even have had its origins as little more than a historical accident, for which a trickster god got the blame – *Beowulf* mentions a prince Herebeald, accidentally shot and killed by his brother Haethcyn.[28] The story also exists in two forms, one from Snorri and a partly contradictory one by Saxo, serving to remind us just how much of the rest of our knowledge of Viking lore issues from the pen of a single, uncontested writer.

Balder is an enigmatic god among the Vikings – if he had

tribal worshippers at any time, they must have died out, perhaps in a genocidal massacre of which his mythological death is a dim recollection. His name is cognate with 'Bright Day', leading some to believe that he was a sun- or sky-god after the fashion of Tiwaz, once highly regarded in Scandinavia, but supplanted by Odin- and Thor-worshippers before the commencement of the Viking Age. In both variants of the tale, Balder's story is one of supposed invincibility laid low. Snorri claims Balder to be Odin's most cherished son (shades here of the Biblical Joseph story) – unlike the bastard Thor, he is a child of Odin's true wife Frigg, who secures a promise from all birds, beasts and plants not to harm him. He is therefore invulnerable to all weapons, save mistletoe, a parasitic growth that escaped Frigg's notice. Consequently, Loki is able to find a loophole, fashioning a dart from the forgotten plant and enlisting the unwitting aid of Hoder, a blind god, whose functions in the saga seems solely to play Loki's patsy on this fateful occasion.[29] Hoder hurls the dart at Balder, who proves to be not so invulnerable after all, and is sent to the underworld, where further intrigues by Loki keep him.

The Saxo story is palpably different, and gives a much more prosaic interpretation. Saxo still spins a yarn, but one that seems much closer to the allegorical tribal feuds that inform so many other Norse tales. In Saxo's version, Balder is a warrior, raised by a race of amazons not named as valkyries *per se*, but with equivalent powers to choose the slain. He is rendered invulnerable by a peculiar diet of food drenched in snake poison, building a gradual immunity both to that and other sorts of danger. Balder is a god, hence one of Us, and keen to win the hand of the fair maiden Nanna. She, however, is also desired by Hoder, a human warrior (one of Them). Hoder realizes that he must fight Balder in order to gain Nanna, but to defeat him he will require a magic sword, guarded by the satyr Mimingus.[30] Saxo describes several battles between the forces of Balder and those of Hoder (suddenly, armies and fleets are involved, inflating the tale from simple argument to some sort of war). At the end of the prolonged conflict, Balder lies dying, wounded by the charmed sword. Hoder marries Nanna, but is later slain by Boe, a child of Odin conceived with the deliberate purpose of avenging Balder's death.

Both versions of the story also include a section in which a god (Odin in Snorri, Hermod in Saxo) must journey into the underworld, accounts whose origins could be anything from outright steals from the *Odyssey* or *Aeneid*, to allegories of spirit-trances, to poetic allusions to mundane hostage-taking and negotiations. Saxo's account is most notable for its lodging of the Balder myth firmly in the real world. Although elements of the tale are undeniably fantastical, Saxo includes details of Balder's tomb, and even the account of one Harald, a tomb-robber who broke into the burial mound in the twelfth century, only to be thwarted in his quest for treasure by subterranean floodwater.[31]

While slightly more believeable and rooted in reality, Saxo's tale lacks the big pay-off of Snorri's, for Snorri's version holds that the death of Balder will ultimately lead to the end of all things. Loki was held responsible both for Balder's death and for the technicalities that kept him in the underworld – Loki, it is assumed, transformed himself into a woman of the Jotnar who refused to weep for Balder, perhaps a reference to botched funereal rites. Rightly fearful of the fate that lay in store for him, Loki transformed himself into a salmon. Inventing the net in order to catch him (an idea the gods appear to have while staring drunkenly at the crossed charcoal twigs in the remains of a fire), the gods tie him to flat stones in the entrails of one of his sons. In an echo of the legend of Prometheus, he is left bound, beneath the mouth of a snake that drops poison on to his face. His wife holds a bowl to catch the poison, but each time she goes to empty it, Loki is left unprotected for a few moments, and his agonized writhing causes earthquakes.

While such an imprisonment represents the end of the road for Loki's troublemaking, it also marks his expulsion from Asgard and his feeling a new hatred for the gods that have treated him so. Next time he appears in Viking myth, it is in the apocalypse, as an agent of the enemies of the gods.

By the time a written record was made of the myths of Viking End Times, it is possible that the mythology had been seeded with ideas and concepts from Christian stories of the apocalypse. But the Viking world-view seems curiously terminal, with many elements aimed not at avoiding disaster, but at meeting it head-on. This may partly relate to a cycle of death and rebirth, a wheel of the seasons repeated on an annual basis. It may also have certain roots in climactic conditions in the Middle Ages. As the long summer of the Little Climactic Optimum began to tail off, the descendants of the Vikings lived amid palpable signs of declining temperature. Particularly in Iceland, where Snorri compiled his sagas, the seas were filling with pack ice at earlier times each year, and to a greater extent. This, then, might have had some influence on Snorri's concept of the *fimbulvetr*, a long period of great cold, in which the world inexorably became locked in ice – if this is the case, then his elaborate apocalypse owes more to his time than that of the Vikings whose myths he hoped to record.

As the climate cooled, the sagas claimed, there would be other signs of the End Times. Three cocks crow, one at the place of execution, another in the halls of the dead, a third in hell – the similarities with St Peter's infamous denial of Christ are too obvious. The world is engulfed in far-ranging wars, brother fights brother and rapes sister. The Fenris wolf either breaks free of its chains or is set free by an evildoer, and rampages through the earth and sky, eventually eating the sun. All chained beasts and monsters somehow escape their cages, and *Naglfar*, a ship made of the nails of corpses, puts out to sea, crewed by angry Jotnar, and helmed by Loki himself, the trickster god finally showing his true colours and defecting to the enemy. Other giants charge across the rainbow bridge of Bifrost, overwhelming Heimdall the faithful watchman, although he is able to blow his horn in warning – there are shades here of Gabriel's trumpet, or the *Song of Roland*, which would have entered popular consciousness a generation before Snorri compiled his *Edda*, but not necessarily of actual Viking myth. The weight of the fire giants causes the rainbow to collapse, and they fall to Earth, ready to join their ice giant cousins in a final battle on Vigrid, the plain of ice.

This, then, is *Ragnarok*, the doom of the gods to which Snorri claimed Norse mythology would strive, as each god meets his diametric opposite in a fight to the death. Odin, the Lord of Hosts, leads his undead warriors out of Valhalla – this is where the Vikings saw themselves on that fateful day, charging towards the hordes of giants with their fellow warriors at their side, amid an unearthly army of screaming Valkyries. Heimdall fights Loki (so much for the ship, and Heimdall's post at Bifrost). Thor fights his nemesis, the mighty World Serpent, smiting it with his hammer but drowning in its poison. Tyr faces Garm, the hound of hell he once bound. Or was it Fenris? No, it cannot be, because Fenris is fighting Odin himself. The wolf kills and eats the ruler of the gods, but Odin's son Vidar has a magical iron shoe, with which he stamps on Fenris's jaw, lifting up with all his strength to tear the wolf asunder. Frey fights Surt, the lord of the fire giants, and seems easily bested by him. But at the end, after the battle to end all battles, only Surt stands, flinging flames to all quarters, consuming the world in a terrible fire, itself only quenched when everything that was once the world of men is engulfed by the sea.

Once again, such an image could owe something to Christian iconography, but the images of fire and water as recorded by an Icelandic scribe offer another explanation. Of all the places in the Viking realm, Snorri's native Iceland was the place where the precarious nature of human existence was most obvious. It is, perhaps, no coincidence that such revelations of the apocalypse should issue from a place where geysers of steam shoot from the ground, and volcanoes push forth molten rock from the earth. As recently as 1965, when charged to come up with a name for a new volcanic island that had suddenly boiled forth from the sea two years previously, the Icelandic government settled on *Surtsey* – 'Surt's Isle'.

But the terrifying end of the Viking world was not complete. As with winter giving way to spring, it offered hope of redemption. Odin and the old gods might all be dead, but Ragnarok, we are told, does not mean the end for all life on Earth. Somehow, a handful of the younger gods have survived – particularly the god Balder, who was thought slain by an earlier trickery of Loki's, but who has now come back from the dead. In the shade of Yggdrasill, the World Tree, a man and a woman come forth, revealing that they have somehow weathered the fire and the flood that followed. In the sky, there is a daughter of the Sun, brighter still than the star that fell. Life begins again, in what could be an analogy of the changing of the seasons, or a faint apprehension that an old way had passed, and now was replaced with a new religion. That was certainly the case in Snorri's Iceland, which had set aside the old gods by vote in AD 1,000. Although pagan elements persisted for several generations, particularly among fortune-tellers and seers, Iceland had become Christian, and Snorri wrote of his ancestors' beliefs only after refracting them through the critical lens of Christianity. There is a certain symmetry in this, since it was through Christian eyes that the Vikings first appeared in chronicles of the west 500 years earlier. However, in AD 793 when they are first mentioned, they are far from the quaint forefathers of Snorri's compilations. To the people of Christendom, they were themselves a sign that the end of the world was nigh.

2

FURY OF THE NORTHMEN

FROM THE FIRST RAIDS TO HARALD BLUETOOTH

The eighth of June 793 was Médard's day, when the monks of Lindisfarne remembered a bishop who had bravely made a stand against paganism.[1] Two hundred years earlier, Médard had helped a Frankish queen flee the clutches of her violent husband, and had supposedly been sheltered from a storm under the wings of a great eagle. Stories led to superstitions, and it was said in some parts of Europe that bad weather on St Médard's day would remain for weeks on end.

The forecast was not good. Northumbria had recently been plagued by terrible weather, such that the *Anglo-Saxon Chronicles* reported 'immense flashes of lightning, and fiery dragons were seen flying in the air'. Earlier that year, superstitious parishioners in York had reported blood dripping from the roof of St Peter's church.[2] St Médard's day looked bad enough, but for many of the monks of Lindisfarne, it was their last. Quite without warning, a flotilla of sleek longships sailed out of the storm and on to the beach at the sacred island.

> They came . . . to the church of Lindisfarne, and laid all waste with dreadful havoc, trod with unhallowed feet the holy places, dug up the altars and carried off all the treasures of the holy church. Some of the brethren they killed; some they carried off in chains; many they cast out, naked and loaded with insults; some they drowned in the sea.[3]

The Vikings were not appreciably fiercer than any of the other races warring for control of Europe in the period. What distinguished them was their willingness to regard the clergy as legitimate targets. Whereas mundane towns and villages boasted defensive walls, forts and local militia, monasteries in particular stood exposed and undefended, their occupants not expecting attack, and consequently unable to put up much resistance. In many places, monasteries accumulated wealth simply *because* they were regarded as safe from attack – who would donate an ornate Bible or silver candlesticks if they expected thieves to carry them off?

It is unlikely that the raiders left their Norwegian fjords, pointed their ships to the south-west, and sailed in a straight line. Even by the late eighth century, navigation was a timid affair. The ships hopped from Scandinavia to the Shetland Islands, then south to the Orkneys. From there, vessels could sail on to the Hebrides and Ireland, or south along the east coast of Scotland and England. The Vikings knew these routes because they had used them for some time. Their earlier presence may not have been recorded because a few bands of roaming foreigners might escape the notice of chroniclers for a generation or more, particularly if they did nothing but sell amber or animal furs. The early Vikings clung to Britain's most distant areas, sheltering behind islands from Atlantic storms, just as they did along the Norwegian coast.

The Sack of Lindisfarne marks the official beginning of the Viking Age, but came after portents far more convincing than the omens of the chroniclers. For some time, there had been scattered whispers of trouble, many only recalled after it was too late. An archbishop in Kent wrote to his son 'of the thick infestations of wicked men in the provinces of the Angles and Gaul', while Irish chroniclers recorded settlers returning home from island colonies, forced to abandon them 'for the sake of the thieving Norsemen'.[4] A shield boss of Norwegian manufacture has been found in the Hebrides and dated to before 750 – it might have been a family heirloom, but its arrival in Scotland could have occurred at any point thereafter.[5]

More concrete evidence is available. Four years before the Sack of Lindisfarne, three longships arrived in the harbour of the Wessex town of Portland. They were met by a handful of horsemen, led by Beaduheard, the reeve of Dorchester. Assuming that they were travelling merchants, he berated them for not landing without the permission (and presumably, taxation) of Beorhtic, the king of Wessex. The strangers killed him on the spot, in what was the first Viking attack mentioned in the *Anglo-Saxon Chronicles*.[6] But even this minor incident does not appear to have been so isolated. The Vikings revealed that they were from Hardanger Fjord in west Norway, (at the time, the Norse and Anglo-Saxon languages were similar enough to permit rudimentary communication), and yet other reports called them merely Norsemen, or indeed Danes, suggesting that the slaying of Beaduheard was mixed with other incidents.[7] The Vikings were already known, as traders and, if one monk is to be believed, trendsetters – a letter of Alcuin mentions that Viking hairstyles were all the rage in Northumbria in the years before the attack.[8]

In 792, a year before the 'surprise' attack on Lindisfarne, the Mercian king Offa had ordered the construction of coastal defences in the east of England – hardly the act of a monarch unprepared for an attack. Mercia's preparation paid off, and kept it safe for many years. Northumbria, however, was not so lucky. In later generations, Vikings would attack in England in forces as big as armies, but there is no need to imagine that these first raiders were anything of the sort. It is, perhaps, no coincidence that Norse traders were already in the Hebrides, where could be found Lindisfarne's parent monastery of Iona. The following year, raiders hit another monastery in Jarrow, south of Lindisfarne, but a substantial number died in a storm.

In 795, significantly emboldened, a different group went on a spree in the Irish Sea, attacking Iona itself, Rathlin Island off the coast of Ireland, and Morganwg in South Wales. Other attacks followed in the same region. A modern-day criminal profiler would triangulate the attacks and look for an epicentre, concluding that these raiders did not sail each year from Scandinavia at all, but were already based somewhere in the west of Scotland. The Vikings always favoured islands just offshore for their winter bases, and the Hebrides seem to present the ideal location. It is also likely that there were more raids that remain unrecorded – large areas of Scotland and Ireland were poorly defended, and one of the Vikings' prime interests was in acquiring slaves – an activity that would have ensured no witnesses were left to report these hypothetical earlier attacks.

It remains possible, although unlikely, that those same three ships that caused the end of Beaduheard were responsible for most of the Viking attacks, including that on Lindisfarne, reported in the period at the end of the eighth century – after all, how many armed warriors would it *really* take to terrorize a church of peaceful scholar-monks? Our sources for the period are primarily the records and letters of the clergy, who felt the terror of the Vikings more than anyone else. The scholar Alcuin, then dwelling at the court of Charlemagne and fully aware of what waited beyond, was even moved to quote Biblical prophecy: 'Then the Lord said unto me, Out of the north an evil shall break forth on all the inhabitants of the land' (Jeremiah 1:14).

Viking life revolved around the war-band, called a *comitatus* by Latin chroniclers, who used the term in their own language for a general's personal retinue. A war-band comprised a leader, often a self-styled 'king', and his cronies. Sometimes barely enough men to fill a single longship, sometimes a veritable army, it was the defining unit of Viking life. A Scandinavian community without a war-band was simply a cluster of huts – it would eventually find itself facing aggressors, and be obliged to submit to someone else's war-band or to form one of its own. The war-band was an organism that lived to acquire possessions – it would roam in search of a territory of its own. It could be destroyed by a more powerful adversary, or it could seize the territory of another, acquiring land, women and wealth for itself. At that point, it would have fulfilled its basic function, and could be expected to fizzle out, losing its vitality. A war-band was not so much a parasite upon a community as an outlet for a community's bad seeds. A generation after the original raiders gave up on the raiding life, their many wives and concubines would have raised another horde of hungry mouths. Eventually, a new war-band would form, and go off in search of plunder, repeating the cycle once more.

To travel, they required the infamous Viking ship. As a community developed, and its wayward sons first turned to trade, a ship would permit them to travel further afield. In lean times, when traders had less to sell, and buyers had less to barter, ships became the vehicles of aggression, permitting the Viking group to remove itself from its own homeland to ruin somebody else's. The raiders of the eighth century were rulers of nothing but their own ships and men, either because they had never had anything else, or, as increasingly occurred, because they had been ousted from their homeland by another group of rivals.

One of the most famous Viking ships is the vessel found in 1880 in a burial mound in Gokstad, south Norway. Sometime around AD 900 a great Viking chieftain had been buried inside his vessel, intact in every detail but for the mast, which was hacked off to fit under the roof of the burial chamber. Whoever he may have been, the middle-aged man was laid to rest with a significant number of sacrificial animals: 12 horses, 6 dogs, and even a peacock.[9] The Gokstad ship was an improvement on earlier vessels from the Dark Ages. It had 16 pairs of oars – enough for a small crew of traders or, doubled-up, sufficient transport for a good-sized war-band. Along the gunwales were 32 shields, implying it was used for the latter purpose. There were, however, no seats for the oarsmen, leading archaeologists to presume that Vikings brought their own sea chests, somehow strapped them down, and used them in lieu of benches.

The Gokstad ship was remarkably preserved, despite the damage done by a party of grave robbers that had hacked through its side. Its state made it possible to seriously contemplate a replica, leading several modern entrepreneurs to build their own versions. The first and most famous was the *Viking*, constructed in 1893 as part of Norway's entry in the Chicago World Fair. The project was led by Magnus Andersen, the editor of a shipping magazine, who was determined to prove that the Vikings were not only superb seamen, but had sufficient technology to allow them to reach America. Some critics accused Andersen of taking a few too many liberties with his 'replica', including adding extra topsails, and giving it a deeper keel than the original Gokstad ship. Nevertheless, the *Viking* would eventually make the crossing to America in less than a month, with relatively little alteration to its ninth-century design.[10]

Actually building and sailing a Gokstad replica allowed Andersen to experience Viking sailing methods first-hand. Perhaps the most remarkable feature of the ship's construction was the use of clinker-building techniques, overlapping planks rendered watertight with tarred rope. Such construction made the ship highly flexible in rough seas, and may have given it precisely the advantage the Vikings required. If a ship could make it from Norway to Shetland, it could make it from there to the Faeroes or Scotland, and from *there* to Iceland or Ireland. The engine of the Viking invasion had been created.

The popular image is of Viking *warships*, fronted by a fearsome dragon's head, but such craft were of less practical use in making a long sea crossing. In fact, in the later days of the Viking Age, some communities deemed that dragon's heads were too frightful for local nature spirits, and had to be removed before a ship was permitted to approach land.[11] Many of the most famous Viking voyages were instead undertaken in a longship, with more capacity for booty, or a craft called a *knorr* – a much more conventional trading ship, with enough space to hold cattle or other livestock. The majority of Viking vessels were much broader at the front, leading to the Norse term of endearment *knerra-bringa* – 'a woman with a chest like a knorr'.[12]

Regardless of whether they moved by oars or sail, in a sleek longship or a rounded *knorr*, another mystery of the Viking expansion lies in their means of navigation. The Vikings did not have compasses, and no evidence has been found to confirm stories of a *sólarsteinn*, a crystal that somehow enabled Vikings to work out the position of the sun on cloudy days. Others have suggested that a broken wooden disc, found in Greenland in the twentieth century, might be the only extant example of the Vikings' secret weapon – a form of sundial that enabled them to compute compass points based on the shadow cast by a central spindle.[13] Such solar compasses were in use in Arab Aleppo in the fourteenth century, but that does not explain how one would end up in Greenland. The use of the solar compass is certainly a possibility, but why are there not significantly more examples? Or was this another of the secrets of Odin?

Towards the close of the Viking Age, civilized by contact with the Christian West, many descendants of the Vikings would attempt to reform their old ways, but the front line of the Viking expansion was undeniably brutal. Even in later medieval Iceland, when the Viking spirit was supposedly somewhat tamed, there were still vestiges of a code based on bravado and at the most basic level, one's willingness to defend one's actions in trial by combat. As Hromund the Lame puts it: 'It's the way of Vikings to make their gains by robbery and extortion, but it's the way of thieves to conceal it afterwards.'[14] Among the belligerent Vikings any argument could be settled by a fight, and as long as no blood was drawn, it was supposed to be forgotten in the morning.[15]

The Vikings often seemed more afraid of slander than they were of violence. Perhaps this is a subjective viewpoint, introduced by enterprising skalds wishing to emphasize the importance of leaving a good saga behind after one's death, but nonetheless, the available sagas are riddled with anecdotes of playful insults that get out of hand. But they are also full of nicknames that somehow stuck, perhaps because their owners rather enjoyed the implications, or admitted that the sobriquets had some element of truth. Names such as Erik the Victorious and Bodvar the Wise recall great deeds; Eyjolf the Lame and Eyvind the Plagiarist are less impressive; others like Halli the Sarcastic and Ivar Horse-Cock beggar belief.

Masculinity seems to have been a particularly sore point with the Vikings – cross-dressing by either sex was grounds for immediate divorce, and the greatest insult one could deliver to a Viking was to accuse him of behaving in an effeminate manner.[16] Homosexuality was not unknown, but talk of it seems to have been repressed. One Viking in a saga is heard to accuse an enemy of submitting to anal sex, while foreign observers occasionally implied that the rituals of Viking sorcery may have involved some form of blurring of gender boundaries. It is still a mystery as to why the grave of one Swedish wizard was found to contain the body of an elderly man from Lapland, clad in women's clothes.[17]

Women were to weave, tend to domestic animals, grind corn, cook and warm the beds. Their objectification in saga poetry reaches remarkable heights – it seems complimentary for a Viking poet to describe a woman as a display unit for jewellery. Viking females are described as 'sleighs for necklaces', as 'guardians of gold', or as 'ring-wearers'. Insult a woman, of course, and you would also insult her man, a permanent threat that led to an uneasy form of etiquette, misogyny held barely in check. The most powerful women are still mainly defined by their male relatives – most women in the sagas have patronymics instead of nicknames, although there are self-explanatory exceptions like Thorkatla Bosom and Hallgerd Long-legs. The most notorious Viking women held power through their children: such as the legendary queens Sigrid the Haughty and Gunnhild Kingsmother. Such women could command indirect respect, through the power inherent in their dowries and marriages. They had the right of inheritance and control over the home, and for the marks of the respect that some might command in the afterlife, we need only turn to contents of some of their graves.

There is no historical evidence for the existence of the legendary Viking chieftain Halfdan the Black, or indeed his mother, Queen Asa, although it has been suggested that this Norwegian lady may have been the occupant of a ship-burial found at Oseberg in 1903.[18] The mound was over 120 feet long and just below 20 feet high, earth shovelled over a ship facing to the south, her prow pointing at the sea. Inside, archaeologists found two skeletons – a young woman whose corpse had been partly tugged away from its resting place by later robbers, and an accompanying older woman. One of them was a luckless slave, accompanying her mistress into the afterlife.

The women were buried with rich accoutrements – beds, pillows and blankets, chests full of supplies, looms and even 'elf-tremblers', rattles designed to scare off evil spirits. The ship was large enough to hold a carved carriage, four sledges and kitchen utensils. Whoever the occupant of the grave was, she was of a family powerful enough to attract fine artisans, in a culture that could support such fripperies above and beyond the harsh demands of subsistence. The Oseberg ship was not built for raiding. It would have lacked the speed, and its oarports were devoid of any means of holding back waves from heavy seas. It was designed for luxury alone, a rich woman's transport, presumably around a peaceful territory.

Our information about Asa and her son Halfdan the Black is dubious, coming in the early chapters of Snorri's *Heimskringla*. For Snorri, however, the story of Halfdan the Black is where his tales of gods and supernatural deeds begin to dovetail with the historical world. Though Halfdan's existence may be difficult to prove, that of his son and grandsons is not.

Somewhere between here and the end of this chapter, the legends begin to fade and we find ourselves discussing people who really existed. Exactly where is still debatable.

According to Snorri, a small chiefdom on the coast of the Vik expanded during the days of one ruler, Halfdan the Stingy, and again under the management of his heir, Guthroth the Generous. Guthroth was able to push his borders up to the site of modern Oslo, by marrying Alfhild, daughter of the king of Alfheim – these 'elves' being one more local people subsumed into the growing territory. Alfhild gave Guthroth a son, Olaf Geirstatha-Alf, but then died, leading Guthroth to marry Asa, beautiful daughter of the neighbouring kinglet Harald Red-Beard. Red-Beard had refused permission, and paid with his life, when Guthroth took the country, and the young Asa, by force.

Asa gave Guthroth a son, Halfdan the Black, but arranged her husband's assassination when the boy was still barely a year old. Official sources claimed that the king had drowned after a drunken banquet, but Asa made no secret of the truth – she had asked for someone to spear him and throw him into the sea. Asa then returned to her homeland, where she ruled in the name of her infant son. Guthroth's eldest, Olaf Geirstatha-Alf, ruled Guthroth's old territory until Halfdan the Black reached the age of maturity. The boys then shared the rulership of the land between them, until Olaf Geirstatha-Alf died in his fifties, leaving the entire area to Halfdan. Reference in *Heimskringla* to a leg disease, and signs of crippling arthritis in the knee-joint of the Gokstad body both point to Olaf as a likely candidate for the man in that ship-grave.[19]

Halfdan's domain increased by traditional means. He fought a brief war with the neighbouring region of Heithmork, and won the land for himself. Before long, his borders had extended all the way to Sogn on the coast of the sea, which he secured for his descendants by marrying Ragnhild, the daughter of Sogn's ruler Harald Goldenbeard. He died barely into his forties, drowning when he fell through the thawing ice on a lake, leaving a ten-year-old heir, Harald Fairhair. Immediately, other neighbouring states sensed their chance to move in, and Fairhair's regents were threatened with a series of attacks. Such was life in southern Norway around AD 860, a petty series of strikes and counter-strikes by war-bands jostling for supremacy.

Things were slightly different just to the south, over the swirling waters of the Skagerrak strait that divides Norway from continental Europe. The feuds and skirmishes of southern Norway were the last remanants of a barbaric tradition dating back through the many tribal conflicts of the Dark Ages. In Europe proper, rulers were thinking on a much larger scale. There was more infrastructure, tax revenues made larger public works possible, and the petty local feuds of olden times had now grown into much larger feuds, albeit just as petty.

While the Norwegians had dealings with isolated islands and forest peoples, it was the Danes who had to deal with the outside world. Denmark was situated on a vital trade route, the only way from civilized Europe into Scandinavia and the Baltic. For two thousand years, Denmark had been the conduit for delivering goods between those two worlds. And Denmark's Jutland peninsula was connected directly to the European mainland, hence witness to the thirty years of war that engulfed Germany at the end of the eighth century. In the distant land of the Franks, peace had broken out, and along with it enough political unity to create a region that fancied itself as an inheritor of Rome. Its king, Charles the Great, *Carolus Magnus* or more commonly, Charlemagne, desired to do what his Roman predecessors could not, and secure the north-eastern border of his empire by conquest.

The fighting began in 772, four years after Charlemagne ascended his throne. His war was fought on military and spiritual fronts, with the Saxons spared retribution if only they would submit to the rule of Christ, and his earthly representative, Charlemagne. He had no truck with paganism; one of the first acts of his soldiers was the destruction of Irminsul, the sacred column that the Saxons believed held up the sky. The impact of the Frankish war on the Saxons was felt in Denmark in the form of refugees, particularly in 777 when the Saxon leader Widukind sought sanctuary with the Danes. By 800, when Charlemagne was proclaiming himself to be the new emperor of the west, his actions had provoked the Danes on to the offensive. The Danish king Godfred led a campaign south of the Baltic against some pagan allies of Charlemagne, destroying the ancient trading post of Reric and, inadvertently it would seem, making the Danish port of Hedeby the centre of the Baltic trading world by default. Hedeby sat inland a way down the Danish peninsula, at the end of a long inlet that cut halfway into the land from the east.

Hedeby was perilously close to the new realms of Charlemagne, behind a remarkable rampart that established a border with the south. In time it was augmented, so that it reached from a river estuary on the North Sea side, all the way to Hedeby's Baltic coast, a construct of earth and wooden palisade known as the *Danevirke*. It also permitted swift access to the Baltic to the Danes and their allies. It was now possible to sail from the North Sea up the Eider estuary and its Trene tributary, unload cargo and carry it a mere eight miles in relative safety, before reaching Hedeby and its access to the Baltic.[20] It was long believed to have been constructed to defend Denmark from Charlemagne, but dendrochronological analysis of the tree-rings of the wood from the palisade reveals that parts of the Danevirke were built considerably earlier than that, around 737, long before the perceived threat of the Franks.[21]

Denmark was a strong enough kingdom by the beginning of the ninth century to have a sense of its own borders and the organization required to define them. It also had a strong enough sense of hegemony to feel threatened by the further encroachment of the Franks. The Danevirke may have established a southern border, but Denmark had interests that lay even further to the south, fanning out from Frisia on the North Sea coast, through Saxony and Germany directly to the south, and to the Baltic tribes to the south-east. As the Romans found, the region presented enough problems to encourage a solution by treaty instead of conquest. With enemies pressing at other points on his vast borders, Charlemagne wanted trouble to go away, and by raiding Frisia in ships, Godfred made it clear that he could make a lot more if he wanted.

The Frankish offensive continued in the spiritual realm. Charlemagne's son, Louis the Pious dispatched missionaries to his frontiers, and, it is said, the first Viking converts were made sometime around 825. In 826, Louis sent a 25-year-old missionary called Anskar, who enjoyed a short-lived period as a Christian preacher in Hedeby, before he was forced to leave by enemies of his patron. Anskar next tried his luck in Sweden in 829. Attacked by pirates, he and his companion lost all their possessions and eventually limped into Birka with nothing but the clothes on their backs. It is no coincidence that these early missionaries concentrated their energies on trading posts, where Christian travellers might be found in greater quantities, and where homesick itinerant traders might be more amenable to tales of a new religion. The backward hinterland could wait until after the missionaries had achieved some success in the more cosmopolitan towns.

Anskar and others like him endured an uneasy relationship

with the pagan Vikings. They were regarded less as messengers of Christianity than as flunkies of the empire to the south, and their presence was often barely tolerated. Nevertheless, the Vikings were not above being impressed by military might, and the claims of the imperial messengers to represent a stronger, more enduring faith than that of the old gods eventually began to influence their hosts, albeit not without a few missionaries martyred at the hands of irate pagans. As far as the empire was concerned, all of Scandinavia was thereafter the responsibility of Anskar, now made the archbishop of the new fort of Hammaborg (Hamburg). As far as Scandinavia was concerned, the Christian missionaries with their messages of humility and an Almighty God were a minor irritation best left unscratched until it was safe to do so.

In 840, Louis died, resulting in a struggle for the succession between his sons Lothar, Charles the Bald and Louis the German. The northern coast of Europe, formerly a risky target for Scandinavian raiders, was left undefended as the Franks warred among themselves. The Danes lost little time in taking advantage of the weakness of their former adversary, pushing south with a fleet of ships to attack and destroy Hamburg. Anskar escaped with his life, and undertook another mission in 849. By now the Franks were, again, no longer an ally to trifle with, and the Danish king Horik, an aging man with strife in his own family, accepted a new mission from the Christians. He may have hoped, or indeed been promised, that openness to missionaries would bring political advantages. When he died, his sons killed each other in a series of bloody conflicts, until a single survivor, Horik the Younger, ascended the throne in 853. Despite pressure from a heathen faction within his kingdom, Horik the Younger not only continued his father's permissive attitude towards the Christians, but even allowed the rebuilt Hedeby church to have a bell, the sound of which was an alien and unwelcome thing to the local heathens.

Each time Christians were in Denmark for any lengthy period, we gain a glimpse of the heathen population from the missionaries' writings. From notes made by Anskar and his successor Rimbert, and from reports made by other Christians, we know that Denmark by the late ninth century was not the monolithic single kingdom implied by earlier dealings with the Franks. In fact, we are not even sure if Godfred was the ruler of all Denmark at the start of the epoch, although *someone* in the region had certainly been powerful enough to organize the construction of the Danevirke. After the death of Horik the Elder, it is far more likely that there were a number of 'kings' not of Denmark but *in* Denmark, and is even possible that Horik the Younger's brothers were not eliminated as other accounts imply.

According to the chronicler Adam of Bremen, Denmark had at least two 'kings' in 873, and they too were supposedly brothers, Sigfred and Halfdan.[22] Wherever they may have reigned, they were at constant odds with other rulers, most likely dotted among the Danish islands, since the prime activity of the rival 'kings' was said to be piracy. In other words, we see Denmark assuming the characteristics for which it was associated throughout the Viking Age: a series of domains ruled by rival chiefs, occasionally giving allegiance to the most powerful overlords, but generally in conflict with each other.

By the 890s, the answer to exactly who was in charge of Denmark eluded the kings themselves. No less an authority than Svein Estridsen, who claimed descent from the kings of the period and in his own time became ruler of Denmark himself late in the eleventh century, was reportedly unable to say for sure which of his ancestors had ruled when when questioned on the matter by the chronicler Adam of Bremen.

There are confused references to a peaceful king called Helgi, soon supplanted by Olaf, a Swede who ousted this rightful ruler. Olaf's two sons split the realm between them, although Sweden seemed to be in other hands by then. Before long, the usurper Hardegon took all Denmark for himself.

Whatever the truth of it, by 900 the Swedes were in a position to take control of certain Danish areas for themselves. They were less interested in the island enclaves and Jutland farms than they were in Hedeby, a centre of trade that many of them would have visited with merchant ships from Gotland and points east. For a while, the area was under Swedish control, but in 935, when we enter a better documented period with some relief, Denmark was back in Danish hands.

When the internecine struggles were finally over and missionaries were able to visit and report once more on Denmark, the land was resolutely pagan, thanks chiefly to its leader Gorm the Old. Gorm had no time for the new-fangled Christians; instead he had purged Denmark of many petty kings and warlords, until, it appears, just one remained, an earl in northern Jutland. Gorm married the earl's daughter Thyri, and their son inherited the lands of them both. Thyri's tombstone at the ancient burial site of Jelling refers to her, or perhaps her husband, as the 'Glory' or 'Improvement' of Denmark, the first time that a Danish source had referred to the region by that name – earlier references had all been in the work of foreign authors.

But while Gorm was a pagan, his son Harald Bluetooth would accept Christianity into his kingdom and his life. By now, the political advantages were impossible to ignore. Christianity was gaining sway all over Europe, and sentiments of Christian brotherhood were much more useful to the beleaguered ruler than yet another round of squabbles. Acceptance of Christianity, even in name only, effectively shut off a number of political conflicts along Harald's southern borders.

Harald Bluetooth also ensured that his rule was strictly enforced. His reign saw the construction of five gigantic circular forts, two in Jutland, one in southern Sweden, one on Fyn, and the last at Trelleborg in Zealand. The design of these 'Trelleborg' forts seemed inspired by similar constructions in the realm of the Franks, massive defensive works, protecting an inner area that formed a military base and place of trade.[23] Most importantly, the Trelleborg forts were an impressive symbol of kingly power, and are thought to have functioned as places to collect the king's tax. Harald Bluetooth had moved away from the old wandering collection of plunder that characterized his ancestors, and instead made a decisive step towards Denmark as a centralized kingdom.

The Christian rulers to the south became his spiritual brothers, everyone was friends, trade flowed and everything was peaceful again, except that is for the dispossessed heathens, who carried out a series of raids on the rest of Europe; Harald could wash his hands of responsibility for them, since they were outlaws and his loyal subjects were Christians. Harald Bluetooth's acceptance of Christianity brought Denmark into the Christian realm; it effectively moved the border of conversion several hundred miles north. The Danes had a new excuse to prey upon the heathens of Norway.

3

GREAT HEATHEN HOSTS

HIGHLANDS, ISLANDS, IRELAND AND ENGLAND

If claims in *The Saga of the People of Laxardal* are anything to go by, the Norwegians had long been raiding the coasts of the Scottish isles.[1] DNA evidence from the Orkneys and Shetlands presents an even clearer indication: these have not only many Scandinavian place names, but also the highest concentration of Norwegian DNA outside Scandinavia. A debate still rages, however, about the nature of the Viking settlement there. Local sheep have interbred with Norse sheep to create a unique strain, but for Norwegian sheep to be on the islands in the first place, they would have to be brought there by ship. Many of the Vikings on the Shetlands and Orkneys not only raided, but also stayed.

The Orkney Islands have given up several ship burials. In 1991, on the north-eastern island of Sanday, excavation commenced on what turned out to be a family ship burial – a man, woman and child. The man was buried with the accoutrements of a warring life, the woman with tools and materials for housekeeping and weaving. Her brooch was a Scandinavian design, dating to the middle of the ninth century, precisely the time when Viking raiders would have had a whole generation to reconnoitre their targets, and perhaps decide to settle in one of them. The Orkneys would have been an especially tempting prospect for a Viking. They were sufficiently distant from the upheavals in Scandinavia, but still within sailing distance should the need arise. They are also islands, and no Viking willingly settled in a location that didn't guarantee him some sense of defensive security.

Much of the scattered signs of Viking habitation in the Orkneys are relatively recent – runic graffiti in a burial mound, for example, whose carvers boast they are on their way to Jerusalem, presumably at the time of the Crusades.[2] *Orkneyinga Saga*, an account of life in the islands until the twelfth century, only recounts bizarre legends for the early period. For the time the first pioneers were building their crofts and appeasing or fighting with the islands' Pictish natives, their later skalds could only discuss a strange creation myth that places the families' origins in the lands of the Finns and the Kainu. By the time the *Orkneyinga Saga* begins in earnest in the ninth century, the Vikings have already been in the region for a generation or so. Runic and circumstantial evidence suggests that they overwhelmed the local population, but not necessarily in an openly belligerent way. Pictish words persisted in the local language, implying that at least part of the next generation was reared by local girls. Unlike many other Viking settlements, however, some of the men in the Orkneys do appear to have arrived with their Scandinavian wives. Orkney and Shetland were colonization attempts, and successful ones, that would eventually form the bridge to points even further east. As time went on, the Vikings would also infest the northern extremities of Scotland – Caithness, Sutherland and, in the west, the Hebrides. From there it was but a short trip to another Viking stronghold the Isle of Man, and then Ireland.

The Vikings found a different kind of world in Ireland – if anything, it was one into which they fitted quite well. Like Scotland, Ireland had been largely unaffected by the Romans. It was a barbarian region of independent crofts and home-steads, widely separated without intermediate places of ex-change that deserved the name of town or village. Instead, local overlords afforded 'protection' (or rather, extorted pro-tection money) from the nearby settlements. The political unit was the clan (*tuath*), and the symbol of local authority was a fortified island (*crannog*) or a ring-fort (*rath*). One 'high king' supposedly ruled over all the others, although such suzerainty was often a subject of some argument among several con-tenders and rival families, often with as many as five simulta-neous candidates. At the time of the arrival of the Vikings, the Ui-Neill clan's hold on power was beginning to fragment, while the rulers of the Munster region were gaining control of an increasingly larger territory.

Christianity already held sway in Ireland, but Irish monks were often as belligerent as their secular countrymen, even involving themselves in battles. In the seventh century, the Ionan monk St Adamnan felt obliged to issue a directive against monks, women and children participating in battles. Nor were the Irish strangers to the idea of plundering mon-asteries. Raiding parties, seeking to rob rival clans of cattle, produce or other wealth, were not merely a known, but an accepted part of the Irish year – in their attacks on their enemies, they were as seasonally predictable as the Vikings themselves. Since monasteries were affiliated to clans, and often used as repositories of wealth, primitive precursors of modern banks, it was not unknown for them to be targets.

Whereas the very idea of raiding a monastery was a terrible sin in the eyes of the Anglo-Saxons, to the Irish it was not an unthinkable idea.[3]

When the Vikings first arrived as isolated plundering parties on the coast, few of the local clans permitted this to distract them from their ongoing family feuds. It was only a generation later, when the raiding parties were transformed into much larger fleets, that the Irish began to take notice. By the 830s, the Vikings were arriving in greater numbers, staying for longer, and even over-wintering in Ireland ready for a second season of raiding. Ireland's rivers and lakes permitted them to travel deep into the country. In a land that had never been conquered by the Romans, roads were all but unknown. The most reliable form of travel was by boat, so monasteries and homesteads clustered by the riverbanks all the way into the interior. The Vikings were able to sail their ships deep into Ireland and take what they wanted, although not without local resistance.

Longships in force plundered Armagh in 832. The following year, they were back in Louth, Columcille and south as far as Lismore in Waterford. By 834, they had clearly decided that pickings were rich in the south, and the *Annals of Ulster* report a series of raids in County Wicklow.

Around the same time in the twelfth century that the saga-writers of Iceland were reaching their literary peak, a similar endeavour in Ireland attempted to chronicle the history of the Irish. The result was the highly unreliable *Wars of the Irish with the Foreigners*, which told the tale of the arrival of the Vikings from the point of view of just one of the ruling dynasties, to the detriment of any role played by others like the Ui-Neill. *The Wars of the Irish* presents the Vikings as vicious raiders descending from the sea, much the same as the English chronicles. But as with the English chronicles, the later

Irish writers only gave one side of the story. The Vikings were not always unwelcome and, in fact, many of them were hired by local clans intent on defeating their rivals, and fought as mercenaries with the promise of plunder and land to settle. Intermarriage between Viking men and Irish women seems to have been commonplace at all social levels, from the lowliest warrior to the highest king. In recent times, archaeologists have been forced to rethink their earlier assumptions – it is no longer assumed that if a Viking grave is found to contain Irish wealth, then that must have been stolen. Some of the Norse killing in Ireland was done at the instigation of and with the approval of some of the Irish themselves.[4]

The Viking assaults increased in the 830s thanks to the arrival of a war leader that the locals call Turgeis, presumed by linguists to have been a corruption of Thorgils or perhaps Thorgest. Had he survived to bring his wealth and power back to Scandinavia, he might have gained himself some fawning skalds and a saga that cleared up such questions. We can only piece together his life from references in the literature of his enemies. Sifting through the contradictory references, comparing rival chronicles and archaeological evidence, we gather that someone with such a name arrived on Ireland's far western shore and sailing deep inland up the River Shannon, plundered the cream of the local monasteries, the inhabitants of which must have regarded themselves as safe from pirate assault, since they were often as much as 100 miles inland.

Whoever Turgeis was, he was in for the long haul. He and others like him founded semi-permanent bases from which to continue their plundering. As in other areas subject to Viking assault, they favoured island retreats at river mouths, or fortified positions on lakes. Around 841, one such base was founded in the wedge of ground where the River Poddle met the River Liffey, at a marshy place the locals called 'the black pool' – *Dubh Linn*. The Viking settlement may have begun as a temporary fortress, but soon became more permanent.

Just how permanent became clear in the 1840s, when work on a railway line uncovered Viking cemeteries at Islandbridge and Kilmainham near modern Dublin. The find is less useful than it would have been if discovered today, since Victorian archaeologists were keener on buried treasure than carefully logging the details of what they found. However, it was catalogued by William Wilde (father of the more famous Oscar) and yielded a rich haul of swords, spears and shield-bosses, mainly from Norway, although some display signs of Frankish workmanship. Certain items had been made locally, indicating that the Viking settlement was permanent enough to have a smithy. The graves were also found to contain women, buried with distinctly Norse jewellery, necklaces and household implements such as spindles, needles and smoothers. Some of the brooches seemed to have been fashioned from book-clasps – in other words, the ornate bindings of priceless Bibles and lost chronicles, levered off before the books themselves were cast into a fire or left to rot in the dirt. The women in the Islandbridge graves were Norse, not Irish, and their presence implies that at least some of the Vikings in Ireland were planning on staying.[5] Other graves contained black-smiths, farmers and merchants, buried with their scales and measures. It would appear that by the end of the ninth century, the Vikings of Dublin were still embarking upon raids and wars, but were also established in a relatively peaceful settlement.

Other place names in Ireland reflect Viking origins: *Vikingalo* (Wicklow), *Veisufjordr* (Wexford), *Hlymrekr* (Limerick) and *Vedrafjordr* (Waterford). The Vikings were still referred to as *gaill* (foreigners) by the Irish, but the use of the term took on a tribal context. The locals had begun to regard the newcomers as part of the scenery – the *gaill* became one more rival tribe to be dealt with, and Turgeis was regarded as their king. After casting out the abbot of Armagh Abbey, the local Irish saw his occupation of the Abbey as a sign of his attempt to set himself up as a religious leader, allowing later writers to interpret his raids as a heathen attempt to spread the religion of Thor. This idea was helped considerably by the blasphemous behaviour of Turgeis's wife Aud, who danced on the altar of Clonmac-noise, and supposedly performed rites of witchcraft there.[6]

By 845, Turgeis and his men were holed up in a heavily defended position on Lough Ree in the centre of Ireland. However, he came to a suitably bad end, drowned in Lough Owel in County Westmeath during a fight with a local clan. A more detailed yet still unlikely story claims that the devilish Aud was not enough for Turgeis, and that instead he lusted after the daughter of a local king Mael Sechlainn. In what could be a garbled reference to a dynastic pact that went awry, Mael Sechlainn sent his daughter to Turgeis, with 15 beautiful handmaidens in attendance. Turgeis arrived with 15 of his companions, clearly expecting a night to remember, only to discover that the 15 Irish beauties were youths from Mael Sechlainn's army. Dressed in women's clothes and with their beards shaven off, the youths supposedly looked good enough to fool the Vikings until it was too late, revealing their true nature only as the Vikings took them in their arms and felt the cold iron of their concealed daggers.[7] Perhaps a confused reference to a thwarted gang rape, perhaps a story wholly invented, the death of Turgeis entered Irish legend, and soon there were others like him.

Around 851, the Norwegian invaders had to fight off an incursion of other Vikings – a group of Danes arrived from England or Scotland, and tried to seize the plunder that the Norwegians had been carefully amassing for themselves. The

Irish were now obliged to distinguish between two groups of foreign invaders – the 'white' Norwegians or *Finngaill*, and the 'black' Danes or *Dubhgaill*. The new arrivals were, however briefly, welcomed by some of the tribes, who were prepared to exploit Viking rivalry to their own ends. The Danes were enlisted to fight on behalf of the Irish, and fought the Norwegians around Carlingford Lough, near County Down. The Danes were victorious, and, when told that Saint Patrick himself had supported them, they even offered gold and silver to the representatives of the saint. This endeared them even further to the Irish, who mistakenly regarded the Viking newcomers as devout Christians, prepared to regard the local people as spiritual brothers.

Before long, the tables were turned. Olaf the White led his Norwegian men in a fierce counter-campaign, chasing the Danes out of the area and firmly establishing himself as a local king – in fact, the first Viking king of Dublin. His victory was so impressive (or, perhaps, threatening), that the locals were swift to accept him, even paying *manngjöld*, Scandinavian-style, in atonement for the death of Turgeis.[8]

Olaf was was not above dealing with the local Irish, and married the daughter of the petty kingdom of Osraige. Olaf, his brother Ivar and their supporters fought on the side of Osraige during his kingdom's brief rebellion against the 'high king' of the southern Ui-Neill, although the Irish soon had cause to regret the presence of the foreigners among them. Deprived of the expected plunder, in 863 Olaf and his fellow Vikings instead decided to rob the grave mounds of the River Boyne, breaking their way into the tombs of ancient Irish nobles. Before long, the clans of Osraige and the Ui-Neill had decided they preferred the devil they knew, and concluded a reluctant peace. Without an excuse for fighting, and facing a united front of local Irish, Olaf led his Vikings in search of easier pickings in Scotland.

The Vikings maintained a presence in Dublin, and Olaf was sure to return to raid Armagh to remind them who was boss, but in 866 it was Scotland that took the full brunt of the Viking offensive. After inflicting a crushing defeat on the Britons at the mouth of the River Clyde, Olaf returned to Ireland for just long enough to profit from the sale of many hundreds of prisoners of war into slavery. He then returned to Scotland, leaving the unsure Irish possessions in the hands of his brother Ivar. Olaf was officially the ruler of the Vikings in Ireland until 871, when he was slain in a forgotten battle somewhere in Norway. His brother Ivar then took on the role of ruler, with a title that implied hegemony not only over the Vikings in Ireland, but also in 'Britannia', presumably Northumbria.

Northern England had fallen to a 'Great Heathen Host' in the late 860s, led by the 'brothers' Halfdan the Wide-Grasper, Ivar the Boneless and Ubbi.[9] They landed in East Anglia, wintered there, and then headed north. Above the Humber, *Northan Hymbre*, was Northumbria, its capital, the ancient city of York – Roman Eboracum. The Vikings occupied the old Roman centre of the town, utilising the ruined walls and fortifications constructed many centuries earlier by the legions. Roman architecture was built to last, and before long the Vikings had jury-rigged an impressive battlement to protect them from the locals.

On 21 March 867, the rival kings of Yorkshire Osbert and Aella agreed that it was best to get rid of the Viking newcomers before they settled their own quarrel. Although some broke into the refortified Roman compound, the Vikings still won the day, and killed both the kings.

With Northumbria now in Viking hands, Ivar's host headed south, where he conquered East Anglia, capturing the local ruler Edmund, tying him to a tree, and using him for target practice. When the time came for the king to be killed, the

Vikings favoured the 'blood-eagle' sacrifice, wrenching his ribs away from his spine and pulling out his lungs. At least, that is what later writers have claimed – it remains possible that Edmund's end, while gruesome, may not have been quite so grotesquely ritualized.[10]

South of Northumbria lay Mercia and Wessex, two kingdoms ripe for the picking. But Ivar and his associates seemed happy with what they had. Northumbria remained in Viking hands, and the Vikings became part of the local population. Ivar's heathen host had tired of warring, and now had won that most important of treasures, land. Furthermore, if they had headed any further south, they would have run into trouble, not only from the Mercians and West Saxons, but also from *another* heathen host. 871 saw the arrival of Guthrum, a new Viking leader with his own band of men in search of English resources. However, the two southernmost kingdoms put up a much better fight.

In April 871, the southern kingdom of Wessex got a new king, Alfred. The youngest son of Aethelwulf (r.839–58), Alfred had enjoyed a far-travelled early life. When he was only a child, he made two journeys to Rome itself, where Pope Leo IV had confirmed him as a godson, and given him the honorary title of a Roman consul. On the second trip, as a six-year-old boy, Alfred had seen European diplomacy in action, as his father concluded an alliance between Wessex and the Franks. One by one, he had seen his elder brothers die during his teens, until, with his nephews too young to rule, Alfred became the king of Wessex.

Alfred's first year as king was not a good start, known as the Year of Battles. For a decade, southern England had been plagued by a roving army of Vikings, first in Kent, then points north, then Reading, then Cambridge. The size of the 'Great Army' is difficult to gauge, although we know from the excavation of a mass grave in Repton that 200 of them succumbed to disease over the winter of 873–4.[11] Some came direct from Denmark, others seem to have arrived via France – the Franks successful in moving them on.

By 876 the 'Great Summer Army' led by the Viking Guthrum had relocated to Dorset, wandering the countryside unchecked. Alfred's warriors followed the army, engaging with it occasionally, but barely controlling its excesses. As the armies headed south, however, there were signs of weariness in both. Alfred and the Vikings made a peace treaty in Wareham on the south coast, and, as a sign of the desperation of the situation, Alfred was even prepared to accept an oath from Guthrum sworn not on the cross, but on an arm-ring sacred to Thor.[12]

Oaths clearly did not mean the same to Guthrum as they did to Alfred. The treaty was soon broken, and the Vikings were on the move again. Eventually, the large war-band reached Exeter, their backs to the sea, and agreed to a second treaty. Guthrum had been hoping to meet up with a second band of Vikings, arriving by sea, and so effect a cunning escape at the very moment Alfred thought he had them cornered. The elements, however, allied with England, and sunk 120 Viking ships before they could meet up with their colleagues.

It was hardly a victory for Alfred. His part of the bargain involved bribing the Vikings to leave – an early precursor of the *danegeld* of later, less feted rulers. The removal of the Viking threat may have brought temporary respite to Wessex, but simply shifted the problem elsewhere. Guthrum's army instead plagued the Mercians north of Alfred's border. Other Vikings, it seems, had given up on fighting – in around 878 many of them began settling in the East Midlands, in a region that became known as the Five Boroughs, the largely Danish settlements of Lincoln, Nottingham, Derby, Stamford and Leicester.

Guthrum still coveted the treasures of Wessex, and seemed to appreciate that the chief barrier to an acquiescent Wessex was the king himself. Accordingly, the Vikings mounted a surprise attack in the middle of winter. A large part of the Saxon army had been disbanded, and the resolutely Christian defenders were coming to the end of their twelve days of Christmas celebrations. Alfred and a small party of his soldiers were wintering in Chippenham in Wiltshire, where they were caught off guard by a Viking assault – pagan Yule celebrations went on for just as long, but seem to have been cancelled in order to allow for hostilities.

With Alfred on the run in the marshes of the West Country, Wessex was effectively overrun. What happened next is mysterious, almost miraculous. Alfred was reduced to hiding in disguise – there is a famous legend that he ended up promising to watch a peasant-woman's baking for her, and somehow caused the cakes to burn. The story, if it has a grain of truth, may have more to do with his role as the provider of 'bread' to the West Saxon people.[13] Somehow, Alfred scraped up an army in the west, waiting until the late spring, when the local farmers would have sown their crops and had more free time. He led his army against Guthrum, who had occupied Alfred's former wintering place at Chippenham. It was a last stand for the Saxons, as final as that once fought in the west by the British against their ancestors.

The West Saxons 'won' the Battle of Edington in 878, although how well they won it is open to debate. Some time later that they signed a treaty, whose terms implied that the battle was not all that decisive after all. A borderline was established between the realm of the Saxons and the area that had been settled by Vikings. It was understood by both parties that the Vikings would not be leaving eastern England, but would instead be settling there permanently. The island was effectively partitioned, along a line that ran up the Thames Estuary, north from the River Lea in what is now east London, and then north-west across what is now the Midlands. The land to the east of it was the *Danelaw*, a place where any remaining Saxons were now obliged to accept that Scandinavians lived among them, and had their own laws and customs. The Scandinavians would never leave.

By acknowledging the extent of Viking incursion into what is now England, Alfred was able to put a temporary stop on the raiders. The next time Vikings attacked (and war-bands were back before the decade was out), the newly settled Danes in the east would have just as much an interest in defending 'their' new home as the Saxons. Alfred's compromise also left the possibility that a later ruler would be able to reassert Saxon control over the Danish lands, incorporating them into a greater 'England'. This, in fact, was what Alfred's son Edward was able to do. Alfred's grandson Athelstan would become the first true king of England.

But Athelstan would be able to accomplish such things partly because by the time he did so, the settlers of the Danelaw were embracing the same religion as him. Alfred had been prepared to give Guthrum exactly what he wanted – a kingdom of his own, so long as Guthrum accepted that Alfred's god was better than his own. Guthrum has evidently thought eastern England was worth the price of Christian baptism. Not everyone believed it. A generation later, Pope Formosus would get extremely agitated at the number of reports he received of pagan rituals persisting in eastern England.

While Guthrum's army may have disbanded after the treaty, there were still other, smaller war-bands roaming England. When one enjoyed some raiding success on the south bank of the Thames, the Danes of the Danelaw were unable to resist the temptation. They marched on Essex, meeting up with the new arrivals on the coast at Benfleet. The threat arose of a Viking assault on London, but then the Viking group broke up, supposedly after arguments on jurisdiction and plans. Alfred, however, could not let the moment go unpunished. A small fleet of English ships sailed to East Anglia and raided the Danelaw coast, wiping out a flotilla of 16 Viking vessels in the Stour estuary. The Danes of East Anglia banded together quickly enough to destroy the victorious English fleet before it could make it back to Kent.

The experience was enough to convince Alfred of the importance of London. Although the city was in Mercia, not Alfred's homeland of Wessex, London was the bridging point of the River Thames. Whoever controlled London controlled the river that ran right into the heart of Wessex, and the 880s saw the city change hands several times, as Alfred fought off successive Danish assaults. Eventually, in 886, Alfred occupied London for good, ordering that the people should repopulate the deserted Roman part of the town. In his desire to hold London against Vikings, he found himself asserting his rule over Mercia, and consequently much of modern England. We remember Alfred for being 'Great' thanks to his mastery not of Vikings, but of other Saxons. Uniting against the Vikings, Wessex and Mercia formed the bulk of what would become modern England.[14]

But this brief history should be told from the Viking point of view. To the war-bands who left Norway and Denmark in search of foreign plunder, the era of the heathen hosts was highly successful – a complete victory for the Vikings. For an outlaw from the Vik, fighting his way around Europe, pillaging foreign lands, and to finally settle down as a farmer in East Anglia with a couple of Saxon concubines must have seemed perfect. It did not matter to him what religious symbol a distant, unseen leader wore around his neck. He had what he wanted, and if he paid protection money to a local ruler, it mattered little whether the cash eventually ended up in the possession of a Saxon or a fellow Dane. From the Orkneys to Essex, the eastern coast of the British Isles was a Viking domain.

In the long perspective, we might call Alfred and the English the ultimate victors. Christianity and civilization did their slow work, undermining the brutal codes of the war-band. The battle-religion of Odin only made sense to roving bands of warriors. Take the Viking out of the longship, turn him into a farmer, and suddenly he worries about crops, disease, trade and family. He welcomes law and order; a war-band is something he wants to be protected from. His children grow up speaking English to their mother, and his grandchildren find his accent hard to understand. When he dies, he leaves barely any sense of his Scandinavian origins, save for a scattering of place names – like *Grimsby*, 'the farm of Grim'. Old age was the ultimate enemy of the Viking hordes – to a culture prepared to play a waiting game, the old enemies eventually faded away.

English history credits Alfred, rightly, with mounting a heroic resistance to the Vikings, and with a diplomacy that saw his greatest enemy accept his religion and his guidance. But that must have meant little to the dead and the dispossessed in the region now known as the Danelaw. To a Dane, laying claim to a stretch of land that used to be Saxon and being allowed to keep it, the Vikings had won.

4

BROTHER SHALL FIGHT BROTHER

HARALD FAIRHAIR AND SONS

The Vikings of the Great Heathen Host and their fellow raiders were fleeing *something* back home, a change in political circumstances that made distant raids seem like a more acceptable option than staying. Debate continues over what caused so many men to leave Scandinavia at around the same time, but is not helped much by the available evidence.

Our chief source, for example, for this period of Norwegian history is Snorri's *Heimskringla*, written some three hundred years after the events it describes, and *Heimskringla*'s chief message about this period is the now contested claim that the rise of king Harald Fairhair irritated enough independent-minded people to make them seek somewhere else to live.[1]

Halfdan the Black's son Harald Fairhair may have been only ten years old when he inherited the lands of southern Norway around 870. The true power rested initially with his regent, his maternal uncle Guthorm, who led the war-band against several incursions. The most threatening was from a nearby war leader called Gandalf, whose forces were eventually routed at Haka Dale, north of modern Oslo. *Heimskringla* graciously implies that the young Fairhair fought in some of these battles, but while he took the credit, much of the hard work must have been uncle Guthorm's.

As Fairhair grew to maturity, he sought other means of acquiring territory. With Gandalf dead and his immediate environs devoid of enemies, Harald sought a union with Gytha, the daughter of the ruler of Hordaland. *Heimskringla* makes much of her great beauty and Fairhair's romantic desire, but we may assume that political expedients governed both his suit and her rejection of it. Her answer was that Fairhair was a petty princeling undeserving of her love, although she might find him more attractive if, instead of clinging to a small fjord in south Norway, he were to make a play for the entire area, as the famous Gorm had done in neighbouring Denmark.

Snorri himself seems surprised at Fairhair's reaction. Instead of railing against a haughty and insolent reply (as many of his descendants would in similar situations), Fairhair took it for the diplomatic offer that it undoubtedly was. He swore to leave his hair uncut until such time as he had conquered all of Norway, a condition that would be regarded as attained when he was able to extort protection money from all the major landholders.[2] The nickname 'Fairhair' was a euphemism for the shaggy mane of the king as he undertook a series of aggrandizing expeditions. 'Tangle-hair' is another reasonable translation. Gytha's reply contained within it an element of truth, that thus far all the 'kings' of Norway were unworthy of the name. Tribal feuds and squabbles over small patches of land might have sufficed in the days when there was no comparison with other regions, but the Vikings were becoming increasingly well travelled. Reports drifted back of far Constantinople and the young kingdoms of Western Europe. *Konung*, in Old Norse, simply meant a scion of a noble (i.e. powerful) family. It is during the reign of Harald Fairhair that it came to mean *king* in our modern sense. But Fairhair, despite the claims of some, was never the king of all Norway. He remained a king *in* Norway, chiefly dominant over the south.

Fairhair's conquest was conducted on a larger scale than before. He rejected the simple rounds of occasional extortion favoured by his ancestors, replacing them with a tax-farming system:

> He appointed an earl [*jarl*] for every district, whose duty it was to administer the law and justice, and to collect fines and taxes. And the earl was to have a third of the taxes and penalties for his maintenance and other expenses. Every earl was to have under him four or more *hersar*, and every *hersir* was to have twenty marks of revenue. Every earl was to furnish the king sixty soldiers for his army, and every *hersir*, twenty.[3]

So claims *Heimskringla*, although the reality may not have been as neat and tidy. Evidence in *Heimskringla* is non-existent, but it is backed up at least in spirit by the later Gulathing Law. This decision, voted on by a Norwegian assembly, agrees that 'free' farmers were nevertheless obliged to provide men and materials for the defence of their homeland.[4] Fairhair and his cronies certainly had a better-organized system of extortion, even to the extent of possibly organizing a ship-levy for 'defence'. He collected a tax on the trade with Iceland and Lapland, and cleverly steered debates at assemblies so that even those who claimed independence from him would support his policies by vote.

The system transformed the king from the most powerful roving troublemaker to a centralized holder of wealth, with an army levied from all over the territory he claimed. It installed his agents at the local level as lawmakers, arbiters and tax collectors. It also contained within it the implication that the land on which the Norwegians lived was not their personal property, but a possession of the king in return for which they had to serve, both directly as soldiers, and indirectly through taxation. In the past, it had been possible for a 'king' to be a distant, unseen figure, whose claims of his own greatness could have little impact on the average farmer or fisherman. Now, a king was a palpable presence in daily life, whose minions were close at hand, with a vested interest in collecting what was their due.

Heimskringla's account of Fairhair's successes has some archaeological support in Kaupang in south-west Norway. Although the original coastline has long since silted up, excavations between 1950 and 1967 uncovered what was once a port, with multiple stone jetties, over 60 lavish burials (of what appear to be successful merchants), and, most notably, no fortifications. Flourishing at the height of Fairhair's power, the town shows evidences of a trade network that, for some reason, did not need immediate protection – the borders lay not at the outskirts of the town, but elsewhere, guarded by Fairhair's ships. The town was called Skiringssal in Fairhair's time – *kaupang* simply means 'place of trade', cognate with *kaupangr* in Icelandic and *kaupunki* in Finnish. Skiringssal is thought to have been the port mentioned as *Sciringes heal* in Orosius' *Universal History*, written in the time of Alfred the Great. Whatever Fairhair managed to achieve, it inspired enough confidence to create a booming economy. The more trade was protected, of course, the more it could be supervised and taxed.[5]

In some places, local leaders relinquished any claim on the term 'king', which, as Gytha had amply demonstrated, didn't mean what it used to anyway. They rebranded themselves as Fairhair's earls, kept their local power, and set about collecting the levies and taxes on Fairhair's behalf. Icelandic farmers might claim that their high-born ancestors had been dispossessed by Bad Men. The truth is less romantic – the wealthy of the Norwegian petty kingdoms likely remained so, and it was the smaller landholders who were squeezed out. Harald's consolidation of the Norwegian coast and hinterland created Norway the kingdom, but it also created hundreds, if not thousands of disaffected Norwegians, unable to pay the protection money, or deposed from their lands for refusing to do so, particularly in the fiercely independent Trondheim region.

Plenty did not like the way the political wind was blowing, and poured across the North Sea to relatives and associates in the Orkneys, Scotland and the Faeroes. Whole communities of Icelanders falsely traced their origins back to those who fled Fairhair's domination, and some sagas paint a picture of mass movements not only west, but also to the Finnmark, Finland, the south Baltic coast and points east.[6] It is better, perhaps, to blame one's presence on a flight from oppression, than to admit one's ancestors took their land from someone else – even if the Vikings were refugees, they were refugees with a sense of self-important entitlement that displaced many original inhabitants. It is also worth mentioning that these very places of supposed 'refuge' were also the sources of much of the trade coming into Skiringssal; far from scaring people off, it might be that Fairhair's reforms encouraged them to *trade* farther afield, and that some of them may have eventually settled in these distant places, their descendants forgetting the more positive impetus that originally led their ancestors there.

However, it would appear that the most troublesome ele-

ment in Norwegian society did not run far enough. To Fairhair's annoyance, a number of Vikings regrouped on offshore
islands and then attacked western Norway. After a time, it
became clear that the main base of these recursive attackers lay
in the Shetlands and Orkneys and that one of the repeat
offenders was a son of Fairhair's associate Rognvald – Hrolf
the Walker.[7] He got his name, it was said, because no horse
was big enough to carry him. Hrolf had devoted much of his
time to bullying the peoples of the Baltic, but had recently tired
of his old hunting grounds and returned to Norway, where
pickings were richer.

Hrolf eventually took his men and ships away, stopping first
in the Hebrides and Ireland, before carving out a new kingdom
for himself on the southern shore of the English Channel. He
found a partly willing ally in the form of Charles the Simple,
king of the Franks, who granted him land around Rouen in
911 if he undertook to keep other Vikings from attacking it –
thereby forming a buffer zone between the coast and inland
France. Hrolf's banishment is a matter of legend, but his
arrival in Frankish lands is a matter of fact, his power confirmed by the treaty of St Clair-sur-Epte.[8]

Hrolf became the head of a new Viking aristocracy in north
France, which swiftly lost many aspects of its Scandinavian
culture. Many members used two names, one 'true' Viking
sobriquet, and a second, more Frankish-sounding one for
dealing with the locals. Under Hrolf's son William Longsword
and grandson Richard the Fearless, the Viking-held lands grew
in prominence until they could play a powerful role in European affairs. The Vikings in the area lost their Scandinavian
language within a few generations, but maintained their prowess in battle and brutal politicking. In a corruption of the
term 'Norsemen', they became known as *Normans*, and their
territory, *Normandy*.

Back in Norway, Fairhair had many women, and the tally of his sons ranges from a conservative nine to a not-impossible twenty. Fairhair's concubines came from all over the Baltic region, and many seemed to dwell in their home regions with their offspring – their 'marriages' to the king enduring only until he headed off to pastures, alliances and bedmates new.

Four of Fairhair's sons were supposedly born of an unwelcome dalliance with a sorcerous woman of Lapland, indicating the continued confusion of pagan beliefs enduring into Fairhair's time. Snorri's *Heimskringla* reports a series of bizarre events one winter solstice. A Finn (i.e. a Sámi) arrives at the door in the midst of Fairhair's feast, and encourages the king to come out. It is implied that the arrival of 'Svasi the Finn' is some sort of fortune-teller or travelling player, but it is his daughter Snaefrid ('Tranquil Snow'?) who holds Fairhair's attention. Supposedly charmed by a magic potion she gives him, Fairhair demands to have sex with Snaefrid, but her father, perhaps playing on his countrymen's reputation for sorcerous vengeance, refuses to allow this unless Fairhair takes Snaefrid as his wife.

Much of *Heimskringla*'s information on the bewitching Snaefrid comprises embellishments after the fact. There may indeed have been an unpopular Sámi woman whose charms caused Fairhair to temporarily neglect his duties, but even if we take *Heimskringla* at face value, their relationship seems to have lasted for some years. The name of their eldest son, Sigurd the Bastard, clearly implies a union out of wedlock, but Snaefrid supposedly goes on to bear Fairhair three other sons – Halfdan Longshanks, Guthroth the Radiant and Rognvald the Straight-limbed. The beautiful Snaefrid then dies, but Fairhair pines for her, refusing to allow any to touch her corpse (which remains miraculously undecomposed), and watching his 'sleeping' wife for a further three years. He is only jarred from his reverie by Thorleif the Wise, who cunningly suggests that it is time to change the bedding of the pretty Finn. The moment her body is moved, the spell is broken, the stench of decay rises and her previously inviolate body yields up 'worms and adders, frogs and toads and vipers'.[9]

The children of Snaefrid remain obscure; while several roaming Viking leaders may have *claimed* to be sons of little-known concubines of Fairhair, that in itself is no reason to believe them. What is clear enough is that the new generation of Vikings took the squabbles that had busied several dozen Scandinavian clans, and transferred them to foreign parts.

Rognvald the Resourceful, supposed father of Hrolf and lifelong friend of Fairhair, was eventually killed in a raid on the Scottish isles conducted by two ne'er-do-wells who claimed to be sons of Snaefrid the Finnish sorceress. It is a testament to Harald's kingship that he was able to calm the situation, when there was every chance that it would erupt into a blood feud and split his new kingdom. He gave his daughter Alof in marriage to Rognvald's son Thorir the Silent, and set Thorir up as the new ruler of the islands. Of the rebellious two half-Finns, Guthroth the Radiant surrendered to his father, and was packed off to the Vik to keep him out of trouble. Halfdan Longshanks managed to get away to the Orkneys, where his arrival took the locals by surprise, and met with little resistance. Thorir the Silent did nothing to stop him, but Halfdan had not reckoned with Rognvald's son Turf-Einar.

Einar was Rognvald's youngest son, the illegitimate and unwelcome offspring of a union with a slave-girl, openly despised by his father.[10] Nevertheless, while his attitude may have annoyed those around him, it was belligerent enough to impress Vikings in general. When unwelcome Vikings had earlier attempted to settle on the Orkneys without Rognvald's permission, it had been the brawling, one-eyed Einar who had led a party to kill them. He had also made the best of his lot, adapting in time-honoured Viking fashion to the particular conditions of the land in which he found himself – his sobriquet 'Turf' came from his early adoption of peat cutting as a viable alternative to burning scarce trees for fuel on the Orkneys.

Einar fled to Caithness to assemble supporters, returning six months after Halfdan had seized the Orkneys. Einar tracked down his father's murderer and exacted terrible revenge. He was a Viking, a worshipper of Odin, and the human sacrifice was intended as recompense for the death of his father. Justice, in Viking terms, had been done, but he knew there would be trouble. The sagas record his satisfaction with the victory:

> Happy am I, keen
> Heroes have spear-hacked,
> Bloodied the king's boy:
> Brave the bold act
> – but hard to hide
> what a howling I've caused [11]

The verse is a triumph of the Viking style, glorying in death and torture, praising Einar's own men (we can see that Einar did not kill Halfdan himself), and crowing in a class-aware manner – the slave-girl's bastard has 'bloodied the king's boy'. In a grisly poetic manner, the verse acknowledges the trouble to come; the 'howling' to which it refers not merely the agonies of the dying Halfdan, but the rage the news was bound to engender back in Norway.

Harald Fairhair, however, seems to have accepted Halfdan's fate with some equanimity. The sagas frame his reaction as kingly wisdom, although if the events described ever happened, it is far more likely that he simply did not care, or even believe that the dead Viking was a son of his at all. Turf-Einar, however, told the islanders that Fairhair had demanded a fine, and that he had offered to pay it on their behalf, on the understanding that he would be their overlord. The result, after much negotiation, was the imposition of a similar system on the Orkneys as Harald had imposed on Norway itself – Einar was sworn in as an earl and left to his own devices, as long as he continued to pay the islanders' tax. How he collected it from them, and what he made on the side, was his own concern.

Even as Fairhair secured southern Norway, the greatest threat lay in the succession crisis that would loom with his death. He had lain with many daughters of local rulers, all of whom had doubtless brought up their offspring to expect future power. Fairhair attempted to impose some sort of system, calling an assembly in eastern Norway in an attempt to establish his will. With the pained composure of a long-suffering father, he assured his sons that they would *all* be kings, and packaged up Norway into a series of satrapies mirroring the petty kingdoms of old. One son, however, would be supreme, and the aging father hoped that all would defer to him in his choice.

One son, Erik, brought with him the hope of future expansion, and it was he who was chosen. Erik's mother was the daughter of a king of Jutland, thereby creating the possibility of expanding Norway's borders southwards into Denmark. But as Erik's sobriquet 'Bloodaxe' suggests, he was a trouble-maker. Another important factor in Erik's desirability as heir may have been his wife, Gunnhild Kingsmother. Snorri, the author of *Heimskringla* and presumed author of *Egil's Saga*, is eloquent on the evils of Gunnhild, claiming that she was universally hated by the Norwegians, and that she was not a Danish princess at all, but a chieftain's daughter from the far north, who had been sent into Lapland to learn witchcraft. It was here that Erik found Gunnhild, cohabiting with two Finnish sorcerers. The faithless witch helped murder her teachers and returned to Norway with Erik – or so claims *Heimskringla*, the truth is likely to have been much more prosaic. The historical Gunnhild Kingsmother is thought to have been the sister of the Danish king Harald Bluetooth. Such a union of Norway and Denmark was a desirable possibility, leading not only to Gunnhild's attractiveness as a bride, but also to the loathing she inspired in her enemies.[12]

In the early days of Erik Bloodaxe's rule, things proceeded calmly. Harald Fairhair, now nearing his seventies, went into calm retirement, while his sons busied themselves with their duties, which chiefly involved keeping half their local income for themselves, and sending the rest on to Fairhair, hopefully to set up a pattern that would be continued after Fairhair's death by Erik.

Erik's brother Rognvald was murdered, supposedly with Fairhair's blessing, when the old king heard that he was dabbling in sorcery. Erik was dispatched to the district, and 'burned his brother in his hall, together with eighty wizards'.[13] This was, apparently, regarded as a good thing by the local people, although Erik's next stab at earning the sobriquet Kinslayer was to prove less popular. He fell out with his brother Bjorn over who ought to take local levies to present to Harald – Bjorn had always done it himself in the past, but now Erik presented himself as the agent of their father. Their disagreement escalated into a full-blown fight, and Erik killed Bjorn as a result. This was not quite as welcome with the locals, or indeed with Bjorn's brother (presumably full-brother) Olaf, who threatened to avenge his death when he had the chance.

Killing and violence continued. Guthroth the Radiant was drowned in a storm at sea, while Erik narrowly escaped death at the hands of Halfdan the Black (not to be confused with his grandfather of the same name). Harald intervened, and forced a reconciliation that favoured Erik's side of the story. Yet even as Erik Bloodaxe was thinning the Norwegian royal line down, the aged Fairhair was building it up again. Eleven wives were clearly not enough for Fairhair, and he managed to impregnate his serving-girl Thora Morstrstong. She gave birth to yet another son, the future Hakon the Good. Perhaps in the knowledge that he would not be around long to protect the newborn Hakon from his brother Erik, Fairhair took steps to ensure he was raised somewhere far away out of trouble. A diplomatic expedition arrived from the English king Athelstan, grandson of Alfred the Great. For the events in *Heimskringla* to match, it would have to have been sometime between 924, the date of Athelstan's accession, and 930, the presumed date of Fairhair's death. The two rulers concluded a diplomatic truce with one another, and as part of the deal Hakon was raised at the English court, safe from his murderous siblings.[14]

Three years after he had officially transferred his power to his son Erik, Harald Fairhair finally died, leaving perhaps two dozen children, almost all of whom were either rulers of parcels of Norway (the boys), or married to earls (the girls). South Norway remained a single kingdom, but with three rulers: Erik the official leader, contending with his brothers Olaf in the Vik area and Sigroth in the turbulent Trondheim. In 934, Erik met them in battle somewhere near the Vik, and emerged from the conflict as the sole survivor. None of his other brothers was prepared to stand against him, and it seemed that Erik Bloodaxe was in charge.

Hakon, however, returned to Norway at some point after hearing of the death of his father, accompanied by a fleet of ships. The exact dates are difficult to match, so we are unsure whether he arrived with the backing of Athelstan himself (who died in 939), or that of Athelstan's half-brother and successor Edmund I. *Heimskringla*'s terse account of Hakon's actions makes it sound as if he simply sailed home on hearing of his father's death, but the decisions involved took a considerable time. When he did arrive, it was as part of a concerted effort to unseat Erik, with the backing of an English crown that liked the idea of a friendly king in Norway. Hakon legendarily wielded the 'finest sword Norway ever saw', a baptismal present from his kingly foster father, named Quernbiter for its alleged ability to slice a millstone in half. Hakon also enjoyed something much more useful and believeable, the full support of the earls of Trondheim.

While Erik still struggled in the south to win over the people of the Vik, the young Hakon went straight to Trondheim, where he and his backers pleaded with the assembly of the farmers to accept him as their rightful ruler. When the people of Trondheim agreed, the news soon made it to the hinterland, where Hakon was hailed as a worthy successor to Fairhair, more likely to see things Trondheim's way. To the majority of the Norwegians, Hakon was a far more acceptable candidate than Erik Bloodaxe. Erik was unable to find enough allies among his earls to field an army, and eventually fled the country, heading for England where he would briefly reign as the king of Northumbria, before his death in battle during yet another raid. His despised wife Gunnhild Kingsmother fled to the Orkneys with her brood of children.

Just as Harald Fairhair had prepared to repel attacks from Vikings overseas, Hakon the Good (or whatever council of Trondheim earls was manipulating him from behind the scenes) also needed to secure his frontiers until such time as the happy news arrived that Erik Bloodaxe was dead, and no longer likely to turn up somewhere off Norway's long coasts with a fleet of his own. His actions as king were limited to some confirmations of Trondheim earls in their positions (no surprises there). Only then, with the chance of further trouble from Erik removed, did Hakon take any new steps.

His first problem was the Danes, who had taken advantage of the unrest in Norway to begin raids of their own in the Vik. Hakon pursued the raiders back to their own lands, and further. Whether it had been his intention or not, he began to advance his father's work, raiding in Zealand and southern Sweden to make it very clear who was boss, and extorting protection money from his victims.[15]

But Denmark, like Norway, was no longer a cluster of semi-independent states. It was now largely united, with its fortresses and the Christian allies of its Christian King Harald Bluetooth. Now that both Norway and Denmark had strong rulers of their own, what would have once been a local squabble, between a couple of dozen ships and their belligerent crews, stood a chance of escalating into a national conflict. The Danes raiding Norway were no longer mere Vikings, but presumed subjects of the King of Denmark. The same applied in reverse to the punitive raids on the coast. Meanwhile, the Danes themselves could argue that Hakon the Good was not a king at all, but a Norwegian rebel against Danish authority.

Many of the 'Danes' raiding the Vik were probably not Danes at all, but an assortment of Vikings under the command of Norwegians. Gunnhild Kingsmother, widow of Erik Blood-axe, had wasted no time in setting up alliances of her own. Erik's daughter Ragnild was now a wife of Thorfinn Skull-cleaver, the ruler of the Orkneys. Erik's sons were now back in the region, first at the Danish homeland of Gunnhild, then raiding along the Baltic coasts, then finally leading parties of their men in raids against their native Denmark.

Despite such annoyances, the rule of Hakon the Good was relatively trouble-free – his nickname does not appear to have been intended ironically. But although Hakon reached manhood and took power to some degree for himself, he was still heavily reliant on his Trondheim supporters. Sectors of Norway were ruled in his name by his two nephews, Tryggvi and Olaf. Other parts were simply beyond his control. There is talk in the sagas of Eystein the Bad, a ruler in the hinterland who so annoyed his subjects that many set out across the mountains that divide Norway from Sweden, in search of new territories in the east – what would become Jamtaland in central Sweden and Helsingaland on Sweden's Baltic coast.

One of Hakon's major achievements was an unforeseen consequence of his formative years spent in England. Like the king of Denmark to the south, Hakon had been raised with full appreciation of events elsewhere in Europe, and of the increasing power of Christianity. Hakon the Good was a Christian himself and, according to later legend, now sought to impose his religion upon his pagan subjects. His supporters remember him for trying in the first place, while his opponents remember him for not trying hard enough.[16]

His decision would have made some sense in the light of events elsewhere, but Hakon was also a practical man, and his main supporters in the Trondheim region were not likely to give up the old gods in a hurry. Hakon made some small attempt to move the pagan Yule celebrations so that they occupied the same slot as Christmas (i.e. that the chief celebration should now be on 25 December, rather than the winter solstice) but otherwise kept his religious beliefs largely to himself. Eventually, believing his position to be secure, he sent for bishops and missionaries from his English allies, only to discover that his subjects were behaving in an irritatingly democratic manner.

There was no divine right of kings in Norway, no heavenly mandate that instructed the people to obey the earthly representative of a god. Particularly in the independent Trondheim region, kings were *permitted* to rule by their assemblies, and woe betide the monarch who did not give orders that had been approved by his subjects. Consequently, when Hakon's missionaries arrived in Møre and Raumsdale to the south of Trondheim, the locals immediately submitted the topic to the regional assembly for discussion.

Of all the places to debate the adoption of a foreign religion, Trondheim was probably the worst. Sigurd, the most powerful local earl, was a staunch supporter of the pagan gods, who proudly cited his many sacrifices to Odin as the source of his power. He was a host in the Odinic tradition, generous with his beer and roast meat to his subjects. He was, quite obviously, not going to submit quietly.

Neither, for that matter, were the farmers who formed the bulk of the Trondheim assembly. How ludicrous it must have sounded to them, that the king they had so willingly chosen would appear before them and reveal alien beliefs that, to the average Trondheim farmer, would have sounded quite unhinged. Hakon the Good, in whom the farmers had placed their trust, now wanted them to submit to a single God, to stop worshipping their old gods, value humility, and (this was the last straw) *abstain from meat and stop working for one day a week*. The farmers refused to believe that a day off was possible, and even the slaves complained at the thought of a day without ample food. Clearly something was being lost in translation.

According to Snorri (although his account is unsupported and probably fictional), the farmers voted to keep their old religion, and *Heimskringla* reports Hakon the Good enduring their decision in an immensely unregal sulk. Perhaps realizing that their ruler was unhappy with their decision, representatives from the assembly even tried to console him with a sacrifice to Odin. Hakon refused to eat or drink the sacrificial foods, and even made the sign of the Cross over his drinking cup, causing Sigurd to hurriedly claim he was making the hammer-sign of *Thor*.[17]

That winter, when Hakon's Yuletide reforms were due to be instituted, a cabal of Trondheim leaders murdered several priests, burned down three churches, and forced Hakon himself to eat some pieces of horse liver (sacred to Frey) at what must have been an intensely unpleasant Christmas dinner. Hakon's anger with the locals' attitude towards Christianity threatened to break into open conflict, and perhaps would have done, had he not faced other threats to the south.

The sons of Erik Bloodaxe continued to plague Hakon throughout his reign, sailing with the open support of their mother's Danish relatives. Hakon the Good approached middle age with no sons of his own, and a single daughter, Thora. His luck ran out in 961, in a battle in which his loyal forces were outnumbered six-to-one by the sons of Erik and their Danish allies. He was wounded in the shoulder, supposedly by the pageboy of Gunnhild Kingsmother, and died later from his injury. His loyal subjects, in a final irony, buried him with full Odinic rites, hoping to ensure their king's place in Valhalla.[18]

5

THE ROAD EAST

VIKINGS, RUSSIANS AND VARANGIANS

Inland from the Swedish coast, amid a network of lakes and rivers, sits Björkö, 'birch island' on Lake Mälar. During the Viking Age, when sea levels were higher, a wide channel led straight from Mälar to the Baltic Sea, affording easy passage for seaborne goods deep into Swedish territory. Around 800, the island became the site of a trading town, founded to replace an earlier settlement that proved to be too small for the needs of Sweden's rising population. The settlement became known as Birka, and it became a magnet for trade from all over the Viking world, from Hedeby, Skiringssal, and points beyond. To the south of Birka, off the eastern coast of Sweden, lies the island of Gotland, another trading centre. Thanks to their positions on the ends of trade routes, these two islands form the centre of the Viking world – Gotland in particular has more Viking treasure than anywhere else. Archaeologists have unearthed the graves of many a fortune-seeker, buried with his hoard of silver coins and the swords that helped him win it.

Not all of the treasures of Birka and Gotland are below the ground. Rune stones dot the landscape, carved with memorials of journeys to far places – Semgall and Courland (Latvia), Wendland (Poland), Virland (Estonia), Gardariki (Russia), Greekland (more particularly, the Byzantine Empire centred on Constantinople), and Serkland, the land of the Saracens. Although some Swedes followed Danish and Norwegian voyages to the British Isles and beyond, Sweden's interest has always lain in the Baltic, not the North Sea. For the Vikings of Sweden, the road to fortune lay not to the west, but to the east.

Early Swedish explorations followed a model similar to that of the Norwegians and Danes. Hopping from island to island, vessels first reached Åland in the middle of the Baltic, then the southern coast of what is now Finland. One saga refers to the region as *Balagard* (Meadow-fort?), implying at least one settlement, and probably more.[1] In Finland, they roamed an archipelago of a thousand islands, and penetrated inland. For those in search of secure, unforested farmland to till, Finland did not offer much, but its lakes were teeming with fish, and its forests with game. Traders were able to meet with the same Sámi who also traded with the Norwegians on the Arctic coast, but also with new peoples, the Suomi (Finns), the Kainuans and the Karelians, whose lands bordered on what is now Russia. The local people asked them what they were, and they replied that they were *rothr*, 'bands of rowers'. The locals called them *Ruotsi*, the Finnish word for Sweden to this day.[2]

In Finland, they discovered an unexpected benefit of the longship. A Viking boat was light enough to be hefted by its crew and dragged out of the water, this much was already known. But in Finland, with hundreds of interconnected navigable lakes, it became possible to sail many miles inland, pulling the ship out of the water and across separating isthmuses of land. The name of Birca had become synonymous with trade, it lent its name to Pirkkala, the 'Birka place' near Tampere in modern Finland.[3] There, the Swedes traded with the locals, mainly in the furs of animals trapped by hunters in Finland's endless forests. To this day, the Finnish word for money is *raha*, 'pelt'.

The Swedes, however, did not keep pushing eastwards. They ran into the Kainu people along Finland's eastern borders, a warlike race who excelled at dragging their own boats across the land to the Arctic Sea, and raiding against the Sámi. The Kainuans were already causing trouble for the Norwegians in the far north, and the Swedes preferred to steer clear. They turned instead to the south-east, and Norse sagas would eventually mangle the Kainu region into *kvenna-land* – the land of the Amazons.[4]

The Swedes found other things to occupy them further to the south. The 'Eastland', southern Baltic countries, Poland and Russia, represented prime raiding territory for early Swedish explorers, whom the locals called *Rootsi*. The legendary King Ivar the Wide-Grasper supposedly conquered an area corresponding to parts of north Germany and the European Baltic states sometime around the seventh century. Whether Ivar really existed, figures like him certainly explored the rivers and estuaries of the southern and eastern Baltic, and at some point, discovered the largest lake in Europe. Lake Ladoga, in the southernmost part of the Finnish peninsula, is today part of Russian territory, about 25 miles east of St Petersburg. This body of water, occupying some 6,700 square miles, was a vital location on the trade routes. It not only made it possible to sail over a hundred miles into the hinterland, it also brought the light ships within transfer or portage-distance of a series of other rivers and lakes. As they had done in Finland, the Swedes were able to sail from one to the other, negotiating a series of minor barriers until they found themselves on much larger rivers that led to the south – the Dnieper and the mighty Volga. Ladoga takes its name from the Finnish *alode-joki*, 'lower river', a root that was also corrupted to form the name of its original settlement, Aldeigjuborg.[5] But the Finnish inhabitants shared the region with Swedes from the earliest days – what archaeologists once assumed to be the Finns' temple is now thought to be a longhouse that sheltered a sizeable community of Norse traders.

Ladoga archaeologists have yet to find any swords, except for several toy ones fashioned from wood in imitation of Norse originals. The area also revealed a significant amount of Norse jewellery, although who wore it is still open to debate. A Rus cemetery on the other side of the river seems to have been used between 850 and 950. Of the 18 identified graves many are female and wearing Norse jewellery, although it is undetermined whether they are local girls or women from the homeland. Linguistic evidence suggests that even if there were an early population of Scandinavian women with the men, their genes were soon crowded out by those of local people.

Ladoga has yielded no inscriptions apart from a few runes scratched on coins and indistinct runic carvings on a stick, the meaning of which still splits scholars – it has been variously described as an elf-summoning wand, a tribute to a fallen Swede, or perhaps even a poem about an arrow or shield.[6]

Tree-ring data on the Ladoga buildings tells us that the first Norse settlement was destroyed between 863 and 870, and replaced a few years later with a stronger stone building. This tallies with a description in the early twelfth century *Russian Primary Chronicle* of a local revolt, in which the new settlers were briefly overthrown, before being invited back:

The Varangians came from beyond the sea and demanded tribute from the Finnish and Slav peoples. They were driven off, but in due course dissension broke out among the people and became so acute that they said 'Let us find a prince who will rule us and judge justly.' So they went across the sea to the Varangians, to the Rus, (for the Varangians were called Rus as others were called Swedes, [Northmen], Angles and Goths), and they said to the Rus 'Our land is large and fruitful, but lacks order. Come over and rule us.' Three brothers were chosen as rulers, and these three agreed to go over, taking all their family and all the Rus people with them. It is further related that the eldest brother, Rurik, came to Ladoga and built there the town of Aldeigjuborg [Old Ladoga]. The second, Sineus settled near the White Sea [at Byelosersk], and the third, Truvor, at Isborsk in southern Estonia. Two years later, the younger brothers died and Rurik assumed full power, after which he went south and build on the shore of Lake Volkhov the town of Novgorod [Holmgard]. From here, the Rus people spread south . . .[7]

The relation of Rurik and his 'brothers' is fictional – it is no coincidence that each chooses one of the three main lake-routes on which to settle. The confused to-ing and fro-ing of the report suggests something else, that one group of Norse settlers was violently supplanted by another, who later claimed to have native support.[8] Whoever they were, they soon established Novgorod and Kiev where they traded with merchants who came up the Dneiper from the Black Sea. There were no offshore islands for natural protection, so the Swedes built heavily defensible enclosures, divided by hundreds of square miles of potentially hostile terrain. The siege mentality led their kinsmen back in Scandinavia to call Russia *Gardariki* – 'the place of fortified towns'.

The Vikings soon headed down the Dnieper to see for themselves. Our sources for their travels are far more reliable than the *Russian Primary Chronicle*: the treatise *De Administrando Imperio*, written in the mid-tenth century by the Byzantine emperor Constantine Porphyrogenitus ('the Purple-born'). It is thanks to Constantine's account that we know of the Byzantines' attitude towards the Vikings, and of the gruelling journey they had to make in order to reach the Miklagard markets.

South of Kiev, wrote Constantine, was the the great forty-mile natural barrier that kept trade to a trickle – seven cataracts where the river surged between forbidding walls of rock, whose names still invoke the sense of terror they must have struck into medieval travellers. The waterfalls and rapids of the Gulper, the Sleepless, the Island-force, and the Yeller, were followed by the greatest barrier of all, *Aifur*, the Ever-Fierce, or simply Impassable. Beyond Aifur lay the Narrow-force, the Wave-force, the Highcliff-force, the Seether and the Courser. No ship could hope to run the gauntlet of the whirling waters, steep drops and rapids, but as the Vikings soon demonstrated, no ship needed to. They brought their ships out on to the land and, as they had done in the north, simply dragged or carried them alongside the dangerous waters. The brave of heart only portaged their ships around the waterfalls, preferring to chance their luck in the rapids. To do so, men had to struggle naked in the water, feeling out the river-bottom with their feet, guiding their boats with long poles, as the white waters thundered around them and threatened to pitch them into oblivion. A rune stone in distant Gotland records four brothers who went 'far into Aifur' and lived to tell the tale, although their friend Hrafn lost his life in the attempt.[9]

Beyond Aifur and the other barriers, the dangers were easier to deal with. A long journey awaited, and occasional difficulties from the local Pecheneg tribesmen, but essentially, the worst was over. The Vikings were able to sail their ships along a river-road that eventually took them to the Black Sea.

This was the famed road to *Miklagard*, the 'Great City' of Constantinople, where the Vikings were able to sell their furs and slaves for silk and the other luxuries of Byzantine civilization. A number of Rus first arrived in Constantinople in 838, and, according to the Frankish *Annales Bertiani*, accompanied Byzantine ambassadors to the court of Louis the Pious. Questioned by the Frankish emperor as to their origins, they volunteered their Swedish ancestry, and the claim that they were friends and allies of the Byzantines at that time. They also asked to be allowed passage through Louis's kingdom to return home, perhaps indicating that they were the first Rus to ever make it all the way downriver to the Black Sea, and did not much like the idea of trying to make their way back up again, through the rapids and the dangerous natives. The Greek-speaking Byzantines also called them something that sounded like Rus, either *Rhos*, 'ruddy', to mark their complexions or, using the term that had once described the attacking Heruls, *Rusioi*, 'blonds'.[10]

An initial trickle of Rus traders was followed by bolder incursions across the Black Sea and eventually an attack on Constantinople itself. Emperor Michael III had conveniently just departed at the head of an army to fight Muslims, leaving the city unprepared for the arrival of 200 hostile vessels. Byzantine sources claim that the attack was only thwarted by divine intervention, when the sacred relic of the Holy Virgin's Robe was dipped in the sea, causing a tempest to rise up and destroy the attacking fleet. This was news to many, who regarded the attack as a Viking victory.[11] Of particular embarrassment to the Byzantines who claimed a miraculous triumph was the later news that several of the 'defeated' Viking vessels sailed past the city to the Princes' Islands, where they had sacked the monastery at Terebinthos. In a textbook re-enactment of the attack on distant Lindisfarne, the Vikings plundered the riches of the holy sanctuary and slaughtered 22 monks. Thereafter, the Rus of Kiev attempted to deal with the Byzantines peacefully, and the Byzantines were happy to oblige, until 941, when a second Viking attack came out of the north, led by one Igor (Swedish: Ingvar), later said to be the son of the legendary Rurik.[12]

Meanwhile, further inroads in Russia and north of the Black Sea brought the Rus into contact with new traders even further to the south and east. The archaeology of Russian Swedish graves tells its own story about the progress of these expeditions. During the eighth century, warriors were laid to rest with grave-goods that reflected their life – a sword or two, a spear, and some trinkets for use in the afterlife. Often, such trinkets include small silver coins, from trading deals by the Swedish Rus with merchants from a distant place the Swedes called Serkland.[13] The coins, or *dirhams*, are marked with strange runes that meant nothing to the Scandinavians. If they had, they would have discovered that one side read: 'There is no god but Allah.' On the other, 'He is Allah, the eternally besought of all, He begetteth not nor was begotten and there is none comparable to him,' and in increasingly cramped Arabic: 'He it is who has sent His messenger with the guidance and Religion of Truth, that he may cause it to prevail over all religion, however much the idolaters may be averse.'[14]

What interested the idolaters of Rus was the silver itself, capitalizing on the sudden flood of the metal in the Muslim world, largely occasioned by the discovery of a rich silver mine in Benjahir, Afghanistan.[15] The Islamic world had silver to spare, and the Vikings had the rich furs and white slaves that the Muslims wanted. By the beginning of the ninth century, there is a vast increase in the number of Muslim *dirhams*, not just in graves of Rus, but in Scandinavia itself, particularly at the trade centres of Gotland, Birka and Hedeby. The Swedes had cut out the middlemen, and established contact directly with the source of the silver. They may have been encouraged by a sharp rise in demand – the first wave of Muslim silver in Rus areas was followed by a second, even larger wave direct to Gotland, implying that the Vikings of the homeland had gone in search of direct trade, and found a market suddenly booming.[16] The years 869–883 saw the catastrophic Zanj Rebellion in what is now Iraq, where thousands of black slaves turned on their masters and set up a short-lived independent state. The incident led to an increase in general mistrust of Africans in the Arab world, particularly since some Muslim soldiers of African origin defected to the rebels. This may have contributed to the improved market for white slaves in the Abbasid Caliphate in the early tenth century, and hence encouraged the Vikings in both their trade and the raids that supplied it.

After Birka and Pirkkala, another 'birch island' was added to the list, at Berezany in the Crimea, where runic inscriptions have been uncovered.[17] Even as some Vikings were dealing with the Byzantines by sailing down the western coast of the Black Sea, others were finding the mouth of the river Don on its northern shores. By 912, they had found the point where it was possible to drag their ships across a narrow neck of land dividing the Don from the Volga, thereby finding the route down the Volga itself, to the trading post of Itil – the Khazar name for the river, transcribed as *Atil* in Arab sources. South of it lay the Caspian Sea. Throughout the tenth century, the south shores of the Caspian were home to the Samanids, Persian Muslims that supported a strong trade network into the rest of the Abbasid caliphate that ruled the entire Middle

East. From the south shores of the Caspian, traders could make their way to Baghdad itself. The journey was not easy but for the merchant with the right merchandise it was worth it – the return journey went back east from Baghdad, north to the Caspian coast, and then up to the environs of Itil as taking around eleven months. Some Muslim traders were prepared to take the risk, and met with the Norsemen who had made the long voyage to Itil.[18]

The Arab impression of them was not altogether positive. In the tenth century, one Ibn Rustah wrote that the Rus were a people of traders and slavers, ruled by a 'Khagan-Rus' (a Rus chieftain) dwelling on an island in a lake, who preyed upon the native population to acquire animal pelts, slaves and other tradeable goods. He also noted that they were intensely quarrelsome among themselves, used to settling disputes through fighting, and prepared to sacrifice human beings to their gods in a ritual that involved hanging.[19]

The writer Ibn Fadlan, who journeyed to Itil himself, observed in 922 that he had 'never witnessed more perfect bodies' than those of the traders he encountered, but also that they were the filthiest of the races created by Allah and 'as stupid as donkeys'.[20] Ibn Fadlan's account also includes an intriguing description of the Rus traders' religious observances. Ibn Fadlan notes that each of the Rus traders leaves offerings and prays to a wooden pole, the image of his god, giving careful accounts of the number of slave-girls and furs he has to sell. Most tellingly, Ibn Fadlan recounts the increasing desperation with which unlucky traders return to their gods on successive days, doubling and redoubling their sacrifices, pleading with their deities for a 'merchant who has many dinars and dirhams, and who will buy whatever I wish to sell'.[21] It is not difficult to imagine the consequences of a truly unsuccessful trip to Itil. A group of traders would have battled their way down the Dnieper from Kiev, wading through the freezing rapids of the cataracts, sailing through potentially hostile Pecheneg and Khazar territory, dragging their ship across a wilderness and into the Volga, and thence to the remote encampment of Itil, only to discover that Arab traders were not in the mood for buying. What use, then, would be their cargo of furs and slaves? Doubtless such lean times, for traders with nothing left to lose, were the origin of 'Viking raids' on the southern Caspian in 864, 910 and 912, when fleets sacked Abasgun, Baku and Azerbaijan.

By 943, the Muslim merchants in Itil were dwindling, and the few remaining were telling stories of a lack of demand back home. Although the Vikings cannot have known it, their traders told the truth – the supplies of the Afghan silver mines were running out, leading to a financial crisis across the Islamic world. Demand fell for luxuries like fur and slave-girls, and for those Rus unlucky enough to make the arduous journey for no reward, the consequences were predictable. That year a Viking fleet captured the town of Berda near Baku, but was defeated by a Muslim counter-assault, and an out-break of dysentery. Their enemies showed them no mercy even in the afterlife, looting their buried corpses of their grave-goods.[22]

The sudden reduction of Arab silver would have an effect elsewhere in the Viking world, and may have ultimately led to Svein Forkbeard's search for new revenues in England (see Chapter Eight). The lean times in the Arab world were also a probable cause of renewed pressure on the Byzantines. In 941, Rurik's son Igor sailed on Constantinople once more. This time, the numbers were serious, with conservative estimates placing the fleet at over a thousand ships. Byzantium was caught, once again, almost unawares, with the army of Romanus I fighting Muslims in the east, and his navy spread thinly across the Black Sea and the Mediterranean. News of the fleet's approach reached Constantinople early, the reward for renewed diplomatic links between the Byzantine Empire and the Bulgars through whose territory the Vikings passed. The Bulgars made no attempt to stop the fleet, but did get a message to Constantinople that trouble was on the way.

With no other option, the Byzantine shipwrights dragged everything remotely seaworthy into service, refitting 15 old vessels that had been earmarked for scrap. The ships were kitted with launchers for Greek fire, and sent on 11 June to block the Bosphorus, that tiny strait which forms the portal from the Black Sea to Constantinople and the Mediterranean. It was a pitiful attempt at defence, but Greek fire was not something for which the Vikings were prepared.[23] Normal fire was one thing, but the Byzantines had a secret ingredient that made their flames impossible to douse with mere water.[24] The front line of the approaching Viking fleet was engulfed in the mysterious flame, and the other ships hastily turned. They headed east, and Constantinople was saved, although the remainder of the Viking fleet wrought havoc along the northern Black Sea coast of what is now modern Turkey, particularly among the inhabitants of the local monasteries, with only occasional resistance.

Before long, the remainder of the Byzantine fleet had been successfully recalled to the Black Sea, and stood in wait for the Vikings on their homeward voyage. The Vikings made the fatal error of trying to return by the way in which they had come, past Byzantium itself, where their fleet was met by an overwhelming mass of Byzantine ships, many armed with Greek fire. Few Vikings made it back alive; Igor himself was only saved by the shallow draft of his ship, allowing him to seek refuge in waters where the Byzantine ships could not follow him. He was back in 944, with an even bigger fleet,

sailing alongside an army that marched on the land – all the
better to present a double-pronged threat to the Byzantines.
But Igor's new attempt never made it to Constantiople –
instead, Romanus met him at the Danube and negotiated a
detailed treaty.

Both sides came away convinced that they had the upper
hand. Romanus had a guarantee that Vikings would only be
permitted on Byzantine soil in unarmed groups of fifty, and
that a tax was to be levied on trade. Igor could be satisfied with
reciprocal military agreements that guaranteed his merchants a
much safer passage south of the cataracts. But posterity would
show Romanus was the true victor, in the spiritual sphere
initially – conditions were now favourable for Byzantine
missionaries to travel to Kiev and Novgorod, and their most
influential convert was Igor's own wife. She is known as Olga
in the *Russian Primary Chronicle*, but was Helga to the
Swedes, another sign of the slow slide of Viking Rus into true
Russian. She came from a rich family in the north, and if
Rurik's younger brother existed, may even have been his
descendant. Soon after Igor's treaty with Romanus, the Viking
leader met with an untimely end at the cataracts, murdered by
Pecheneg tribesmen of the Drevljane.[25]

The Drevljane were attempting to grab for power like the
Vikings, hoping to control the rivers and thereby trade between the Black Sea and Baltic. With that in mind Mal, prince
of the Drevljane, made a proposal of marriage to Igor's widow,
hoping thereby to bring the lands of the Rus within his own
control. So, at least, claims the *Russian Primary Chronicle*, in a
story that grows progressively less believeable, but which has
stayed with us because it became incorporated into hagiogra-
phy.

Mal soon discovered the true nature of his bride-to-be, when
he heard of how she ordered his ambassadors thrown in a

trench, and asked them if they found her honour to their taste, even as her men shovelled earth and buried the Drevljane alive. Olga then embarked on a campaign of revenge herself, ending in a year-long siege of the Drevljane capital. Eventually, she consented to a truce, asking only for a tribute of six live birds per household. When this strangest of taxes was handed over, she had her men wrap sulphur tapers to the birds' legs and sent them flying home to their nests under the eaves, causing a terrible conflagration.[26]

The story is doubtful, of course, not the least because it is one of several bird-arson tales to be found in Viking legend. But other elements ring true, particularly Olga's decision in the aftermath to leave many of the Drevljane free, all the better to tax them. For it was in the regency of Olga, as her son Svyatoslav reached maturity, that the Swedish Rus began to institutionalize the collection of revenue from the conquered areas. Each autumn, as the trading season came to an end, the rulers of the Rus would begin their *polyudie*, a progress among the peoples of the surrounding area to collect tribute, be it in money, furs, slaves or services. In typical Viking style, the ruling class of nascent Russia would leech off their neighbours when times were hardest, returning to their bases of Kiev and Novgorod in the spring, ready for a new season of trading with the south. Olga put a stop to the charade, instead setting up a system of government-salaried tax inspectors, extorting her protection money in a more civilized manner.

As for Olga, she began paying tribute to a higher power. After ruling in the name of her son Svyatoslav, she found a new faith in the Christian God, and set aside her warlike ways. At the instigation of her mentor, a missionary called Father Gregory, she even made a pilgrimage to Constantinople, there to be baptized in the cathedral of Hagia Sophia itself. But Olga had a rude awakening on her arrival in Constantinople. She expected to be feted as a visiting dignitary, bearing gifts of gold plate, and proclaiming that her baptismal name was to be Helena, in honour of the current empress. But the emperor Constantine VII, son-in-law of Romanus I, had a different view, assuming that Olga was coming to pay tribute to Constantinople as a representative of a vassal state. In his eyes, he honoured her by permitting her to dine with the ladies-in-waiting. Olga returned to Kiev, still a Christian, but embarrassed enough at her treatment to send envoys to Germany in search of Catholic priests, hoping perhaps to have better treatment from them than at the hands of the Eastern Orthodox nobility.

Despite the occasional disagreement with her son, Olga did not have to endure an outright challenge from him – the closest they came to an argument was over his pagan polygamy, of which Olga sternly disapproved.[27] But after Olga, later Saint Olga, was laid to rest in 969, her son did not wait long before renewing war with Constantinople.

Svyatoslav himself led a campaign along the river Volga to Itil, where he destroyed the centre of the Khazar people who opposed Viking passage to the Caspian Sea. That, at least, was the official excuse – it is more likely that the Khazars were getting the blame for the drop in the flow of Muslim silver. When this led to no appreciable improvement in trade with the Muslim world, Svyatsolav did what any self-respecting Viking leader would, with a financial crisis looming and a large number of unoccupied warriors – he marched on Constantinople, with an army of Rus alongside tributary battalions from the conquered Pechenegs, Magyars and Bulgarians.

With Constantinople ruled by the usurper John Tzimisces, Svyatoslav sought restitution – he believed, or at least it was his excuse, that Tzimisces had reneged on an earlier Emperor's offer to pay Svyatoslav to fight the Bulgarians. But when

Tzimisces offered to pay his predecessor's debt, Svyatoslav made it clear that there would be no negotiation:

> If you reject my proposals, you will have no choice, you and your subjects, but to leave Europe forever, where you have scarcely any territory left to call your own and where you have no right to dwell. Retire then to Asia [Minor], and leave Constantinople to us.[28]

Tzimisces had hoped that the sight of supremely disciplined Byzantine troops would be enough to put Svyatoslav to flight. His generals were able to win small victories against some of the auxiliaries. The battle against the Rus themselves, fought at Arcadiopolis (modern Lülebargaz), was a tougher affair. But the Byzantines, hardened in countless battles in the east, eventually won, forcing the surviving Rus to retreat. In 972, John Tzimisces pursued Svyatoslav into Bulgaria, 'liberating' the region from its conqueror, and besieging the former invaders in Dristra (modern Silistra). After a three-month siege, Svyatoslav made a desperate attempt to hack his way through the Byzantine army, but failed. Humiliated, he called for a meeting with Tzimisces, who was of Armenian descent, short of stature with dark-blond hair and a red beard. Svyatoslav, despite his Slavic name, still had Viking genes – his head was shaved, but for two long locks of blond hair, the mark of rulership in his Rus culture, and a long Scandinavian-style moustache. Suitably cowed, the Rus leader politely expressed his hope that the old treaty would continue to be honoured, and then rowed back to his people.

However, Svyatoslav was not so lucky on his return journey. The Pechenegs had permitted his army to pass through their territory unhindered on the promise of a cut of the loot, and Syvatoslav was returning home empty-handed. The locals allowed him and his starving men to get as far as the cataracts of the Dnieper, where they ambushed them during the vulnerable portage process. Svyatoslav was killed, and the rulership of the Princedom of Kiev passed to his sons Jaropolk and Oleg.

It was a third son, Vladimir, overlord of Holmgard (Novgorod), who became the eventual ruler of Russia. Since he was the bastard offspring of Svyatoslav and a guard-captain's daughter, this outlying, unimportant town seemed suitable for him. Its northerly position, however, put it much closer to Scandinavia. Novgorod, it is thought, was the place of exile where Vladimir's contemporary Olaf Crowbone grew to manhood (see Chapter Six), and sagas relate several tales of the young Vikings' friendship.[29] It was thanks to Vladimir's proximity to the old country that he was able to call on Viking aid. In the inevitable power struggle that ensued between him and his brothers around 978–80, Vladimir arrived in Russia with an army of fresh recruits from Sweden, killed his brothers, and became the ruler of many pagan peoples. Vladimir's coup may also have revitalized the population with more Scandinavians and allowed it to preserve its Norse identity for another generation or so. The original 'Rus' had largely gone native by this time, replaced by semi-Slavic descendants. Vladimir's mercenary 'Varangians' from Sweden, many of whom stayed, brought stronger connections once more to the motherland.[30]

Vladimir was not a pagan for long. In far Constantinople, the new emperor Basil II, 'the Bulgar-Slayer' invoked the terms of his predecessor's treaty with Svyatoslav, and Vladimir was obliged to send 6,000 Viking soldiers to serve him. Beleaguered by no less than three challengers, themselves backed by reinforcements from Baghdad and Georgia, Basil II badly needed help. Vladimir insisted on a terrible price for his aid – the hand in marriage of the emperor's sister Anna. Contemporary writers present this as a mismatch of almost horrific proportions, a 25-year-old beauty, led weeping to the altar where waited a savage Viking beast who already had four other official wives and, it was later said, 800 concubines. Vladimir was, after all, the man one German chronicler called *fornicator immensus et crudelis*, whose second wife, Rogned, became his when he raped her in front of her terrified family in Polotsk.[31] Princess Anna accused her brothers of selling her into slavery, and her fears seem well founded.

But Vladimir was most insistent. He had kept his end of the bargain, and his 6,000 warriors turned the tide in Basil II's war. Many of them were to stay and form units within the household troops, the first of the famous Varangian Guard. When the weeks turned into months and there was still no sign of his new bride, Vladimir showed the Byzantines what could happen when treaties were broken – he attacked the Crimea, in blatant defiance of another of Svyatoslav's promises.[32] Realizing that the Crimean campaign was a prelude to yet another Viking assault on Constantinople itself, Basil II caved in, although he did insist that Vladimir set aside his allegiance to the Thunder God, and instead accept Christian baptism.

If it was an attempt to call Vladimir's bluff, it failed. Vladimir was no stranger to Christianity, having grown up in the shadow of his grandmother, Saint Olga. He accepted, the extremely reluctant Princess Anna arrived with a group of priests, and Vladimir was baptized in Kiev. The marriage and attendant conversion was, says one authority, 'perhaps the most fateful religious ceremony in Russian history'.[33] It linked the fate of the Rus with that of the rulers of Constantinople and it led to the conversion, over a long period, of thousands of Vladimir's subjects. Most importantly of all for posterity, it locked Russia into the orbit and influence of the Eastern Orthodox Church.

6

ADVENT OF THE WHITE CHRIST

FROM HARALD GREYCLOAK TO OLAF CROWBONE

In 961, the oldest surviving son of Erik Bloodaxe was Harald Greycloak,[1] who became the nominal ruler of western Norway after the death of Hakon the Good, although his mother Gunnhild and, we may assume, her other Danish relatives had no small say in her son's decisions. He had four surviving brothers, who were also clamouring for areas of their own. Meanwhile, other parts of Norway belonged to non-relatives. Trondheim stayed in the hands of Earl Sigurd (who recognized the authority of Harald Greycloak, so long as he kept his nose out of Trondheim business), Tryggvi Olafsson still had the eastern coast of the Vik, and Guthroth Bjarnarson hung on to the western area.

The conflict over Norway became one of pagan independents versus the Christianized descendants of Harald Fairhair – or, from a more secular point of view, it was a matter of increased interference from the Danes. Unlike Hakon, Harald

Greycloak was determined to force Christianity on the Norwegians – possibly as a result of an agreement made with Harald Bluetooth in Denmark. Envoys of Greycloak interrupted sacrifices and despoiled places sacred to the gods of the Vikings, and did so with bad timing. The farmers began to wish for the more flexible days of Hakon, while a series of poor harvests and bad weather convinced both sides that their gods were angry.

On that much, historians are agreed, although Snorri pushes into more dubious ground in his *Heimskringla*, preferring to continue his one-man vendetta against Gunnhild Kingsmother.[2] Gunnhild, so claims Snorri, was incensed that such large sectors of Norway were not under the direct rule of her sons. Tryggvi and Guthroth in the south she could understand, since they at least had some claim to royal blood and some relationship with the departed Harald Fairhair. But these earls of Trondheim had no right to throw their weight around. Either through chance, or Gunnhild's sorcerous influences, depending on whom one believes, strife broke out among the earls of Trondheim. The weather in Norway continued to be very bad, such that it became unfeasible to leave cattle in the open, causing a skald to complain that: 'like the Finns, have we our bud-eaters bound in barn in middle summer.'[3]

Sigurd's brother Grjotgarth, a younger sibling unlikely to ever gain the title of earl through natural causes, was won over as Greycloak's man on the inside, and participated with the sons of Erik Bloodaxe in a surprise attack on the incumbent ruler of Trondheim. Sigurd perished in the flaming hall, but Grjotgarth did not gain the earldom for which he had hoped. Instead, he was forced to defer to Sigurd's son, Hakon the Great. Hakon had the full support of his region and the Uppland hinterland, which had often voted in favour of paganism and still supported its prime candidate. He fought

Harald Greycloak to a standstill, and the king was forced to accept that Hakon the Great had the same dominions as his father before him. Harald Greycloak was eventually lured to Denmark and killed by an agent of Hakon, who ensured that he himself then captured the 'criminal' and sent him off to the gallows.

Gunnhild Kingsmother and the survivors of her brood fled for the Orkneys. Although the remaining sons of Erik Blood-axe would continue to raid the coasts of Scandinavia and points beyond for another 20 years, they no longer presented any firm candidates for kingship in Norway.[4] In purging the powerful earls and kinglings of southern Norway, Harald Greycloak and his brother had cleared the way for an un-expected alliance of their bitterest enemies. Hakon the Great struck a deal with Harald Bluetooth, reclaim his title of earl, and no more. Meanwhile, the fleet of the Danish king arrived among the strongholds of southern Norway. On either side of the Vik, the depleted earldoms saw little choice but to swear allegiance to the Danes. Southern Norway was given to Harald Grenske, an obscure great-grandson of Fairhair – he took the title 'king' but ruled as an agent of the king of Denmark. Norway was split between the Danish puppet and the earl of Trondheim, and would remain so for a generation. *Heimskringla* reports a series of scuffles between Hakon the Great and a few fractious kinsmen, but essentially, he had what he wanted. Norway's sea coast belonged to Trondheim, and the southern districts were now, at least in theory, ruled by a descendant of Harald Fairhair. What Harald Bluetooth had to say about Norway's continued pagan status is not recorded – it seems that he would rather have peaceful heathens on his northern frontier than Greycloak and his covetous Christians. Possibly, Bluetooth had other plans for the Norwegians, but he was soon ousted by a series of misfortunes to the south, and by a betrayal from amongst his allies, and possibly from within his own family.

With Norway shakily secured, Bluetooth encouraged his son-in-law Styrbjorn to lead an attack on Sweden, then ruled by Styrbjorn's uncle Erik. Erik earned his nickname 'the Victorious' from this ill-fated venture, since the Danish army and its Baltic allies was soundly trounced near Uppsala. Harald Bluetooth then turned to his other available border, expanding south-eastward into the land of the Wends. All the while, he made sure to pay extravagant homage to Otto I, the ruler of Germany, although the two-faced nature of this loyalty became immediately apparent on Otto's death. His son Otto II was barely on the throne before Danish raiders conducted a series of attacks on Germany's north coast. Although Bluetooth denied all knowledge of it, he was surely somewhere behind it all, testing the new ruler's resolve. Unfortunately for Bluetooth, Otto II was resolute, not wasting any time listening to Bluetooth's protestations of innocence, but immediately launching a massive offensive against Denmark's southern border. Bluetooth was forced to call upon every available ally to held defend the Danevirke. Hakon the Great, embroiled in several local disputes with argumentative subordinates, was obliged to send a large force of his own men down to help, a case of pagan and Christian Scandinavians fighting side by side, and a sign, if ever there was, that blood ran thicker than holy water.

Several Viking sagas detail the attempts by the Germans to break through the invulnerable walls and moats that defended the land. This would have been news to the German chroniclers, and indeed it contradicts archaeological evidence from the location itself, both of which make it rather clear that the Danes and their Norwegian allies were severely beaten. German troops made it through the Danevirke, the port of Hedeby suffered a brief period in German hands, and the twilight years of Bluetooth's reign were spent as a German vassal. It was a humiliating descent from the heyday of the 960s, when Bluetooth stood a fine chance of becoming the master of all Scandinavia. His forays into Europe had cost him dear, and now Hakon was suddenly less willing to lend support from Trondheim – ready to plead he was busy on other matters, knowing that Bluetooth was no longer able to force him to comply.

Harald Bluetooth made one last attempt to bring the pagans to heel, sailing north to the Trondheim with a mighty fleet – so the saga claims, although this national 'navy' was still probably no more than 60 ships. Hakon was waiting for him with a fleet of similar size, jointly led by himself and his successor Earl Erik. Bluetooth's fleet was repulsed, and the aging Danish leader retreated to his native domains, never to trouble the north again. During the closing years of Bluetooth's reign, the Danes finally regained some of their honour, but did so without the help of the aging king.

Instead, Bluetooth's final years appear to have been dogged by an unexpected nemesis – his son, Svein Forkbeard, who, if the sagas are to believed, was instrumental in deposing him. A fort built by Otto II on the Danevirke was captured and burned down in 983, and soon Hedeby itself was recaptured after a siege. The Germans beaten away, at least for now, one might have expected the Danish leaders to congratulate themselves, but it was now that Bluetooth retreated too, supposedly to die from his wounds somewhere on the southern Baltic coast. The Christian king had been defeated by his pagan son – Svein Forkbeard was firmly devoted to the savage ways of Odin, trusting more in battle than in diplomacy. He did, however, tolerate a minor Christian presence if it prevented the Germans from finding another excuse to attack. Attempts by Forkbeard to orchestrate takeovers in Norway and Sweden were foiled, since the earls or Trondheim and Olof Skötkonung were strong in their respective realms. Consequently, with Germany strong to the south, and Norwegians and Swedes uncooperative to the north and east, Forkbeard turned his attentions west, to England.

England had enjoyed a long period of peace under King Edgar (r.959–975), a monarch with the support of several powerful Scandinavians and Celts. Through the early and unexpected death of his brother, Edgar had come to be the ruler of Mercia *and* Northumbria, and enjoyed relatively good relationships with the large Scandinavian populations in both his kingdoms. Squabbles among the English managed to ruin that state of affairs with Edgar's death. His son and heir was murdered before he made it out of his teens, by supporters of his younger brother, known to history as Aethelred the Ill-Counselled (*Aethelred Unraed*, or more popularly, 'the Unready'). The term 'supporters' is perhaps misleading – much was done in Aethelred's name without his consent. Whoever was running England from behind the scenes operated on the foolish assumption that the new waves of Viking invaders could be bought off.

Parties of Danes were raiding the coasts of England, often with the tacit and not-so-tacit support of their countrymen in the Danelaw, and of their cousins in Normandy. Christian envoys tried to broker some kind of deal based on shared spiritual beliefs with the Normans, but a treaty between them and the English failed to stop Normandy being used as a rest stop and hiding place for raiders on their way across the Channel.

If anything, the English attempts to buy off the raiders only encouraged even more of them. The term used at the time for the protection money was *gafol* ('tribute') although later writers would call it *danegeld* ('Dane-gold'). Once they started in 991, the English would be forced to pay such bribes for almost two hundred years, either directly to their enemies as *danegeld*, or to their supposed kingly protector as *heregeld* ('army-gold') a tax levied to fund the army that was supposed to make the paying of *danegeld* unnecessary.[5]

While the English came to regard their *danegeld* as an insurance policy against further raids, the Danes themselves saw it as a tribute not dissimilar from that collected in Scandinavia – not a one-off payment, but instead a form of protection money that could be extorted anew. Where more than one attacker was in the neighbourhood, such extortion often afforded very little safety, as the new outlaws in town would first raid to prove they could, and only then collect their *danegeld*. By the time the protectors' protection was actually needed, they were often long gone, and the cycle repeated itself with a new set of raiders.

Sources are largely quiet as to why Svein Forkbeard, the king of Denmark, should suddenly turn up at the head of a Viking raiding expedition in England in AD 994 – although a simple search for ready cash is not unlikely. Most contemporary references to his alleged conflict with his father, while mentioning that Harald Bluetooth was dead by 987, neglect to discuss a third party who temporarily seized Denmark from Forkbeard himself for a few years. But the chronicler Adam of Bremen claims that Denmark was invaded by King Erik the Victorious of Sweden, leading an army 'as innumerable as the sands of the sea'. The same period, claims Adam, also saw Denmark attacked from the south by Saxon war-bands intent on plundering the beleagured country.[6]

There are signs here of a forgotten conflict involving Swedes and Danes at the very least, either as invaders or forces supporting a pretender, with the likely involvement of non-

Vikings, too. It is, perhaps, no coincidence that the highly doubtful tale of derring-do, the *Saga of the Jomsvikings*, revolves around a group of raiders from what is now Germany/Poland, and their involvement in a conflict in Svein Forkbeard's Denmark.

The fact will not have escaped the reader that the family ties of the Norse world had become rather complicated by this point. The family trees in this book make some small attempt to demonstrate the dynastic connections that bound the Viking leaders together, but do not even come close to the whole story. Svein Forkbeard may have been the son of Harald Bluetooth, but he was also the nephew of Gunnhild Kingsmother. His sister Thyri was the widow of Styrbjorn, who led the ill-fated raid on Sweden repulsed by Erik the Victorious. Svein himself would eventually marry the widow of Erik the Victorious, making him the stepfather of King Olof *Skötkonung*, the 'tributary king' who came to the Swedish throne in AD 995, and paid Forkbeard to leave him alone. Forkbeard's own daughter Gytha would marry Earl Erik of the Trondheim, and there were several other, lesser alliances that firmly joined Svein to the other rulers of Scandinavia. When one finally untangles the web of marriages, in-laws, cousins and obligations, Forkbeard almost appears as the single figure most likely to rule Scandinavia with, if not the blessing of its inhabitants, at least a fair amount of toleration. The operative word, however, is *almost*. There was another.

His name was Olaf Tryggvason, nicknamed Crowbone for his hobby of reading the omens, an interest that he supposedly retained even after his conversion to Christianity. Crowbone's father was the same Tryggvi who had been killed in battle with Harald Greycloak. His mother, Astrid, had been a scion of the Swedish royal house. When Tryggvi was murdered in Greycloak's purges, Crowbone was not even born. His pregnant mother Astrid had somehow eluded capture. The sons of Erik Bloodaxe scoured the countryside looking for her, all the more desperately when they heard that she might be carrying Tryggvi's heir. But their ongoing troubles with Hakon distracted them, and Astrid was able to make her escape.

This, at least, is the *Heimskringla* version, although the sons of Bloodaxe must have been remarkably stupid if they truly failed to locate Astrid in her hiding place, her father's house. *Heimskringla*'s highly entertaining but also highly dubious version of events has Astrid and her infant son fleeing to the court of Sweden's King Erik the Victorious, eluding pursuing soldiers sent by the irate Gunnhild Kingsmother. From there, supposedly, they head for Russia, only to be intercepted midway by Baltic pirates,[7] and sold into slavery. Crowbone, claim his sagas, was then sold for the value of a single goat, and grew to manhood as a farmhand in what is now Estonia, before being rediscovered and freed by his uncle Sigurd.

If there is *any* truth in such a rags-to-riches fairytale, it may lie in its use as a legal defence later in Crowbone's life. For the first we hear of the adult Crowbone is in Russia, where he killed a man with an axe in a Novgorod marketplace, later claiming that his victim was the same pirate who had killed his mother's guardian Thorolf Lousebeard (too old to fetch a good price as a slave). Crowbone's legendary exploits then took him from Russia to the land of the Wends (Poland), where he enjoyed an all-too-brief marriage to the doomed princess Geira, daughter of the Wendish ruler Boleslav.

With that lady's early death, Crowbone supposedly headed west, first to his great-uncle Erik Bloodaxe's old haunts in Northumbria, before completing an impressive (and some might suspect, poetically neat) circumnavigation of the British Isles, raiding Scotland, the Hebrides, Man, the coasts of Ireland, Wales, and then somewhere on the coast of France.

Heading back for England, he stopped over in the Scilly Isles, close to the south-western tip of Cornwall, where a soothsayer, claims his epic saga, told him that he was destined for kingship, and to 'find the true faith.'[8]

Such is the idealized portrait of sagas, though the repetition of the word 'raiding' gives the game away. Luckily for the historian, Crowbone's enemies provided a wholly more believeable account of his deeds off the coasts of Britain. We see increasing evidence of Crowbone, or at least men very like him, in the British Isles in the *Anglo-Saxon Chronicles* in 981. It tells of a raid on Padstow in Cornwall, and seven ships (perhaps the same group) attacking Southampton. By 987, Anglo-Saxon records imply that the Vikings were raiding in far greater numbers, with Goda, the ruler of Devonshire, falling in battle 'with a great slaughter'.[9] It is around this point that the *Chronicle* records the first instance of paying off raiders from Dublin – an apparently simple solution, to a Christian bishop, which backfired almost immediately. In 993, the small raids of previous years were replaced with something much larger:

> Here in this year Olaf [i.e. Crowbone] came with ninety-three ships to Folkstone, and raided round about it, and then went from there to Sandwich, and overran all that, and so to Maldon.[10]

It was Maldon where the Anglo-Saxons would mount one of their most famous stands against the Vikings. Regardless of the unpheavals at the centre of the country, there were still local leaders who were able to put on a resistance. In Essex, the land of the East Saxons, the locals had managed to resist most attempts by Danes to settle, largely by organizing themselves on similar lines. The Vikings were not the only war-bands in the area – waiting for Crowbone at Maldon was the white-haired Saxon earl Byrhtnoth. The Vikings followed their time-honoured strategies, picking an offshore island for protection. The Maldon area, however, is notorious for its mud flats and shallows; when the Saxons arrived, they climbed down off their horses and simply waited on the shoreline, while the Vikings on Northey island glumly stared down at the receding tide. A thin causeway joined Northey to the mainland, and neither side felt like wading through the mud on either side of it. Someone would have to attack along the causeway, and whoever did would be at a great disadvantage.

If we are to believe the surviving fragment of the English poem *The Battle of Maldon*, there was considerable confidence to be found on both sides. The Vikings on the island called out to Byrhtnoth, asking him if he was the richest man in the neighbourhood, thereby hoping to work out whether he was in a position to offer them money. Pointedly, the Vikings in the poem refer to the bribe they demand as 'tribute'. But Byrhtnoth was not one of the Saxons who believed the Vikings could be bought off. His use of terms and phrasing in the poem implies that he stood with a force of several hundred men, easily the equal of the Viking numbers, and with the upper hand for as long as he stood on solid ground.

The standoff continued until the proud Byrhtnoth allowed the Vikings to come ashore. He had little choice – if he had forced them to remain on Northey, they would eventually have simply sailed away to raid elsewhere. By permitting them to come ashore along the narrow causeway and draw up in battle formation, Byrhtnoth hoped to settle things once and for all. Unfortunately, after granting them equal footing, he met his own death, as did many of his men, in a hard-fought battle on the shoreline. The progress of the battle was regarded with some bitterness by its poet, who took care to list the names of those who fought bravely, even after Byrhtnoth was cut down, as well as those who fled from the Vikings, particularly one Godric, who galloped off on the dead Byrhtnoth's horse, thereby giving some of the other men the impression that Byrhtnoth himself was running away. Although later sources would claim that the battle of Maldon was a pyrrhic victory for the English, Byrhtnoth's last stand was not damaging enough to prevent Crowbone conducting further raids that season, and the Vikings were also able to demand crippling tributes from the people of Essex that year.

In 994, Crowbone returned with 94 ships, some of which were led by his brother-in-law Svein Forkbeard. Forkbeard had greater plans than a mere series of assaults – in a banquet with his allies, he swore that within three years he would invade England and seize the country for himself, driving out King Aethelred or killing him. The hordes of Swedes and Danes who had once sailed east in search of fortunes, now turned west again. Forkbeard was one of them, realizing that with the coffers of the Muslims empty, the next best source of ready coin at the edge of the Viking world would be among the wealthy English.

Forkbeard may have had another reason. Svein Forkbeard was the son of Harald Bluetooth, but Forkbeard's modern sources are not even sure which of Bluetooth's wives or concubines was Forkbeard's mother. The Icelandic *Tale of Thorvald the Far-Travelled* baldly states that Svein only '*claimed* to be the son of Harald Gormsson [Bluetooth] . . .' and that 'Svein was not settled in Denmark at that time because [Bluetooth] would not admit his paternity.'[11] Is this a later slander by enemies of Svein? If true, it would certainly help explain his strange relationship with the 'father' he supposedly overthrew, and his long-term association with outcast war-bands like the Jomsvikings. It also casts new light on Forkbeard's willingness to simply take England by force, without any acknowledged right of kingship. If Denmark had not been his by birthright, why not steal England as well?

So it is that we have Forkbeard and Crowbone, raiding the coasts of England either to bolster Forkbeard's Danish regime, or to raise enough funds to win it back from a forgotten usurper, or possibly simply because they felt like it. For outlaws intent on plunder, there had not been a better time to attack the English. No Alfred the Great appeared to unite the shires; instead, the hapless country was saddled with Aethelred Unraed and his coterie of self-interested nobles. As 'England', that confederacy of Angles, Saxons and Britons threatened to tear apart, Aethelred and his advisors were prepared to consider anything, appearing to blow hot and cold towards the raiders quite unpredictably.

Aethelred might have ordered the deaths of entire communities of Danes, but he also seemed keen to establish alliances with other Vikings. The *Saga of Gunnlaug Serpent-Tongue* goes out of its way to describe him as a 'good ruler', always ready to help his Viking associates – he even bestows Gunnlaug with the trusty sword, Kingsgift, after Gunnlaug sings a song comparing him to God Almighty.[12] Christian Vikings, it appears, were friends that Aethelred was prepared to tolerate. He would even marry one, in a manner of speaking, when he wed Emma, the daughter of the Norman ruler Richard the Fearless in 1002. The marriage, it was hoped, would bring England and Normandy closer together, perhaps even into a union that might block the Channel and bottle up the Vikings in the North Sea. But there were other implications. Queen Emma was of Viking ancestry – her great-grandfather was the raider Hrolf the Walker, and she probably spoke reasonable Danish.[13] Emma was not the only new arrival with possible pro-Danish leanings. Other nobles in and outside the Danelaw took the hint, and tried to deal with the Vikings on their own terms. The presence of the Danes in the midst of the English would eventually prove to be the most insidious assault of all – over the generations, the fearsome raiders from the sea gained a human face. The end result of Aethelred's haphazard attempts at inclusion was to make Danish alliances, and ultimately Danish kings, seem acceptable to the English.

Another of Aethelred's new allies was Crowbone himself. At some point in his adventures, Olaf 'Crowbone' Tryggvason became a Christian. *Heimskringla* suggests that he had a sudden conversion after hearing the ravings of the old man in the Scilly Isles. Possibly he was coming to realize the political advantages of tolerating Christians. Supposedly, after his conversion, Crowbone stopped raiding the coasts of Britain. He was baptized at Andover, in modern Hampshire, with King Aethelred himself serving as his godfather, a symbolic adoption, alliance and treaty that bore great similarities to the conversion of Guthrum by King Alfred. But unlike Guthrum, Crowbone did not appear to have any obvious designs on the British Isles. He seemed ready, like Hakon the Great before him, to acknowledge a friendship with the Anglo-Saxons that would allow him to return to Norway with his rear sufficiently guarded. As for Aethelred, although history famously records that he was badly advised, perhaps he was copying the actions of some of his forerunners on the French mainland. Had not the Franks successfully halted the Viking advance by setting other Vikings like Hrolf the Walker upon them? If Aethelred was prepared to do a deal with Crowbone for this reason, it could only mean that there was a Viking somewhere else in the world he feared more. In a textbook case of preferring the Christian devil he knew to the pagan devil he didn't, Aethelred formed an alliance with Crowbone, thereby hoping to keep Forkbeard away.

His friendship with the English established, Crowbone had

begun a slow procession back to his native Norway. Now supposedly a Christian, he did his bit for godliness on the way, stopping off in the Orkneys and Hebrides en route, and threatening to put the locals to the sword and burn their houses to the ground unless they were prepared to submit to the love of Christ. Although hardly a Church-approved method of evangelizing, it did bring fast results, and Olaf sailed for Norway with newly Christianized territories at his back, hoping for similar results in Norway.

When matters of Christian evangelizing among Vikings are discussed, it is important to remember that for the early Church, the end often justified the means. Mass conversion under threat of execution hardly represented the acceptance of Christianity into a people's hearts, but it did pave the way for further missionaries. Christian priests and bishops accompanied Crowbone in his later travels, and if any of them had any reservations about his bluntly barbaric methods, their complaints are not recorded. But the Church has always been able to think in the long term. While the reluctant promises of threatened farmers were unlikely to change their characters all that much, their children would grow up in towns with churches at their centre. Christianity had a toehold, and Europe would be fully Christianized within a few generations, thanks in part to the atrocities of men such as Crowbone.

Forkbeard, meanwhile, was making other plans. He married the widow of Erik the Victorious, a woman unnamed in the contemporary chronicles, but who may have been the Sigrid the Haughty of saga legend, who had seen off several earlier suitors, including the hapless Norwegian king Harald Grenske, by burning them alive.[14] She had also, according to legend, even rejected the advances of Crowbone himself, or rather, been rejected by him when she refused to give up her pagan ways.

The Gokstad longship

Fragment of a painted stone showing
Odin on his eight-legged horse Sleipnir

Carriage from the Oseberg grave

Oseberg ship

Wooden post with
carved animal head

Trelleborg Fortress

Reconstruction of the Viking barracks at the fortress of Trelleborg.
It is considered to have been built by Harald Bluetooth

Interior reconstruction at Trelleborg, built following
the pattern of the original foundation post holes

St Olaf, patron saint of Norway

Smith's mould for casting both Christian crosses and Thor's hammers

L'Anse aux Meadows National Historic Park, Newfoundland, Canada

A berserker, chewing on his shield, from the Lewis chess set

The Lindisfarne stone, depicting a raiding party of Vikings

Norway was unstable once more, and Crowbone arrived in the hope of winning a kingdom for himself. Trondheim's Earl Hakon had not helped matters by imposing his own variant of the *droit de seigneur* on a couple of prominent locals. *Heimskringla* recounts at least two occasions when the pagan lord decided to borrow another man's wife, sending his warriors over to the lawful husband, and demanding that his spouse be handed over like a common whore for his use. The placing of the stories by Snorri Sturluson immediately invites suspicion – they crop up at exactly the moment that Crowbone returns with his Christian message, as if Crowbone himself was using them as reasons why the Trondheimers might find Christianity to be a more appealing religion than the 'old ways'.

Whatever the truth regarding Earl Hakon's behaviour, the farmers were in open revolt by the time Crowbone arrived – whether to avenge their stolen womenfolk, or to depose a leader who had lost Odin's mandate depends on one's sense of story. Crowbone was welcomed by a large sector of the population, and promised riches to whoever brought him Hakon's head. According to *Heimskringla*, a disguised Earl Hakon heard this proclamation, and decided to hide in a pigsty, accompanied only by his faithful servant Kark, who, realizing which way the wind was blowing, knifed the old earl in the throat, hacking off his head and bringing it to Crowbone. For technical reasons, however, Kark's reward for his betrayal was to be beheaded himself.

Crowbone became the ruler of Trondheim, causing Earl Hakon's relatives to flee to Sweden. As a descendant of the famous Harald Fairhair, Crowbone also enjoyed a good claim to southern Norway, and with Grenske dead, it fell to him by default. Undoubtedly, there would be resistance from the Danes under Forkbeard, and Crowbone had a brief window of opportunity to establish himself before war broke out again.

Crowbone began his campaign of Christianizing Norway, marching from the Vik up to the west and north, accompanied by his army. In each new township, he presented the case – accept the love of the Christian God, or die resisting. While the sagas present Crowbone's march as a largely religious venture, it also mopped up a lot of political resistance, firmly establishing the new order along with the new beliefs. There are reports of fights and skirmishes, but also of mass conversions and treaties sealed by marriages. Crowbone smartly targeted not just the wielders of temporal power, but also their allies in the pagan religion. A proclamation went ahead of him, demanding that all 'sorcerers' leave the country. It was, at least, a witch-hunt that permitted the victims a chance to escape. Those that chose to remain were burned at the stake or otherwise executed. Among Crowbone's victims was a distant cousin, Eyvind Kelda, a descendant of Harald Fairhair, left to drown on a tidebound skerry.

Even though Crowbone's achievements are lovingly recounted by later Christian authors, there are still some strange contradictions. His habit of observing the omens and other pagan beliefs seems to have stayed with him for his whole life. Even *Heimskringla*, the work of the pious Snorri, recounts a folktale that grew up around one particular visitor – an old one-eyed man who entered the hall at Ogvaldsness, where Crowbone was staying. Crowbone found him to be an entertaining conversationalist, and with no skald around to sing stories of times past, Crowbone talked to the old man through the night. The one-eyed stranger seemed to have an answer for anything; he was even able to provide a detailed account of how Ogvaldsness got its name.

It was only late in the night that Crowbone was ushered to bed by the Christian bishop who had been at his side through the long campaign, but even then, he woke in the night and asked where the stranger was. The stranger could not be found, although the bemused kitchen staff reported that he had admonished them on leaving for the meagre fare they were preparing for the king's table. He offered them two sides of beef and was never seen again. Crowbone ordered the meat destroyed, claiming that it was surely a gift from the pagan Lord of Hosts, Odin, and not to be accepted by good Christian folk.[15]

The tale of Crowbone's mystery visitor may have been a bad dream given shape and meaning by later scribes, but if it has any roots in the real world, it could also be an allegory of Crowbone's own doubts. There is certainly something suspicious in the behaviour of the bishop, who all but orders Crowbone to bed – was this famous figure less a soldier of Christ than another puppet? The tale of the one-eyed man hints that Crowbone still had some hankering for his old religion.

It did not come as any surprise to Crowbone that true resistance awaited further to the north, in Trondheim. Ahead of Crowbone's arrival, assemblies met and decided that they would treat his attempt at conversion with the same indifference as they had that of Hakon the Good. Crowbone's attitude demonstrates how little had changed. He was happy, he claimed, to sacrifice to the old gods with the people of Trondheim, as Hakon the Good had done so reluctantly in the past. But since Crowbone was a great king and this was an event of supreme importance, it would have to be the greatest sacrifice ever made in the region. The old gods, said Crowbone pointedly, were no longer happy with a few chickens, the odd dog and a couple of horses. The situation (presumably the blessing of his kingship and the brewing war with Denmark) required full-strength human sacrifice. But Crowbone wanted to take things even further. This time, he claimed, it would not be enough to bump off a couple of slaves or prisoners-of-war, nor would it be acceptable to execute some criminals in the name of Odin. These sacrifices would require the noblest of blood, the deaths of leaders, not followers – and he proceeded to list the names of twelve of the most powerful men in the region. In a matter of moments, the assembly changed from discussion into standoff, with Crowbone's warriors seizing twelve eminent hostages.

Further north, in the heartland of the Trondheim region, he faced a similar assembly of recalcitrant heathens. This time, one farmer in particular, Járnskeggi, whipped up the crowd into support of the old ways. Faced with greater numbers than in the last location, Crowbone feigned acceptance until he was inside the temple. Once inside, he personally smashed Thor's idol, while his associates destroyed the other gods. In the riot that ensued outside, Járnskeggi was killed by Crowbone's men. None stepped forward to take his place, and the remaining farmers accepted the decree of Crowbone that they would all be baptized and turn into good Christians. Just as extra insurance, he took many of their family members hostage, and threatened to kill them if anyone stopped behaving in a Christian manner.

The treatment received by Trondheim was a textbook case of Crowbone's methods. He arrived with threats and destruction, and then, once consent was at least theoretically obtained, did what he could to make his reign appear to bring benefits. On the banks of the Trondheimfjord he founded a new town, first simply called 'the trading place', *kaupang*, but later known as Nitharos, and long after the Viking Age was over, as the *city* of Trondheim. The town would form a new centre for the Vikings in the outlying areas, a place for them to gather that had no association with the pagan assembly or temples of old. At its centre, of course, there would be a church.

The crucifix began to compete with the hammer of Thor as the must-have fashion accessory, and missionaries soon followed behind the trendsetters. In distant Iceland, for example, where missionaries had been visiting the remote communities since 980, the news of the conversion of Norway as a whole led many of the diehard heathens to believe they were missing out on something.[16] When Thangbrand, a Saxon priest in Crowbone's retinue, was dispatched to Iceland to spread the word, many Icelanders began to seriously consider converting.[17] Others, however, spoke out against the Christians in the same manner as the Trondheimers of old. One Hedin the Sorcerer was slaughtered by Thangbrand the Christian soldier, along with all his retainers. A similar fate awaited Veturlidi the Poet, who composed a satirical verse about the missionary, for which he was cut down in front of his son.[18] Thangbrand met his match when his ship, the *Bison*, was wrecked on the eastern coast near Bulandness. There, he got into an argument with a devout heathen lady by the name of Steinunn, who asked him where his Christ was when Thor was causing his ship to be smashed on the rocks. According to Steinunn, Thor had challenged Christ to a fight, but Christ had not shown up.[19]

Thangbrand eventually headed back to Norway around 999, leaving behind him a confused mix of Christian converts and zealous heathen resistance. Although many Icelanders had accepted Christ, there were still many like Steinunn. Thangbrand had killed a few himself, no doubt on the understanding that they could be better convinced by God himself, but he certainly could not kill them all. The Icelanders, let us not forget, were largely the descendants of those who had left Norway during previous troubles up to and including the imposition of the rule of Harald Fairhair. They were, to a large extent, like Trondheimers, but *difficult*.

Back in Norway, Crowbone hit the Icelanders where it hurt.

After allowing them to enjoy relatively free trade for two years, he closed the ports of Norway to heathens. Icelanders found their newfound trading route cut off, and with it the bulk of their contacts with Europe – Trondheim was the point of departure for most vessels heading for Iceland. Crowbone did not merely enforce his will indirectly; his men seized ships with Icelanders on board, and held any prominent Icelanders hostage. Possession of a ship fit to travel to Norway was a likely sign of a man being high indeed in Icelandic society, and Crowbone found himself with relatives and associates of many of Iceland's most powerful families. Crowbone sent word back to Iceland that if the families wanted to see their sons and cousins again, then it was time to welcome Christ into their lives. If they resisted again, he promised maimings and executions.[20]

News of Crowbone's behaviour caused exactly the upheavals he had hoped for. The growing Christian faction in Iceland immediately redoubled its efforts at conversion. Resistance to missionaries dropped drastically when preachers were backed by the threat of harm to loved ones. Some strongholds clung even harder to their heathenism, but there was enough discord for the already Christianized areas to seriously consider forming a breakaway society – holding their own Christian assemblies. The prospect threatened to divide Iceland along sectarian lines, and to destroy the democratic system that had endured for a generation. A boatload of Icelandic Christians reached Norway, its passengers intent on pleading with Crowbone for more time. They would do what they could, they said, to persuade their more reluctant fellow islanders. Crowbone gave them a little more time, but he knew that he was winning. Iceland could not survive without the shipping link to Norway.

7

BEYOND THE EDGE OF THE WORLD

ICELAND, GREENLAND AND VINLAND

There are some who claim that Gotland, with its hoards of silver, is the treasury of the Viking Age. But it is Iceland that preserved the most valuable relics of all – the words of the Vikings themselves. Cut off from Europe by long distances across treacherous seas, the colonies of Iceland first became a haven for fugitives, both well-intentioned and criminal. In the centuries after the Viking Age, the isolated Icelanders chronicled the activities of the Viking Age in the many sagas that are our main literary source for the period. The conservative, exclusive society of Iceland maintained heavy restrictions on change, leading to a homogenous population and a language that has changed little from the medieval Norwegian tongue spoken by the original settlers. The precise identity of the original settlers, however, is more problematic.

According to the ancient Greek writer Pytheas, six days' sail north of Britain, mariners would reach the Arctic island of

Thule. There, the local inhabitants lived a peaceful farming life, and drank a beverage made from grain and honey – a forerunner perhaps of Viking mead. Pytheas paints a bleak picture of life in the frozen north, claiming that the barbarian farmers of Thule brought their harvest indoors so that they could thresh their grain out of the wet, sunless weather. Considering that Pytheas's other descriptions of the far north include what appear to be several descriptions of the Baltic, it is likely that the Thule to which he referred was a location somewhere on the coast of Norway. For some, however, his comments are the first known reference to Iceland.[1]

Although popular wisdom credits the Vikings with the discovery of Iceland, that distinction belongs to the Irish. It was, after all, Irish monks that explored the coasts of Ireland and Scotland right round to luckless Lindisfarne, in search of remote places to set their hermitages and monasteries. As part of the contemplative life, some of the early Christians ascetics would set out in wickerwork boats clad in skin, or *curachs*, in search of a 'desert in the ocean'. It was the ultimate leap of faith, a 'wandering' or *peregrinatio*, in which the monks would steer a course into the unknown, trusting in God to bring them to a safe landfall. Such blind sailing may indeed have brought monks to Ireland in the first place, from Gaul.

It is likely to have been Irish monks, sailing into what they believed to be open sea, who first witnessed the *hillingar* effect, the 'uplifting' or 'looming' of an arctic mirage. When significantly colder air underlies a layer of warmer air, as can happen at northern latitudes particularly in the summer months, objects on the ground can be refracted so that they appear higher than they really are. Distant ships may appear to float inverted in the air, and distant lands may suddenly become visible, even though they are over the horizon. Although Iceland lay beyond the normal range of ships of the pre-Viking period, its phantom image may have encouraged early sailors to seek it out.

When Viking sailors 'discovered' Iceland, the Irish were already there. The sagas of Iceland's colonization, written long after the event, attempt to revise history to exclude the Irish presence. Norse tradition tells of the legendary Gardar the Swede, who sailed west from the Scandinavian mainland, hoping to reach the Hebrides, where he expected to pick up his wife's inheritance. Gardar was blown far off course in a gale, missed the Hebrides by miles, and reached the easternmost part of Iceland – tellingly, this is exactly where two communities of Irish monks were trying to eke out an isolated existence. Rather kindly for the sake of prosperity, Gardar then sailed clockwise along the coast of the 'new' land, all the way around to the secluded cove of Husavik ('Houses-bay') on the northern shore. After a winter at Husavik, Gardar then supposedly completed his circumnavigation of the island, which he modestly named Gardarsholm, before heading back to civilization.

If Gardar truly had relatives and colleagues in the Hebrides, then his accidental trip to Iceland probably owed more to stories heard from the Irish and those who associated with them. The tale of his journey seems to exist for one reason only, as a means of retroactively crediting a Norseman with the first circumnavigation of the island, and thereby its ownership.[2] Gardar supposedly spread the word about his discovery, but even so, the next Viking arrived in Iceland by crashing into it. His name was Naddod, and he was supposedly a Viking of some high standing, forced to leave his native Norway for reasons undisclosed. Hitting a storm somewhere off the Faeroes, Naddod and his crew were blown to Iceland's eastern coast, once again, close to the sites of earlier Irish settlement. Naddod, it is said, put ashore with his men and climbed the hill of Reydarfjall, hoping to see the smoke of cook-fires, or some other evidence of human habitation. Conveniently for later claimants, Naddod and his men reported no sign of human life whatsoever, and set off back to the Faeroes amid a punishing snowstorm. Unhappy with their experience, they chose to call the putative Gardarsholm by a new name – Snowland.

Despite such unpromising beginnings, the place soon attracted another sailor, this time intentionally. Floki Vilgerdason later gained the name Raven-Floki for his legendary assistants – a trio of ravens cast out from the ship, whose flights were closely watched for signs of land sighted. The first raven, set free early in the trip, turned and flew back to the Faeroes. The second, released later, returned to Floki's ship, unable to find another place to land. The third (and we may wonder why the second raven was not reusable) flew ahead of his ship, confirming that land lay beyond the horizon. Like so many other sagas, the tale of Raven-Floki seems too neat to be taken at face value – with its avian navigational aids, it bears too close a resemblance to the story of Noah. However, other elements of the Raven-Floki tale ring true, such as the miserable time he had once he arrived.

Raven-Floki and his fellow Vikings eventually made landfall in the north-west of the island, and spent the summer clubbing seals and netting fish. They were obviously planning on staying for the long haul, since they had brought a considerable amount of livestock with them. But they were fooled by the deceptive Arctic summer – on a coast warmed by the Gulf Stream, and with long days to offset the cold latitude, Raven-Floki's group made poor preparations for the turn of the seasons. When the autumn arrived, its severity took the Vikings by surprise. Raven-Floki's livestock all died, supposedly for lack of fodder. After a bitter winter, Raven-Floki decided to return home, but was forced by spring storms to put back to land and wait another year. When he did finally make it back to Norway, he had nothing positive to say about his trip at all, and gave the place of his torment the name it bears today – Iceland.

Despite such unpromising beginnings, Iceland was colonized. Perhaps it was thanks to Raven-Floki's more positive associate Thorolf, who claimed that Iceland's pastures were so rich they dripped with butter. Possibly there were other pressures, political and logistical, that led large numbers of colonists to arrive between 870 and 930. Iceland's sagas of settlement mention good Vikings wrongly accused of crimes, or fleeing the land reforms that accompanied Harald Fairhair's consolidation of power in Norway. The age of the great land-rush to settle Iceland is also roughly contemporary with Viking difficulties elsewhere – defeats in France, Ireland and Scotland, and internal strife in the Orkneys, for example. Iceland was a chance for a new beginning, a fresh start far from the warring troubles of Old Europe. In later generations, the descendants of the first settlers would mythologize their arrival as a triumph of liberty, telling tales remarkably similar to those of later colonists who would flee further west on the *Mayflower*.

The Icelanders, so say the stories, fled the tyranny of Harald Fairhair, although he was not even born when the migrations began. The most famous of their number were Ingolf Arnarson and Leif Hrodmarrson, relatives who had become embroiled in a bitter vendetta over Leif's rivalry with an unwelcome suitor for the hand of his betrothed. When the two kinsmen ended the feud in traditional Viking style, by murdering the suitor and his supporters, their estates were confiscated. With nothing to lose, they went in search of Raven-Floki's Iceland.

For some reason, they had a lot of Irish people with them.

Despite their Norwegian blood, the brothers appear to have spent a while pillaging Ireland – indeed, Leif was the proud wielder of a sword he had personally liberated from the tomb of an Irish warrior. Supposedly, their Irish slaves revolted, stole their remaining possessions and women, and set up on the *Vestmannaeyjar* – the Isles of the West Men to the south of the Icelandic coast. Ingolf killed them all in revenge, although the story sounds suspiciously like a rationalization for the removal of earlier Irish settlers, or perhaps even a joint colonization effort that went sour with the Norwegians emerging on top.[3] The remaining Irish monks on the island soon quit their scattered hermitages, often in such a hurry that their religious paraphernalia was left behind to inspire later stories among the Icelanders.

The Icelanders' own records mention around 400 original settlers, over 50 of whom had names that implied mixed Irish ancestry, or Celtic nicknames denoting considerable time spent outside Scandinavia. Their slaves and concubines (the mothers of many later generations) were also predominantly Irish, some of impressively noble birth. *The Saga of the People of Laxardal* mentions a haughty slave-girl with no appreciation of her duties, brought to Iceland already pregnant with the child of her Viking captor. She is eventually revealed as Melkorka (Mael-Curchaich?), the daughter of the Irish king Mýrkjartan (Muircertach?), kidnapped at 15 years of age. Faced with feuding women and clearly unable to control his Irish mistress, her owner eventually installed her in a homestead of her own across the river, recorded as the now-deserted site of Melkorkustadir.[4]

Not all of the Irish who accompanied the first settlers were ill treated. The Norse matriarch Aud the Deep-Minded, who figures large in the Icelanders' tales of the first settlers, brought many Irish slaves with her from Dublin where her late husband

Olaf the White had been king.[5] After unsuccessfully relocating to Caithness, where her son Thorsteinn the Red was killed, Aud and her entourage gave up on the harsh life on the Hiberno-Scottish fringe and set out for pastures new. Aud would eventually free several of her slaves and set them up on their own – freedmen including Vifil, whose great-grandson would become the first European to be born in America, and Erp, a thrall whose mother was supposedly Myrgiol, an Irish princess sold into slavery in Britain.[6] Although such tales often have the ring of truth, it is important to remember who was telling them – later generations of Icelanders hoping to put a polish on concubine ancestors by inventing noble backgrounds for them. Irish names certainly persisted among the Icelanders for many generations, including Njall, Kormakr, Brjan and Patrek.

Such was the place where agents of Crowbone arrived, spreading the word of God, or, more properly, the news that Crowbone was boss in Norway. Sources on the conversion of Iceland are, as with so much about the Viking Age, chiefly written long after it was over, and by the winning side. Although numerous medieval documents, contracts and church materials were collated during the nineteenth and twentieth centuries into the *Diplomatarium Islandicum* collection, there are very few extant sources from the first couple of centuries of Christianity in Iceland. We do, however, have Ari the Learned's *Íslendingabók*, written by a man who claimed to have heard stories of the conversion from old men who had been children at the time. Ari's version, even though it was written down a hundred years after the event, is the closest we have to a reliable account – if *Heimskringla* matches it, it is perhaps only because *Íslendingabók* was there for Snorri to use as reference.[7]

According to *Íslendingabók*, by the summer of 1000,

heathens and Christians in Iceland were preparing to fight over their religion, in what would likely become only the first skirmish of a religious war. The one chance to head off the disaster came at the summer assembly meeting. The 'law-speaker', Thorgeir Thorkelsson was the master of ceremonies, the arbitrator of disputes, and had been so since 985. With impressive wisdom and foresight, he realized that if he made no attempt to settle the dispute, the 1000 assembly would be the last time that Icelanders could claim to be self-governing. If he failed to come to a solution, the following year would see two rival assemblies, and before long they would be at each other's throats.

Somehow, Thorgeir's agents managed to bring both sides into negotiations. He heard the arguments for and against, and took over a day to reach his decision. A heathen himself, Thorgeir nevertheless had enough support among the Christians to still command their respect.

Thorgeir demanded assurances from both sides that they would abide by his decision, to which they agreed. He then decreed a compromise that pleased everybody. Iceland, as a nation, would accept baptism *en masse*. Crowbone would be assured that the entire country was now Christianized. Meanwhile, the Icelanders also remained free to practise the old ways. Thorgeir specifically assured the heathens that the exposure of children and the eating of horseflesh were still permitted – a tantalizing reference to two particular sacrificial practices that may have formed part of the worship of Frey, Thor or Odin. As for actual heathen religious ceremonies, they were to be declared illegal, but only if accusers were able to produce witnesses to verify that such heathenism was taking place. Crowbone had his assurances, and unless he spied on the hearthside activities of every Icelandic family, he would never hear that anyone was not as Christian as their baptism implied.[8]

Thorgeir had done it; he averted the crisis. He was replaced as Law-Speaker by 1001, so probably had had to call in every single available favour. The Christians were fully aware of the nature of the compromise, and that pagan ways continued in secret, but such was the conversion experience all over medieval Europe. A few years after Thorgeir's landmark decision, the 'old ways' were officially criminalized by a larger Christian majority, and the new religion was the victor.

But Iceland was not the last bastion of Viking culture. Restless settlers were soon looking beyond it, particularly after 930, when the initial land-rush had claimed the best settlement sites. On Iceland's western tip, on the promontory of Snaefellsness, it is possible to climb the towering 1,446 metres of an extinct volcano that looks out to sea. On the rare clear days when it is not surrounded by clouds, it is sometimes possible to another coastline in the distance – floating upside down above the horizon in an arctic mirage.

Early in the tenth century, the mariner Gunnbjörn Úlfsson overshot Iceland in a storm, and turned his ship around at a series of remote rocks known thereafter as Gunnbjörn's Skerries. He was, however, convinced that there was land even further to the west. For those living in the west of Iceland, the existence of further territories became a matter of faith. Others may have reported similar looming lands in the distance on remote fishing trips, and many noted the flights of migrant birds that periodically headed beyond the western horizon.[9]

One family in particular was to become instrumental in the colonization of points even further west, partly through their roving Viking spirit, but mainly through their habit of getting into trouble. Their patriarch was Thorvald Asvaldsson, a man from Jaeder in south-west Norway, forced to relocate to Iceland 'because of some killings', as the sagas bluntly put it.[10] With him went his son Erik, known to prosperity as Erik the Red, for his flame-coloured hair and beard, and as he reached manhood, his inheritance of his father's belligerent ways.

Although Erik tried to settle into the peaceable life of an Iceland farmer, bad luck seemed to follow him. He reached maturity during a period when Iceland suffered one of its harsher famines, and tempers among the farmers were frayed. Icelandic conservatism was already settling in, with the earlier settlers established on the best land, and unwelcoming towards newcomers, particularly those with doubtful pasts. Erik's slaves somehow caused a landslide that destroyed the farm of a fellow Icelander, Eyjolf. Eyjolf killed the slaves, causing Erik to kill Eyjolf himself sometime later. His saga also mentions offhandedly that he also killed someone called Hrafn the Dueller – Erik was clearly getting out of hand.[11]

The local population took limited action, and were happy merely to banish Erik from the area. He resettled in another part of Iceland, where he soon quarrelled with his neighbour Thorgest over the loan of some bench-boards. When Erik took back his furniture by force he was pursued by Thorgest's sons, two of whom he also killed. Perhaps it did not escape the attention of the local Assembly that Erik's crimes, although murderous, had not been without provocation. He and his men (who had also fought in the skirmish) were banished from Iceland for three years, leading Erik to turn his ship towards the west, and go in search of the fabled land beyond Gunnbjörn's Skerries.

Erik was not even the first. Around 978, one Snaebjorn Galti had led a disastrous attempt to settle the coastline beyond Gunnbjörn's Skerries. The small party of colonists did not last the first mercilessly harsh winter, and ended up slaughtering each other. Erik, however, had more time on his hands to go exploring, and ignored the forbidding, glacier-strewn east coast of the new land. Instead, he sailed down the coast and around the southern tip, to discover the far more welcoming lands of the western coast. Warmed, like Iceland, by the Gulf Stream, and with long fjords penetrating deep inland, the new area seemed deceptively like Erik's native Norway. It was also apparently deserted, with land for the taking, meadows of green grass, and plenty of fish. Erik and his men spent their three-year exile exploring the new land, realizing that it presented the ideal settlement opportunity for the younger sons and newer arrivals of Iceland. If the old settlers in Iceland were refusing to budge, then this new island would be an excellent site for colonization. Erik even decided to help things along by picking a name that suggested a far more hospitable climate – he called it Greenland. He also may have neglected to widely publicize another important fact – although he and his men had encountered nobody in Greenland, they were patently not the first people to visit it. Scattered all around their new 'discovery' were the tell-tale artefacts of previous visitors, people who had arrived in small boats made from animal skins, with no metal but enough skills to make spearheads and arrowheads of stone.[12]

Erik and his men did a good job of talking up their discovery. After a triumphant return to Iceland and a grudging reconciliation with those he had wronged, Erik set out again in 986, in a fleet of 25 ships. These were not only longships but also wide-beamed high-capacity *knorrs*, loaded with livestock. It is a testament to the perils of navigation at the time that only 14 of the ships made it to Iceland – many of the knorrs were unable to make it through the cross-currents, and it is assumed that the vessels with more oars were more successful in the journey than the ones with larger cargoes.[13]

Approximately 450 people formed the initial Greenland colony, scattered across the fjords of the western settlement in two main locations. They explored their new land as far north as possible, to the point where the stony ground gave way to endless ice, and they soon formed a loose-knit community of homesteads in imitation of the Icelandic model. The colony prospered slowly, and the people were forced to adapt to the absence of some basic necessities. Although there were attempts to tease crops from the soil, grain was in short supply, and bread all but disappeared from the Greenlanders' diet. Trees were also thin on the ground, and there was no metal to be had locally. The Greenlanders were forced to improvise, and to trade with the Icelanders across the dangerous strait. Perhaps the greatest lack of all was people – they had found Greenland to be 'deserted', without a local population that they could prey upon, trade with, and ultimately marry into.

But for all Erik and his fellow colonists knew, there would be yet more lands further on, with yet more space for colonization. Although Greenland was destined to become the farthest edge of the Viking world, there was one more shore further to the west that would also briefly be visited by the Vikings. Our sources for it comprise two sagas, which unhelpfully contradict each other – each seemingly an attempt to assign credit for certain discoveries to a different person. They have, however, become the two most discussed sagas in the English-speaking world, because of their subject matter, and because later, tantalizing scraps of archaeological evidence have revealed them to be true, at least in their general narrative.

The existence of this new land was first mooted very soon after the initial settlement of Greenland, as usual by a sailor who had got lost. Bjarni Herjolfsson was a young merchant who plied the seas between Norway and Iceland on a two-year cycle that allowed him to sail in seasons when drift ice was not a hazard. He would load up with goods at his father's farm in

Iceland, and make the long voyage back to his ancestral home in Norway. There he would spend the winter selling his wares, before loading up with materials likely to sell back in Iceland. He would set off the next year and then repeat the process. Bjarni was thus rather surprised to arrive back in Iceland to discover that his father had left. He was told that Herjolf had tired of the declining state of Iceland, and decided to seek new lands with Erik the Red, to the west.

The news, so reports the *Greenlander Saga*, was a surprise to Bjarni, but his merchant's mind was already working.[14] Rather than unload his cargo in Iceland, he decided it would be more prudent to head after his father – presumably reasoning that colonists in Greenland would be pleased to find a ship of Norwegian luxuries turning up on their shores. Bjarni's men were in agreement, although they did note that the route to Greenland was unknown to them, and that it might prove difficult.

Bjarni's ship overshot Greenland by several days, possibly due to his ignorance of the route and currents, although his saga is swift to plead poor weather conditions. Beset by a severe fog that made it difficult to get their bearings by sun or stars, Bjarni sailed ever onwards, and when he did eventually sight land, it did not fit the description he had heard of Greenland's eastern coast. Bjarni's ship was the first European vessel to record a sighting of the place now known as North America, although Bjarni did not put ashore. Realizing that he was significantly to the south of his chosen destination, he sailed north along the strange shore for a further two days, but at no point did he see the glaciers that would identify the coastline as Greenland. His men did, however, note that the coastline was thickly forested – a fact that would encourage later explorers to seek it out from tree-starved Greenland. The exact location of Bjarni's voyage is unknown – he never dropped anchor, but merely tracked the Canadian coast north. Somewhere in the region of Baffin Island, he stared out at the icy shore and pronounced it worthless.[15] Turning back to the east, Bjarni sailed for several more days, until he reached a coastline that did indeed turn out to be Greenland. He found his father's new homestead and supposedly turned to a farmer's life, although by the next paragraph the *Greenlander Saga* reports that he began trading once more, with Norway.

It was 14 years after Bjarni's historic voyage that the unknown coastline began to renew its pull on Vikings. The prime mover in the new venture was Erik the Red's son, Leif the Lucky, the foolhardy pioneer of new sea routes. It was Leif who first sailed direct from Greenland to Norway, bypassing completely the staging posts of Iceland and the Faeroes, and instead pointing his ship directly at Scandinavia. Leif's route headed due east from Greenland's southern tip, and, if sailed properly, would pass neatly between the Faeroes and the Shetlands, steering with the former to port and the latter to starboard. Sailors might not arrive immediately at their destination port, but Norway was a large target and difficult to miss.

Leif bought the aging Bjarni Herjolfsson's ship, and attempted to organize an expedition to the unknown coast at the turn of the eleventh century. He even tried to enlist the help of the venerable Erik the Red, but although the old Viking agreed to go, an injury from a fall as preparations were finalized caused him to excuse himself. It is therefore Leif the Lucky who is credited with leading the first party of Europeans to set foot in the New World. Deliberately retracing Bjarni's trip homewards, Leif reached a flat, unpromising shore that was probably Baffin Island.[16] Regarding himself as the rightful namer by virtue of actually making a landfall, he called it *Helluland* (Slab-land). Sailing further to the south,

Leif's crew sighted another land, covered in dense forests. This, too, matched Bjarni's earlier descriptions, and was dubbed *Markland* (Forest-land) by Leif.

Another two days further south, they found an even more promising region, where they decided to spend the winter. The exact site of Leif's base is unknown – although the most likely site is a Viking camp excavated at L'Anse aux Meadows in north Newfoundland. Constructed somewhere between 1000 and 1020, the site appears to have been a base suitable for up to 90 men with the facilities for heavy-duty ship repair – a hollow for use as a dry dock, a smithy, and a kiln. At several points in the site, modern archaeologists have unearthed butternuts, which are not known to grow north of the St Lawrence river – whoever stayed at the L'Anse aux Meadows site had sailed further south, as confirmed by other information contained in *Greenlander Saga*. Leif reported the length of the day at winter solstice, which tallies with a latitude somewhere south of the Gulf of St Lawrence, but north of New Jersey.

The most famous feature of the land was discovered by Tyrkir the Southerner. Separated from the group while foraging, he returned babbling excitably in his native German, and had to be calmed down enough to speak intelligible Norse. Tyrkir had found some kind of berry (probably a cranberry) that he regarded as a grape, suitable for the making of wine. Leif took his word for it – they do not appear to have known much about wine themselves, and relied on Tyrkir's hazy memories of vineyards from his childhood.[17] Leif dubbed their new land *Vinland* (Vine-land), wherever it may have been.

Triangulating the solstice length of day, with the butternuts and the 'grapes', it appears that Leif's wanderings took him somewhere near Prince Edward Island, Nova Scotia, or perhaps even further towards New England, somewhere north of

Cape Cod. Even back in the warm summers of AD 1000, true grapes did not grow in America north of Maine. After a winter in the new lands, and some brief further explorations, Leif set sail back for Greenland, his ship loaded with lumber from the Canadian forests.

The *Greenlander Saga* also reports an encounter that Leif made on the way home with a group of 15 fellow Vikings wrecked on a reef. He rescued them and brought them safely back to Greenland, before returning to the place of their wreck to retrieve their cargo. The saga implies that the ship was on its way from Norway, but it may have been *another* mission to America, specifically for the purpose of gathering timber. However, *Erik's Saga*, a less reliable account that includes the same incident, makes no mention of the ship's destination, instead noting that one of the rescued sailors was the first Christian missionary to reach Greenland. Considering that all the Icelandic sagas were committed to books long after the events they describe, it remains possible that the shipwrecked Vikings may have played a far greater role in the discovery of America than *Erik's Saga* lets on. There is certainly a bizarre jumble of incidents concerning the survivors, which the suspicious-minded might interpret as signs of a whitewash. Among the rescued party was a woman called Gudrid, 'a woman of striking appearance' and the wife of the ship's captain Thorir.[18] Without a place to stay in Greenland, Thorir's crew lodged among the locals, and the couple were invited to stay at Erik the Red's homestead in Brattahlid. For some reason, Thorir did not survive the ensuing winter – the saga implies that an outbreak of disease did for several of the new arrivals, as well as causing the death of Erik the Red himself. But Gudrid had no trouble finding a new man; she married Leif the Lucky's brother Thorsteinn, and was to play an important role in later explorations of America.

Whatever the truth behind Leif's luck and Thorir's peculiar lack of it, Leif did not return to America. With the passing of Erik the Red, Leif was the inheritor of Brattahlid, and had other responsibilities to concern him, chiefly his *de facto* position as the senior colonist. His seafaring days were over, but he passed his well-travelled vessel on to his brother Thorvald. Thorvald wasted little time in preparing another trip to Vinland, fired possibly by the desire for new conquests, but more probably by increasing tensions in Greenland. Whether the story of the missionary rescued by Leif was true or not, Christianity had begun to take hold in the Greenland settlements, and was leading to tensions between the new religionists and the pagan old guard. Quite possibly, the Christian Thorvald was searching for a new place for fellow Christians to settle.

Thorvald was able to sail across the Davis Strait and down the coast to the place where Leif's crew had previously wintered – wherever it was, it was in a sufficiently prominent position to be easy for other sailors to locate if they knew what they were looking for. After a winter spent at Leif's old camp, Thorvald ordered further explorations in the spring. On one such trip, his men found evidence of human habitation, a wooden stack-cover.

After another winter at the camp, further explorations led them to a heavily wooded promontory between, as the sagas quaintly put it 'two fjords'. Wherever it was, it was idyllic enough for Thorvald to decide he had found a place to settle. However, someone else had beaten him to it – three anonymous lumps on a beach in the distance were found to be upturned animal-skin boats, each hiding three Native Americans.

The Norsemen called them *Skraelings*, a word thought to evoke elements of 'wretches' or 'savages', and possibly related to the pejorative prefix *Skrit*, used in earlier times to describe the inhabitants of Lapland.[19] The exact identity of the Skraelings is impossible to determine from the limited saga descriptions; they could have been Beothuk or Micmac Indians. Whoever they were, they appeared sufficiently threatening for Thorvald's men to kill them. After a scuffle on the shoreline, the first recorded encounter between Europeans and Native Americans ended with eight Indians dead, and a lone survivor paddling in fast retreat towards a distant cluster of huts. He soon returned with heavy reinforcements, and in the ensuing battle between Viking ship and kayak flotilla, the Vikings were victorious. Thorvald, however, was shot through the armpit by a Skraeling arrow, and died in the aftermath, becoming, in a day of many firsts, the first European to perish on American soil, buried at at unknown location recorded as Crossness.

Thorvald's crew made it back to Greenland, dismayed at the loss of their leader, but still optimistic about the potential offered by Vinland. They arrived back at Eriksfjord to discover that the sons of Erik the Red had suffered a second tragedy – in their absence, Thorvald's brother Thorsteinn had also perished of an unknown disease, leaving his widow Gudrid an exceptionally rich woman, with inheritances from two departed husbands.

Although by now she must have seemed remarkably unfortunate, Gudrid remained an attractive marital prospect. She was still young, famously beautiful, rich, and related by marriage to the celebrated Leif the Lucky, unofficial headman of the Greenland colony. The sagas report a strange incident that could refer to a failed love affair or courtship with another man,[20] but by the time the Vinland explorers returned, Gudrid had found a third husband. He was quite literally fresh off the boat from Norway, a wealthy ship's captain called Thorfinn

Karlsefni. Leif brokered the marriage himself, functioning *in loco parentis* for his bereaved sister-in-law, and Gudrid's groom soon found himself pestered into initiating another expedition to Vinland, this time with the intention of settling.

Karlsefni set out to colonize Vinland, but was expressly told by Leif that he could only 'borrow' the campsite where Leif and his brother had wintered. Leif clearly intended to maintain his claim on Vinland by reminding all successive travellers exactly who had reached it first. Karlsefni's party was expected to find land of its own; certainly if it was a colonization mission, it was intended merely as the spearhead – only five women accompanied the settlers.

Karlsefni's group had been at Leif's camp for some months before they had their first encounter with Skraelings. A group of natives approached the settlement from the woods, bearing packs loaded with furs. This is in itself a strange occurrence – how did they know what the Vikings would want to trade? If this truly was the first peaceful encounter between the Skraelings and the Vikings, it is not likely to have been as sudden as the saga reports.[21] Despite a complete lack of shared language, trade was made possible by accident. In a gesture of hospitality, Karlsefni sent the women out with milk for the skittish new arrivals, but the Skraelings regarded the simple drink as such a delicacy that they were happy to trade their wares simply for more of it.

The incident gave Karlsefni pause. He ordered for a wooden palisade to be erected around the camp – hardly the act of someone not expecting trouble. Some of his companions grew restless, reportedly angry at the complete absence of the much publicized wine-grapes; one, Thorhall the Hunter, setting off back to Europe in disgust.[22] But in time, Gudrid gave birth to a baby boy, Snorri, the first European to be born in America.

The next visit from the Skraelings came when Snorri was

still in his cradle. Trade went on in a similar manner to the previous occasion, but more Skraelings arrived, and may have even overwhelmed the little camp. *Greenlander Saga* reports an encounter between Gudrid and a mysterious woman, described by most commentators as an 'apparition', although if we look at the information revealed in the text itself, she is nothing of the sort:

> . . . a shadow fell across the door and a woman entered wearing a black, close-fitting tunic; she was rather short and had a band around her chestnut-coloured hair . . . She walked up to Gudrid and said, 'What is your name?'
> 'My name is Gudrid. What is yours?'
> 'My name is Gudrid,' the woman replied.[23]

Surely this is no apparition, but merely an inquisitive Indian girl repeating the first Norse phrases she has heard. Meanwhile, a fight broke out among the men when one of the Skraelings attempted to make off with a Viking sword – Karlsefni had expressly forbidden the trading of weapons with the inhabitants of Vinland. The would-be thief was killed, and the others fled during the struggle. Since none of the other Vikings remembered seeing Gudrid's 'apparition', it is possible that she was one of a second party of Skraelings that had been detailed to pilfer the camp while the traders caused a distraction.[24]

The Skraelings were soon back in greater numbers, and openly hostile. The Vikings killed many of them in the ensuing battle, and witnessed a Skraeling chief hurling a captured Viking axe into the lake – purportedly in fear of its magical properties. The saga reports no further trouble from the Skraelings, but Karlsefni was clearly not prepared to take any more chances. Like Thorvald before him, he had successfully queered his pitch with the locals, and was unwilling to stay in Vinland waiting for the Skraelings to return with reinforcements. The following spring, the Vinland expedition broke camp and sailed back to Greenland, with a cargo of pelts and lumber, but still with no permanent settlement established.

Greenlander Saga recalls one further attempt by the descendants of Erik the Red to establish a colony in Vinland, this time by his illegitimate daughter Freydis, who may have been one of the women on the Karlsefni expedition. The year after Karlsefni's return, Freydis convinced two brothers newly arrived from Iceland to join her and her husband on a trip back to Leif's camp. The Freydis mission, however, went swiftly wrong in what was either a series of highly unfortunate misunderstandings, or the resurgence of the belligerent genes of Erik the Red. Freydis implied that the brothers would be allowed to stay at Leif's camp in Vinland, but refused to allow them in on arrival, claiming that Leif was renting the base to her crew alone. Although the brothers grudgingly moved to a different camp, an attempt at reconciliation at a sports meeting went similarly sour and ended in a brawl. A final attempt at reconciliation led to a pitched battle between the separate crews; a self-contradictory account in *Greenlander Saga* suggests that Freydis either falsely accused the brothers, or was assaulted by them in the midst of negotiations. Whatever the truth of the matter, Freydis was able to goad her husband and crew into killing their rivals. When only five women remained as witnesses, Freydis dispatched them herself with an axe. The Freydis expedition returned to Greenland the following summer, its survivors clinging to a carefully constructed alibi that the missing Vikings had remained as colonists. Word eventually got out, but Freydis remained unpunished – the aging Leif limiting his retribution to a curse on her descendants.

The disastrous Freydis mission is the last reported attempt at colonizing the area known as Vinland, a land whose historical significance was not truly appreciated until recent times, when its relation to the New World that Christopher Columbus reached in 1492 became apparent. To the people of the eleventh century, Vinland was merely one more place where they could find furs and wood, but simply too dangerous and remote to justify increased attention. In the time it took to reach Leif's fabled Vinland, a Greenlander vessel could make it all the way to Europe, where Vikings could expect to find a much better price for their pelts and wares. To a trader, it also made sounder economic sense – a merchant could return from Europe with a cargo of even greater value: books, new devices and technology, news itself and fine cloths. A journey to Vinland merely meant an arduous trip to a land populated by potentially limitless numbers of hostile people. Even if the Vikings found someone with whom they could trade, they would only be buying more of the same things they could acquire elsewhere. The discoveries of Leif and his family faded from consciousness. Vinland was still referred to in Icelandic sagas, but it seemed to interest the Icelanders little. Leif, let us not forget, was regarded as headstrong and lucky by the Vikings themselves; we know that he was setting out in an antique ship. As later generations of Greenlanders clung to their increasingly precarious colony, they became more cautious. With ships in dwindling supply, and the children of the original sailors and explorers becoming increasingly land-bound, the Greenlanders developed other priorities.

As the Viking Age gave way to the High Middle Ages, the north Atlantic population was periodically thinned by plague, and the need for new colonies to relieve population pressure never became as great as it had been during the first settlement of Iceland and Greenland. Later Greenland records of America do not refer to Vinland at all, but merely to Markland, to which occasional trips across the Davis Strait were made to obtain timber, as late as 1347.

8

LONDON BRIDGE
IS FALLING DOWN

FROM SVEIN FORKBEARD TO OLAF THE STOUT

We know that King Svein Forkbeard had secured alliances that gave him Denmark, Sweden and allies in Trondheim and what is now Poland. We know that Olaf Crowbone had other ideas, and that the forces of the two warlords were destined, inevitably, to clash. Snorri's *Heimskringla*, however, chooses to frame their confrontation as a monstrous family feud, beginning with the image of a weeping Danish bride, dragged to a pagan ceremony in a foreign land, perhaps allowing latter-day notions of chivalry and romantic love to influence his account.

As Snorri tells it, the girl in question was Forkbeard's sister Thyri, promised to Boleslav of Wendland (Poland) as part of a dynastic alliance. But Snorri, unable to resist a good story, claims that Thyri was a devout Christian, who celebrated her unwelcome betrothal to a pagan with a seven-day hunger strike, before fleeing with her Danish retinue in search of sanctuary. Supposedly, she chose to run to Crowbone, who not only welcomed her as a Christian bride, but resolved to regain the tracts of Poland that had gone to Boleslav as part of her abortive dowry. This is highly unlikely as a motive, and may have been manufactured in later centuries by writers intent on buttressing Crowbone's good Christian values. Certainly Adam of Bremen and Thietmar of Merseburg seem never to have believed in Crowbone's conversion, and see no romance or heroism, merely another skirmish over wealth and power.[1]

After sailing his 60 ships through Danish waters with miraculous lack of incident, Crowbone concluded a treaty with Boleslav for the handing over of Thyri's lands. Boleslav may have known than any deal he made was unlikely to last all that long, or perhaps the deal was genuine, but Boleslav changed his story in the light of later events. Crowbone still had to sail home between the coasts of Sweden and Denmark, and the combined fleets of Forkbeard, his stepson Olof Skötkonung, and the dispossessed earls of Trondheim, were laying in wait.

The preamble to the battle and the battle itself, fought near the unknown island of Svold, occupy the sagas for some time – Snorri, in particular, steals several highly doubtful stories from other times and other wars, all designed to build a sense of the crushing finality of the great naval battle. There were representatives from every part of Scandinavia: independent Trondheimers, heathen Swedes, Christian Danes, the religiously mixed Norwegians, and warriors from other races. Men of Wendland fought on Crowbone's side, while Snorri reports the presence of a Finnish archer with the Trondheimers, whose lucky shot shattered the bow of one Einar Paunch-shaker. At the time, Einar had been aiming at Earl Erik of Trondheim, whose life was thereby saved.

The battle went on so long, claims Snorri, that the combatants ran out of arrows and spears, and even their swords were too blunt to do much damage, so that Crowbone was forced to hand out fresh weapons to his men. But even though Crowbone's fleet wrought significant damage on the Swedes and Danes, it was the men of Trondheim who fought most fiercely. In the closing moments of the conflict, the last battle for the right to rule Scandinavia was fought chiefly by Norwegians against Norwegians – the exiled Trondheimers against the man who had usurped their land. Crowbone was wounded in the shoulder, and kept fighting, but his giant warship, the *Long Serpent*, was completely surrounded by enemy vessels. Crowbone was last seen leaping, not falling, over the side of the *Long Serpent*, and disappearing beneath the waves.

There were rumours that he somehow survived, slipping off his mail shirt and swimming for his life, or perhaps escaping on a Wendish vessel that chose that moment to flee the battle. Snorri's *Heimskringla*, perhaps unwilling to accept an unchristian suicide, cannot resist reporting a folktale that the 32-year-old Crowbone headed south to Byzantium, hoping to reclaim his fortune, but died anonymously in an unknown battle. Whether Crowbone died at the battle of Svold or somehow survived to live a new life under a new identity, he was never seen again by the Vikings. The battle of Svold marked a victory for Forkbeard, and the division of the spoils along familiar lines.

Olof, the son of Erik the Victorious, took Sweden, including the southernmost districts that had previously owed allegiance to Norway. Earl Erik of Trondheim received his father's lands, while his brother Svein ruled the area to the south – Norway now belonged to Trondheimers. Among the allies of the new rulers was Einar Paunch-shaker – it is a sign of the flexibility and transience of Viking alliances that the bowman who had supposedly tried to shoot Earl Erik at Svold would soon become his brother-in-law.

Svein Forkbeard now ruled Norway, Sweden and Denmark, either directly or through his allies and relative. The line of Greycloak, Bloodaxe and Fairhair was now all but extinguished, and Forkbeard was able to turn his attentions to the prize he had coveted for almost a decade – the largest concentration of Danes to be found outside Denmark itself. For the next 60 years, England was to become the battleground for the children of the Vikings.

Danish raiders had in fact been constantly harrassing the coasts of England throughout the 990s. In 991, agents of the Pope had tried to enforce a sense of Christian brotherhood between Aethelred Unraed and the Norman leader, Richard the Fearless. However, Richard seemed to prefer the company of his heathen cousins to his English neighbours, and continued to look the other way while Viking fleets put in to Norman ports to restock with provisions, sell their plunder and evade the ineffectual English fleets. Although Crowbone and Forkbeard had gone home to fight over their birthright, others continued to plunder Wessex and East Anglia, and Aethelred Unraed's attempts to organize resistance were a failure. The *Anglo-Saxon Chronicles* reported particular troubles in Devonshire, Cornwall and Wales in 997, and from a party of Vikings that sailed up the coast the following year, wintering at the Isle of Wight, before following the Kent coast in 999 to the Thames Estuary and heading up the River Medway to attack Rochester. There, the Kent army was supposedly prepared to meet them, but soon fled when faced with superior numbers. On the English side, there were operational disputes among the defenders. Aethelred Unraed had previously raised funds to pay off the Vikings. Now he wanted to raise funds to repulse them, but the monies do not seem to have been used in the right place. The Peterborough manuscript of the *Anglo-Saxon Chronicles* notes sourly that the Kentish army was forced to retreat because 'they did not have the help they should have had,'[2] while the Canterbury variant, presumably written with much greater knowledge of local issues, speaks in detail of the money wasted assembling a navy, and marines who arrived late, and watched helplessly from the sea as the Vikings plundered deep inland, where the local armies were now at half-strength. In the end, wrote the chronicler: 'the ship-army achieved nothing, except the people's labour, and wasting money, and the emboldening of their enemies.'[3]

As in the days of Guthrum's Great Host, the new raiders benefited from longer stays in their target areas. Instead of random attacks at points of presumed worth, they were able to spend months, even years reconnoitring the best places to attack.

The opening movements of the Danish seizure of England began in intrigue, with a supposed conspiracy against the ill-advised English king, Aethelred Unraed. We do not know if Forkbeard was behind it, or if it was simply the result of increased paranoia. Athelred's efforts to buy off Danish raids had only served to encourage further attempts at extortion by other Vikings, and at the same time the number of Danes living within England was swelling. Whatever the reason behind it, Aethelred reacted by ordering the Danes to be removed. As he put it:

A decree was sent out by me with the counsel of my leading men and magnates, to the effect that all the Danes who had sprung up in this island, sprouting like weeds amongst the wheat, were to be destroyed by a most just extermination.[4]

The ethnic cleansing began on St Brice's day, 13 November 1002. There is little evidence of how widespread the killings actually were – we do know that there were still Danes living in England after the massacre, although in some places entire communities of them were killed. In Oxford, some Danes sought sanctuary in the church of St Frideswide, only to have the bloodthirsty locals burn it down around them.

Another victim, presumably with the full knowledge of Aethelred, was one Gunnhild, a high-born Danish lady who had been left with the English king as a hostage. Her killing was regarded as an abrogation of the treaty, and an atrocity that required vengeance. According to legend, she was a sister of Forkbeard – another luckless (probably non-existent) sibling used as an excuse, like Thyri, for another war.[5]

Forkbeard arrived in England at the head of a fleet of ships in 1003, determined to avenge his alleged sister's death – the murder of a Danish princess, we can assume, would require a hefty *manngjöld*, and one that would be most usefully spent in securing Forkbeard's newly acquired territories in the Baltic. Nowhere is the folly of Aethelred's actions more clear, not only in the vengeance it inspired from Forkbeard, but also in what followed. For the strongest resistance to Forkbeard's fleet came from the Danes themselves, that sector of the population Aethelred most feared. Although the Danelaw may have made Aethelred uneasy, there were still Danes who called it home, and did not take kindly to attacks by sea-raiders. After attacking places in Devon and along the coast, he made the made the mistake of attacking East Anglia.

His nemesis was Ulfkell Snilling, a man of Anglo-Danish descent, a local leader in the Norwich region and powerful enough for some Scandinavian sources to refer to East Anglia as 'Ulfkell's Land'.[6] Faced with Forkbeard's oncoming fleet, Ulfkell had initially been prepared to pay the tribute demanded, realizing that he did not have time to assemble his own men. In theory, Forkbeard's men should have waited by their ships for the money to arrive, but clearly tired of it, and decided to attack anyway. Ulfkell immediately mustered what little manpower he could. The Vikings were taken by surprise at the resistance, and might have even been completely defeated had Ulfkell's victory not been ruined for him by his own allies. As in other cases alluded to in the *Anglo-Saxon Chronicles*, disorganization was the worst enemy of the local defenders, and Ulfkell's order to them to destroy the Viking ships was ignored. The failure of his associates to act on his plan gave the Vikings an opportunity to escape. As had so often been the case in other parts of the Viking world, they simply fled in search of easier pickings, and Ulfkell could not be everywhere at once.[7]

Forkbeard's fleet left for Denmark in 1005, because that year England was struck by famine (probably thanks at least in part to the previous year's fighting), and the starving locals had little worth stealing. In 1006, Forkbeard was back in force, establishing a base on the Isle of Wight and plundering the Wessex heartland. Forkbeard's fleet was packed with a new generation of Vikings; Scandinavia was divided between the victors, all the best land in Iceland was taken, news of Greenland had yet to spread, so England it had to be. The men with Forkbeard included one Olaf the Stout, a short but powerful teenage Viking whose father was that same Harald Grenske who had been legendarily killed by Sigrid the Haughty. At least for now, the old Viking feuds had been put to rest, while they united against a common foe.

Forkbeard's assault was a military exercise in depopulation and despoiling. The Vikings set up guarded supply dumps in Reading, allowing them to conduct missions further inland, before returning to recuperate. They may have even been encouraged in this by English bragging, since in an outbreak of Alfred-style patriotism, it had been widely boasted that if the Vikings ever dared to advance as far as Cwichelm's Barrow (Cuckhamsley Knob in Wiltshire), they would never make it back to their ships alive. Such a challenge was too good for Forkbeard to resist, and he not only made it to Wiltshire, but also saw off the English army that had been waiting for him there. We get a sense of disorganization prevalent in England. Even as Denmark became ordered enough to mount an invasion on a national scale, England was reverting to a cluster of small states, each unwilling or unable to cooperate with its neighbour. Forkbeard met resistance, but the forces that ranged against him seemed consistently unable to work with each other towards a common good. By 1007, a shaken Aethelred scraped up another small fortune to pay Forkbeard off, and for two years there was peace.

Local legend in some parts of England holds that captured Danes were skinned alive and their flayed hides nailed to church doors. In Copford, near Colchester, and Hadstock near Saffron Walden, fragments of this supposed Daneskin survive, and the Hadstock piece still sports grey-blond hairs. However, the gruesome local legends have their doubters – another 'Daneskin' from Westminster Abbey was found to be perfectly normal leather, a completely mundane and everyday protective covering for a door. The precise origin of the Hadstock and Copford skins are unconfirmed; the Hadstock fragment only survived because it sat under the hinges, and, far from being nailed to a church by irate locals after a Danish attack, it appears to have been carefully laid in as part of the door's original construction. Hadstock church itself was founded by a Dane, King Canute in fact, making the presence of a Daneskin unlikely, to say the least. Even more damagingly for the Daneskin legend's believers, the first documented mention of one is by Samuel Pepys in 1661, when the noted diarist recorded a visit to Rochester cathedral, '. . . observing the great doors of the church, as they say, covered with the skins of the Danes.' There is already a sceptical note here, perhaps because it would take a very rotund Dane, roughly the size of a cow, to cover such a door.[8]

Sometime around 1005–6, the dire situation in England led to a quiet revolution. Although Aethelred remained the nominal ruler, a number of the powers behind the throne lost their influence in a palace coup. The largely South Saxon clique that had previously 'helped' Aethelred run the country so badly was replaced by a largely Mercian group, who were to find a number of entirely new and original ways of failing. Most notable among them was Eadric *Streona* ('the Acquisitor'), a power-hungry nobleman who soon proved to be no less corrupt than his predecessors.

Whoever really held the reins of power, the problem remained the same. Forkbeard would be back the next time he needed silver, whether or not Aethelred and his 'advisors' provoked him by another massacre. The Normans across the Channel were uncooperative and untrustworthy, so Aethelred's marriage to Emma of Normandy had achieved little. The Danes, at least, were not attacking, but Aethelred had bought himself nothing but time, which he devoted to preparing a better resistance against the next assault. It is likely that his attempts to find the money to fight the Vikings were almost as extortionate as the Vikings themselves. The unit of taxation was the *hide*, an area of land thought to be large enough to support a peasant family, but more likely to support several by the early eleventh century. Every 310 hides had to come up with enough money to construct a warship, and every eight hides had to raise enough funds to provide armour for a single soldier. By these means, it was hoped, England might defeat the Vikings by fighting fire with fire, and destroying them on the sea.

England's new navy was ready in 1009, and was immediately mired in squabbles over who was in charge – the exasperation in the *Anglo-Saxon Chronicles*'s reporting of events is clear to this day.[9] One nobleman of the new faction, Beorhtric, made a series of accusations against the West Saxon leader Wulfnoth, who had control of another part of the fleet. Since Wulfnoth's father had been one of the previous 'advisors' to Aethelred, we may assume that Beorhtric's attack was an attempt to edge the old guard out once and for all. Whatever Beorhtric may have accused him of, Wulfnoth took great exception, absconded with much of the fleet, and conducted a series of his own raids against the south coast.

The one and only significant battle of the new English fleet was thus fought against itself, as Beorhtric's squadron pursued the breakaway faction. Beorhtric went aground in a storm, and his ships were burned on the beach by Wulfnoth – a third of the new navy was thus destroyed before it had even seen a Viking.[10] With civil war threatening to break out between Wessex and Mercia, Aethelred and his 'advisors' hurried to London for safety, taking the pitiful remains of their fleet with them. It was thus nowhere to be seen when the Vikings landed in Kent on 1 August 1009.

The new arrivals were followers of Forkbeard, but Forkbeard was no longer with them. He was otherwise occupied in Denmark, and had delegated the next round of extortion and pillaging to a party of lesser Vikings, led by one Thorkell the Tall. The Vikings of 1009 were not the old-style traders, wheeler-dealers, ne'er-do-wells, and criminals. Instead, they were professional soldiers, many of them Danes, with a significant proportion of Swedes. We know this from the number of rune stones in Sweden that commemorate their deaths.

There were no hoards of Muslim silver in Scandinavian graves of the eleventh century; instead, old Vikings were buried with coins that bore the face of Aethelred Unraed.[11]

The people of Kent bought off the raiding party for 3,000 pounds – enough to protect a county, but not its neighbours. Abandoned by Aethelred, the people of south England did not make any attempt to hold off the Vikings from their next target: London.

Dates in contemporary accounts do not match each other for the period 1009 to 1014, but we can still work out a progression of events from the contradictory sources. The *Anglo-Saxon Chronicles* for the period sees only undifferentiated Vikings and fierce resistance in London. The Norse sagas are more forthcoming, albeit less trustworthy, and reveal that there were at least two distinct groups of Vikings in the area – possibly four. Moreover, the battles in the south of England were fought not only between English and Vikings, but between Vikings themselves.

Both before and after the death of Forkbeard, several groups of Vikings were already choosing to serve his enemies. Among them was Olaf the Stout, the eldest descendant of Harald Fairhair, who seems to have chosen this moment to rediscover his family vendetta against the Danes. Norwegians, fighting in the name of England, attacked a fortress of Danes, nominally loyal to Denmark, on the south bank of the Thames. *Heimskringla* reports fierce fighting in 'Súthvirki' (modern Southwark) around the site of London Bridge, a heavily fortified structure that not only crossed the river, but permitted archers, catapults and the like to threaten any passsing ships.

What happened next, doubtful though *Heimskringla*'s account may be, lives on in a nursery rhyme, and indeed in the name of a London street. Just as Vikings of an earlier age had been thwarted by fortified bridges over the rivers of France, the

Norwegians serving in the English army found their passage barred by London Bridge. In a conference between Aethelred and his generals, Olaf the Stout volunteered a plan that would make him forever famous on both sides of the North Sea. Olaf led a river assault on the bridge, using mastless longships roofed over with 'soft wood' – wicker and unseasoned green planks that would be more resistant to fire. Amid a constant hail of rocks, spears and other missiles, Olaf's ships attached strong cables to the wooden pilings that supported London Bridge. The rowers then propelled their ships away from the bridge, no doubt using the current's momentum and their own brute strength to pull down the wooden pilings. The old wooden bridge now collapsed, other forces were able to land at an undefended portion of the south bank, seize Southwark and regain control of London. The location of Olaf's alleged adventure is marked today by the hidden London alleyway, St Olaf Stairs.

According to Olaf's own saga, his forces continued to fight on Aethelred's behalf, in the internecine conflict that continued to destroy many of the best men in England. At some point, Olaf's fellow-Viking Thorkell the Tall transferred his allegiance to the English as well. Some historians see Thorkell's sudden defection as a sign of his newfound ambition – a desire to win a kingdom for himself as his predecessors had done in Ireland, Scotland, Northumbria and elsewhere. Certainly, with England left in ruins by attacks both within and without, Thorkell does not seem to have had much trouble convincing the Anglo-Danish population of East Anglia that he would make a good ruler – he even married a daughter of Aethelred.[12] What difference would it make to them if they were paying 'tax' to Saxons or 'tribute' to Vikings?

Other sources regard Thorkell's change of heart as something more spiritual. In 1012, his army took Canterbury, with the aid of a traitor. One of the Vikings' prize prisoners was the archbishop Aelfheah, for whom they demanded a ransom.[13] Aelfheah, however, would not allow anyone to pay it on his behalf. The 58-year-old clergyman was dragged along with the Viking host as far as Greenwich, where, in what seems to have been a banquet prank that turned deadly, he was pelted with bones, offal and heavier missiles, until his captors tired of their sport and buried an axe in his skull. Thorkell, however, attempted to stop his followers from torturing their eminent guest, and even offered to pay the ransom himself. It is claimed that this may have been the last straw for him, deciding him to abandon Viking ways.

For some years, England had been a battleground, source of revenue, and ultimately a pressure valve for Viking ambitions. For as long as England was plundered and exploited, Fork-beard's Scandinavia remained at relative peace. But with Thorkell and Olaf the Stout defecting to Aethelred, it did not take a genius to see what could happen next. 'Ill-Coun-selled' or not, King Aethelred now had the chance to follow in his predecessors' footsteps. Just as his great-uncle Aethelstan had done in the case of Earl Hakon the Good, he could deal with his local Viking problem by sending it back. Instead of cowering before a series of assaults from Scandinavia, Aethelred now had the opportunity to cultivate his newfound Viking friends, perhaps suggesting to Thorkell or, more sen-sibly, Olaf the Stout, that their true destinies lay in Norway and Denmark. Unless Forkbeard did something quickly, every Viking in England, and a fair number of English reprobates, might suddenly invade Norway with Aethelred's kingly bles-sing. Whether his next move was provoked by fear or merely the culmination of a long-hatched plan, in spring 1013 Fork-beard arrived at the head of his fleet, to invade England.

The Danelaw welcomed him. The northern regions of

Northumbria, Lindsey and the Five Boroughs took one look at his fleet and proclaimed their allegiance. Forkbeard's fleet did not begin raiding until it reached the south. Establishing a base at Gainsborough on the Trent under the command of his son Canute, Forkbeard took his army south, through Oxford, to Winchester and then west to Bath. London remained safe, defended by soldiers under Thorkell the Tall. Others, however, deserted the beleaguered Aethelred – Olaf the Stout took himself off to France, and so did Aethelred himself. Realizing that London would be unable to hold out much longer, Aethelred and his family fled for Normandy, abandoning England to Forkbeard.

In 1013 Svein Forkbeard proclaimed himself the King of England by right of conquest. Five weeks later, in what the *Anglo-Saxon Chronicles* boldly describes as a 'happy event', he dropped dead.[14]

His son Canute, a youth in his late teens, received pledges of allegiance from the other Viking leaders in Gainsborough. As far as the Norsemen were concerned, Canute was the rightful heir, and tragic though Forkbeard's death was, England remained a part of the Danish hegemony. The English, however, had other ideas – Forkbeard had been 'king' for only five weeks, and had never been crowned.[15] Claiming Forkbeard's demise to be caused by the wrath of God, the ruling clique swiftly dispatched ambassadors to Normandy, where Aethelred was living in exile among his in-laws. Within two months, Aethelred was back, promising a new order and a better deal for the English. Enough locals believed him to flock to his banner again, and the restored English king marched with an army on the traitorous region of Lindsey.

Canute faced an army of Englishmen, bolstered once more by Viking mercenaries – Olaf the Stout was back in Aethelred's service, and Thorkell the Tall continued to serve the English.

He also faced trouble back home; he was the king of the English, but not of Denmark, since that role was reserved for his elder brother Harald II. Meanwhile in Sweden, King Olof Skötkonung signalled his defiance by appointing a bishop whom Forkbeard had vetoed. Canute gathered up his fleet and set sail, pausing at Sandwich to order the mutilation of the hostages he had inherited from Forkbeard. Having set the luckless individuals ashore, Canute sailed to Denmark, where he struck a deal of some sorts with his elder brother. It was in Harald's interest to get Canute out of the way in a kingdom of his own, and England presented the ideal opportunity. The kings appear to have agreed some kind of joint authority (Danish coins were struck in Canute's name), and a year after he arrived in Denmark, Canute was ready to head back and claim England for himself.

In the intervening period, Aethelred Unraed had not enjoyed much luck. His eldest son, named Aethelstan in honour of the great English unifier of old, died in June 1014. In September of the same year England suffered some of the worst flooding in record. Fully expecting Vikings to return, Aethelred organized a conference designed to reassure all parties that, regardless of whether or not they had been *willing* to pledge allegiance to Forkbeard, all would be forgiven if only they would pull together and resist any further attacks.[16]

The conference was a disaster. Some allies, it transpired, were trustier than others. Two northern leaders, in-laws of the absent Canute, were murdered by another earl, kicking off another vendetta among the English nobles. Edmund Ironside, one of the sons of Aethelred's first marriage, seized much of the north of England for himself and married the widow of one of the murder victims. Aethelred might have been the nominal king, but England was still a divided nation. The behaviour of Aethelred's son in the north verged on rebellion – Edmund

Ironside received pledges of allegiance from the lesser nobles, and issued proclamations in his own name. Meanwhile, the south coast was largely in the hands of Wulfnoth, the infamous noble who had once stolen half the English fleet. Upon Wulfnoth's death sometime around 1014, the region passed to his son Godwine.

Aethelred died in 1016, after a long but troubled reign. No more than a child when he became king, he had been buffeted by the interests of his regents as England tore itself apart. In his attempts to play Vikings off against each other, he had only served to encourage more alliances between his feuding nobles and their sometime enemies. When Aethelred died, leaving England to the disobedient Edmund Ironside, Canute was back with 160 ships and an avowed intention of regaining control of the country. Sources, once again, are contradictory, but he seems to have enjoyed the support of Thorkell the Tall for his attack on London. With London Bridge apparently repaired after the supposed assault of Olaf the Stout, the Vikings seized Southwark again, and bypassed the bridge – either by dragging their ships along the bank, or through a newly dug channel. With Edmund Ironside trying to raise an army in the west, the defence of London fell to his stepmother, Queen Emma, a remarkable woman who saw seven kings rule England in her lifetime, two of whom were her husbands, and two her sons. Trusting more to the support of the Mercians than the West Saxons (i.e. keeping to the north of the Thames), Edmund Ironside finally caught up with the Danes at Brentford, where he crossed the Thames and dealt a crushing blow. The Danes regrouped in the east, marching through Essex, and fought the Saxons again at the disputed site of *Assandun* (either modern Ashingdon in south-east Essex, or Ashdon in the north-west). The list of combatants includes an impressive number from far-flung parts of Edmund's kingdom, from Dorset in the west to the faithful Ulfkell Snilling in the east. Assandun may, finally, have brought the English together, but only for them to experience defeat there at the hands of the Danes.

Scattered skirmishes continued, with the tide now turning in favour of the Danes. Eventually, their armies fought to a standstill, the two rival kings agreed to meet on an island in the River Severn. There, they agreed that the land would be split between them in a similar power-sharing arrangement to that which Canute had with his brother in Scandinavia. The lands north of the Thames were Canute's. South of the Thames (i.e. the ancestral domain of the Kings of Wessex) was in Edmund's hands. It was enough of a compromise that both parties could call themselves the victor – both held large areas of land under a kingly title, and both agreed that the other would inherit the lands of whoever died first.

Edmund Ironside suddenly passed away on 30 November 1016. Although there is no mention of foul play, it certainly seems suspicious – the young king was barely in his twenties, and Canute was not above skulduggery when the opportunity presented itself. Whatever the reason, Canute was now the ruler of all England – Canute the Great, as he is remembered, a local translation of the Danish *Knud den Store*.

Wanting no part of the squabbles that had so hobbled the reign of Aethelred, Canute put his own people in charge at all places of strategic importance. Thorkell the Tall was rewarded for his double defection with the earldom of East Anglia, while Earl Erik of Trondheim, the aging son of Hakon the Great, acquired Northumbria. A couple of local turncoats were given brief roles in Canute's government, but many were purged, either through their own misdeeds or through Canute's machinations. Canute, whatever the methods he employed, was remarkably successful in reconciling the disparate factions of his kingdom. He is, after all, the king who supposedly ordered his throne to be set on the seashore, so that his courtiers might observe that he was unable to command the rising tide. Canute's legendary paddle, a folktale which comes to us through the twelfth-century *History of the English* by Henry Huntingdon, reminded the assembled nobles that, although they might be Angles, Saxons, Danes and Swedes, all of them, their king included, were subject to the Christian God, whatever gross flatterers might say.

In an attempt to establish a link with the previous dynasty, Canute sent for Aethelred's widow Emma, who had so boldly resisted his army in London. Emma became the wife of Canute the Great, in a match decried by a contemporary satirist as a bull ravishing a queen.[17] Canute and Emma, both together and separately, would somehow be the parents of several monarchs, until the ruling dynasty of England crashed to a messy end with the death of Edward the Confessor. After the battles, mutilations, banishments and natural attrition of several generations, only one of the secret cliques behind Aethelred's throne survived to see the latter half of the eleventh century, and that was the family of Wulfnoth, the man who stole half of Aethelred's fleet. Wulfnoth's son Godwine ensured that his daughters married into the royal family, and after the Confessor, his eldest surviving male heir, Harold Godwinson, was ideally placed to seize the throne for himself.

Canute paid off the Vikings in his entourage, causing most of the raiders to return to Scandinavia or leave England in search of plunder elsewhere. When his elder brother died, Canute sailed for Denmark with an Anglo-Danish fleet that enforced his sovereignity over the old territories of Forkbeard.

Many in England might have considered the new king's reign to be a return to relative peace. The period saw the establishment of communities of Danes in London itself – the

Thames riverbank or 'Strand' gaining a *Densemanestret* and Westminster gaining a *Denscheman* parish, both eventually with churches sacred to St Clement of the Danes.[18] Canute kept the English free of most Viking predation, and enacted new laws, many of which were slightly polished old laws, written up for him by the Saxon bishop Wulfnoth. However, peace restored in one area only caused pressure elsewhere in the Viking world. Canute was forced to lead an army against his sometime ally Thorkell in 1023, when East Anglia attempted to exhibit a little too much of the old Viking spirit. He may have secured a series of advantageous tributary treaties with the kings of Scotland, but faced increasing unrest back in his homeland. While Canute could legitimately claim to be the overlord of a North Sea empire that stretched from Cornwall to Sweden, it was also *over*-stretched. He suffered a military defeat against Swedish rebels in 1026, and was forced to make a prolonged expedition to Norway in 1028 to deal with a predictable return of old enmities.

With the Earl of Trondheim busy with his new possessions in Northumbria, Trondheim itself was open to seizure by anyone who could offer the locals a better deal than the incumbent Danes. Even as Canute had set sail with his invasion fleet for England, the eldest surviving heir to Harald Fairhair was making plans of his own. Deprived of his main source of mercenary revenue, Olaf the Stout embarked on a couple of raids on the English coast before returning home. *Heimskringla* strains credulity by reporting him taking the remarkable step of abandoning his longships in England, and instead packing his followers into a couple of converted merchant ships. Olaf, now nominally a Christian, was giving up on the raiding life and setting off home with a small army, not a raiding party, intent on conquest. For Olaf, the voyage back to Scandinavia was intended as a one-way trip to reclaim his birthright.[19]

He announced his intentions to take back Harald Fairhair's kingdom from Canute at the point of a sword. His stepfather Sigurd called an assembly of south Norwegian headsmen, capitalizing on Olaf's ancestry and his kinship with them. Olaf the Stout was decreed to be the ruler of Norway by common acclamation, gaining further support from many of the places through which his retinue passed. He met little resistance until he reached the north, where, predictably, Trondheim and its outlying regions rebuffed any who claimed to be its lord. Olaf was obliged to put down the Trondheim resistance by force, fighting Earl Erik's brother Earl Svein, who enjoyed ominous support from Olof Skötkonung, Sweden's ruler and Canute's stepbrother.

Despite minor resistance, Olaf the Stout was able to consolidate his rule. With the north pacified, he enforced his domain as far as the border with Sweden, and with it brought Christianity to the populace. While Olaf did little that had not been tried before by Crowbone or Hakon the Good, had the benefit of a further generation of missionary influence. Faced with the prospect of violence or conversion, many acknowledged Christianity as their belief, even in the ever-resistant Trondheim region. Olaf reputedly put an end to 'many heathen customs', although undoubtedly they still persisted.

Sweden was next on Olaf's list – unless he did something swiftly, he might find the same Swedish-Danish resistance in Scandinavia that had destroyed his predecessor Crowbone. But *Heimskringla* would have us believe in yet another romantic intrigue – if Snorri had his way, every Scandinavian princess would doubtless be a lovestruck damsel waiting for a heroic rescuer. Even as the aging Olof Skötkonung railed against 'that fat man' in Norway, his own daughter Ingigerd supposedly considered the possibility of marrying Olaf the Stout. The story probably conceals a more prosaic truth – that

Sweden was torn between the prospect of alliance with Russia or Norway. When faced with the prospect of a marriage alliance between Norway and Sweden, or continued tit-for-tat raids across their territory, the landholders of southern Sweden preferred the former option. But the Swedish king had already promised Ingigerd to Jaroslav the Wise in Russia. Olaf the Stout, however, eventually got a princess of his own, Ingigerd's sister Astrid.

Norway was back in the hands of a descendant of Harald Fairhair, and the Swedish border was finally quiet. Olof Skötknonung seems to have been a most unpleasant father-in-law, and the passing of the Swedish crown to his son Onund Jacob in 1022 on his death was probably a large contribution to peace in the region.

Olaf busied himself with the spread of Christianity, either for genuine reasons, or simply as a handy excuse to unseat any incumbent local lords who refused to do his bidding. The 1020s passed with occasional skirmishes over religion or land (or both), but to many in Norway, it was a good time – there were constant whispers from further to the south that life under Olaf the Stout was preferable to life under Canute, and several outlying regions volunteered to join Olaf's Norway, such as the distant Orkney isles, and Norway's far north, where the Viking world receded into that of the Sámi.

Olaf the Stout is one of the more famous kings of Norway, and yet his reign was not all that successful, chiefly remembered for the lasting impact of Christianity. His saga recounts several incidents of unrest among his men, including an assassination attempt on their king. With Canute's empire blockading the west, and Sweden only nominally supportive to the immediate east, Olaf the Stout was forced to seek aid at the only border available to him – the bleak regions of Halogaland and Finland to the north-east. There, Snorri speaks of a disastrous 'tax-collection' expedition into Finland, which ended in fighting between Olaf's men, and the desecration of a local temple. Although he was ready to play the simple, local ruler with the people of Trondheim, Olaf the Stout was not above demanding tribute from elsewhere, particularly distant Iceland. Like Crowbone before him, he probably hoped to squeeze the Icelanders by exerting pressure on their shipping route to Trondheim, but they refused to pay up.

More worryingly for Olaf, two closer regions refused to acknowledge him as their king. Jamtaland and Helsingaland, founded several generations earlier by Norwegian exiles, had long been nominally parts of Norway. They had paid tributes to previous Norwegian rulers, and maintained relationships with the Norwegians across the Keel mountains. Now, in the mid-1020s, the people of Jamtaland and Helsingaland changed their minds. Instead of acknowledging the rule of a man over the mountains, they preferred to pledge allegiance to Onund Jacob.

Canute seemed ready to accept Olaf the Stout as the ruler of Norway, on the condition that he came to England, swore allegiance, and acknowledged that Canute was the rightful owner of Norway, and that he was merely looking after it. Efectively, Canute was demanding a form of *danegeld* from Norway itself, since Olaf would be obliged to collect taxes on his ruler's behalf. A more pragmatic man might have seen it as a good opportunity to avoid conflict, but it wasn't good enough for Olaf, who may have also regarded Canute's offer of a treaty with healthy suspicion – was Canute really intending to ignore the claims of the earls of Trondheim, or was the offer simply a ruse to lure Olaf to his death?

Olaf told the ambassadors that Denmark belonged to the Danes, and Norway to the Norwegians, and that Canute should be more than pleased with the extension of his lands to include England and large parts of Scotland. According to Snorri, Olaf even laughed that Canute should surely be happy with all the cabbage he was getting – England's vegetable produce being something of a joke in medieval Europe. But Olaf would not send any portion of his revenues to any other king. Norway belonged to him, and he was prepared to fight for it.[20]

Canute began preparing a fleet to retake Norway and reinstall the earls of Trondheim. It is likely that this was his plan all along, but a ship of ambassadors, a ship to carry Olaf to England, and then an assassin's dagger in the dark were an altogether cheaper means that he had been prepared to try first.

Knowing that Canute was on his way, Olaf sent word to his brother-in-law Onund Jacob, the king of Sweden. He urged the ruler of the Swedes to consider the implications of an Anglo-Danish attack on Norway, and that Canute's ambition was unlikely to stop at the Swedish border. Onund Jacob sent his reply that he was prepared to agree a treaty with Olaf, stating that each would send aid to the other in the event of an assault by Canute. Canute had himself already sent an embassy of his own to Sweden, laden with gifts for Onund Jacob, and assurances that Sweden would be quite safe from Denmark, and that only Norway and her allies need be concerned by his plans for war. Onund Jacob treated the ambassadors to an icy reception, and made it plain that he placed greater value on the simple, homespun aims of Olaf the Stout than he did on the imperial ambitions of Canute the Great.

With an attack by Canute seemingly inevitable, the kings of Norway and Sweden decided it was time for a pre-emptive strike, and led a double-pronged assault on Denmark. They may have also attempted a more diplomatic form of attack, since Canute's regent, his sister's husband Ulf, may have switched sides at least once during the conflict. Canute's long-awaited fleet caught up with the raiders on the Baltic coast of southern Sweden. Onund Jacob escaped with his life and dignity intact, while Olaf the Stout was forced to abandon his ships. Remembering the unhappy end of his predecessor Crowbone, he preferred to walk home rather than risk a further encounter with the Anglo-Danish fleet.

Olaf the Stout's golden age was coming to an end, largely because Canute cut a much more impressive figure. Olaf the Stout spoke of an independent Norway and the benefits of Western civilization, but even as he limped home with his supporters, Canute was doing everything in his power to win the Norwegians over with similar promises. And Canute was not an old war hero, returning with booty and tales of raids in the west, he was an acknowledged king of several countries, bolstered with the wealth and prestige of his adopted English home. Where Olaf the Stout spoke of Christ's power, Canute could brag of his pilgrimage to Rome itself – his trip there had won him the Pope's approval, and also secured Denmark's German border with the betrothal of his daughter Gunnhild to Henry III, son of the emperor Conrad.

Olaf's talk of 'Norwegian independence' meant little at the grass-roots level, merely that he wished to hang on to more of the tax revenues himself. To farmers in Trondheim, it mattered little *who* was collecting the taxes, as long as they were left to themselves. Although Olaf had done what he could to promote the idea that Canute was evil incarnate, the Danish king's arrival in Norway killed many of those rumours for good. Canute was conspicuously generous with his gifts and grants and soon had won the people of Norway over.[21] In 1028, with supporters deserting him in droves, Olaf the Stout was forced to admit that Canute had the upper hand. The Trondheimers proclaimed Canute a fitting person to be their king, and Olaf the Stout may have sneaked away to Russia, where he hoped to impose on the hospitality of Princess Ingigerd, his former betrothed, and her husband Jaroslav the Wise.

Canute turned out to be almost as wily as Olaf had painted him. News drifted in from the Pentland Firth that Earl Hakon, the strongest of the Trondheim rulers, had met with an unfortunate accident. The Trondheimers Kalf Arnarson and Einar Paunch-Shaker both now put themselves forward as possible replacements – and each believed himself to have the support of Canute. Imagine, then, their surprise when Canute favoured neither, and instead announced that the vassal-king of Norway would be his own son, Svein, in spite of promises he had initially made for home-rule in Trondheim.

The Trondheimers did not greet the news with much relish, particularly when it transpired that the newly arrived King Svein was only a child, and that the reins of power would actually be in the hands of his mother. To make matters worse, King Svein's mother was not even Canute's acknowledged wife before Christ, Queen Emma, the widow of Aethelred Unraed. Instead the new *de facto* ruler of Norway was Aelfgifu (Álfífa), regarded by the Norwegians as a highly unwelcome, interfering floozy who was not even Scandinavian, but instead from Northampton in England.

Canute had his reasons for keeping Aelfgifu at arm's length – he intended to eventually leave England and Denmark to Harthacanute, his son by Queen Emma, and thereby pre-empt any succession wrangles among the Anglo-Saxons. Since he already had two elder children by Aelfgifu, they would need to be packed off somewhere out of the way, and Norway must have seemed ideal. Some sources claimed that Canute and Aelfgifu were 'hand-fasted', or married in the pagan sense. This, of course, was of little concern to the people of Norway, converts, however grudgingly, to the Christian faith.

News of all this eventually reached the court of Jaroslav the Wise, where Olaf the Stout was in exile. Leaving his infant son Magnus (named after *Carolus Magnus*, Charlemagne) in the care of his in-laws, Olaf gathered his war-band once more and prepared to take back his kingdom. He was eager enough to have begun his travels in the dead of winter, traversing the frozen rivers of Russia and waiting at the Baltic coast for the ice to break up. His initial band of only a couple of hundred men was doubled in size upon his arrival at the court of his sometime ally, Onund Jacob of Sweden. He marched into southern Norway, offering the unhappy locals a choice between a foreign mistress or a Norwegian master. By the time he faced his enemies on 29 July 1030 at the Battle of Stiklastad, he had perhaps 3,600 men in his retinue, including Norwegians, Swedes, Russians and Finns. Unfortunately for Olaf, he faced an army in excess of 14,000. By the end of the day he was dead, although the legends of 'Saint Olaf', patron of all Scandinavia, were only beginning.

9

THE THUNDERBOLT OF THE NORTH

THE LIFE AND LEGENDS
OF HARALD THE RUTHLESS

Olaf the Stout's half-brother, Harald, would be known in later life as Harald *Hardraada* – if Aethelred had been *Unraed*, 'ill-advised' then Harald was 'severe in counsel', 'hard-ruling' or simply Ruthless. His life was the pinnacle of the Viking Age, his infamous defeat the beginning of its end. Harald's story also unites many of the separate strands of the Viking experience. Although his main area of interest was Norway, his travels took him throughout the world known to the Vikings, as far south as the coast of North Africa. One source even claimed, however doubtfully, that he ventured in search of Vinland, and even beyond, to the 'dark failing boundaries of the savage world'.[1] Although a man of 'noble birth', he spent much of his life as a mercenary, and much of his reign in a 'war' with Denmark that often seemed little more than a succession of pirate raids. Although he was one of the most well-travelled of Vikings, his raids and battles for a dozen years were fought not against foreigners, but against fellow Scandinavians. His last campaign united his destiny firmly with that of England.

We are fortunate in that Harald's remarkable life has been recounted in several works, most notably Snorri Sturluson's saga, which itself records poems about his deeds that had been sung in his presence. Snorri wrote about all Norway's early kings, but on Harald he is particularly rich in detail and anecdotes. Two of Harald's closest companions, Halldor Snorrason and Ulf Os-paksson, who fought at his side and even shared his brief incarceration in a Byzantine jail, were the descendants of notable Icelandic families. In later life, Halldor would return to his native land and insist on regaling the assembly there with tales of his time with King Harald, a habit that fixed many of Harald's adventures firmly in the mind of other skalds. Snorri Sturluson was one of Halldor's descendants, and much of his biography of Harald in *Heimskringla* draws, we may assume, on tales told and retold in his own family.

Harald grew up in Norway, and was occasionally visited by his half-brother Olaf. By the time Olaf commenced his cam-paign against Canute in 1030, Harald was 15 years old, still quite young by Viking standards, and certainly not expected to serve in Olaf's army. Harald, however, accompanied Olaf's forces, perhaps as an observer. *Heimskringla* reports his argument with Olaf on the eve of the battle of Stilkastad, with Olaf suggesting that he was too young to fight, and Harald protesting that he was old enough to lift a sword, even if the hilt had to be tied to his wrist.

Olaf relented, and Harald was among the men to hear Olaf's pre-battle address, a reminder that the bulk of his forces comprised hardened soldiers, while the Canute loyalists they faced were primarily conscripted farmers. Although Olaf was outnumbered, he was still confident that he could win, and called upon almighty God to ensure an outcome 'that He deems right for me.'[2] Despite predictable pleas to the Christian god for aid, Olaf's pre-Stilkastad speech shows the Viking mind still very much in evidence – he advocated a quick and terrifying charge, hoping to cause the less seasoned enemy soldiers to flee before they realized the inferior numbers of their attackers. His speech also made it clear that his grab for the crown was inspired by the traditional desire for more land – when all the talk of God had passed, he assured his men that their true rewards would not be in heaven, but paid in land and chattels taken from the vanquished.

Heimskringla reports Olaf's final moments, as he and his henchmen were approached by Thorir the Hound, a warrior supposedly shielded from harm by 'the mighty magic of Finns.'[3] As Olaf's henchmen fell, the king stood alone against a crowd of enemies, notably Thorir, Thorstein Shipbuilder and Finn Arnarson, who between them hacked him down. Thorir reported that contact with Olaf's blood caused his own wounds to heal. It was the first of several miraculous events associated with Olaf in the afterlife, leading to his later canonization.

The boy Harald, grievously wounded in the battle, was borne to safety by Rognavald Brusason from the distant Orkneys. Rognavald managed to smuggle the injured boy away to a remote house in the forests, and ensure that he was tended until he was able to travel farther afield. Needless to say, Harald's saga stresses that he *did not* run away, but had to be dragged from the battlefield by his associates, *gravely* wounded. Such behaviour befits a glorious hero, although a poem supposedly written at the time by Harald himself is notably lower key, makes no reference to wounds, and instead mentions Olaf's brother creeping '. . . from wood to wood with little honour now.'[4]

Whatever the circumstances surrounding his escape, the fugitive Harald rejoined Rognavald and a handful of other men by picking his way across the mountains that formed the spine between Norway and modern Sweden. With Scandinavia closed to them and their fortunes in decline, the last supporters of Olaf sought refuge with their relatives in Russia.

Saga sources are suspiciously reticent concerning the next three or four years. Although there are hints of wars and campaigns, and glories won, even Snorri whisks through the Russian years in barely a page. The *Russian Primary Chronicle*, however, fills the period with a series of internal and external conflicts among the Rus, into which a band of job-seeking Vikings would have fitted quite snugly.

Vladimir, the son of Saint Olga, had died in the year of Harald's birth, and his domain was now ruled by his son Jaroslav the Wise. Jaroslav's rise to power had been precarious, involving conflicts with several of his siblings, but he had secured his position with the aid of Viking mercenaries. Now he shared power with a handful of his surviving brothers, and already plotted to seize their lands when the opportunity arose. With Pecheneg tribesmen on the offensive again, Jaroslav was more than willing to take on new recruits, particularly those with whom he had a family connection – his wife Ingigerd was Olaf's sister-in-law. Dates are difficult to match, but it would seem that the arrival of Harald and his fellow exiles was contemporary with the final moves in Jaroslav's grab for sole rulership of the region. By 1036, with the help of his new recruits, Jaroslav was the sole master of the Rus domains.

For the teenage Harald, his service in Russia was the true test of his military abilities. He fought on Jaroslav's behalf for several years, against rebellious tribes in Poland, Estonia and regions beyond.[5] He also developed a close relationship with Jaroslav himself, such that Jaroslav may have even conceded that he might make a good choice of son-in-law. That, at least, is how Harald seems to have understood it; a closer reading of the sources rather suggests that Harald's request for the hand of Jaroslav's daughter Ellisif was gently declined. The young Viking was assured that he *might* be an ideal candidate, once he had gained further experience and, more pointedly, regained his lost wealth and inheritance.

Harald's saga paints the tale as one of frustrated romance, but although it is an entertaining fiction, there are no star-crossed lovers here. Harald offered Jaroslav a deal, and Jaroslav simply named his price – Ellisif was around ten years old at the time, giving Harald a small window of opportunity to find the required wealth and fortune – by the time she reached her late teens, he could reasonably expect her father to have found another husband for her. Returning to Scandinavia was still out of the question, so he took the next best option: Byzantium.

Ever since Vladimir had first sent a company of Viking warriors to the aid of Basil II (see Chapter Five), the emperors of Constantinople had come to place great reliance on the barbarian recruits. The Vikings, known in Constantinople as Varangians, formed an indispensable part of the empire's military might. They were, of course, expendable, but also highly reliable in battle. Sworn to serve the emperor himself, and without land-holdings that might influence their willingness to obey orders, they were often more trustworthy than local troops, who were too often riddled with factionalism and partisanship for other potential emperors.

Nevertheless, the Varangians were often uncontrollable. One Byzantine writer left an unhappy account of his attempts to lodge in a room near their quarters, where the noise made it impossible to sleep. The Varangians traded on their fearsome reputation, and revelled in their indifference to the high-level ceremonial they were there to guard. A slang term seemingly common among the Byzantine nobility referred to them as 'wine-bags', denoting disgust with their consumption of alcohol.[6] The relics of the Byzantine world still bear the scars of their passing, from the runic graffiti that was carved into a lion in Athens' Piraeus harbour, to the name 'Halfdan', etched into a balcony in Constantinpole's cathedral of Saint Sophia, presumably by a Varangian bodyguard tired of standing through yet another interminable Greek Orthodox ceremony.[7]

Power in Constantinople lay in the hands of Basil the Bulgar-Slayer's niece, the Empress Zoe, who was to be the wife of three emperors, the adopted mother of a fourth, and eventually a ruler in her own right. When Harald arrived in Constantinople, he did so around the time of the accession of Zoe's second husband, Emperor Michael IV. Taking the assumed name of Nordbrikt to avoid association with the ruling dynasy of Norway, Harald joined the Varangians as an officer, leading a squadron of men who knew his true identity.[8] He was first assigned to clear up a series of pirate attacks in the eastern Mediterranean, leading a Viking fleet against these Arab raiders. Although Harald may have sailed in longships, extant sources specifically refer to his vessels as *galeidir* ('galleys'), so it may also be the case that the Vikings were forced to use Byzantine ships in their naval battles.

Harald did not take well to a subordinate role, clashing often with his superiors, particularly the Byzantine general George Maniakes. Although the Muslim raiders had been able to defeat Byzantine shipping, they were no match for Vikings honed by several generations of raiding in northern Europe, and were soon retreating to their strongholds. The Varangian assault continued on land, and as the leader of a detachment, Harald is thought to have fought in Asia Minor, possibly accompanying a mission to Jerusalem itself, where he may have stood watch during the restoration of the Holy Sepulchre, and supposedly bathed in the waters of the river Jordan. This journey was made possible by a newly signed 30-year treaty between Byzantium and the Fatimid Caliphate, although some of the sagas preferred to report it as a military victory for Harald. Snorri's account is not even sure if Harald fought in Anatolia or Libya.[9]

Harald, it is said, took part in 'eighteen fierce-fought battles' in Serkland, 'the land of the Saracens', a term which then unhelpfully encompassed everywhere from north Africa to Turkey. The years 1038–41 supposedly saw him campaigning against Saracens in Sicily, and Lombard invaders in southern Italy. By this point, he had risen high enough in the ranks to be given command of two battalions – his own Viking followers and a group of Normans. Not all of Harald's soldiers were party to his secret, although rumours seem to have been rife – sagas report attempts by suspicious soldiers to unearth the true name of the mysterious Nordbrikt.

Snorri's account describes in detail some of Harald's most cunning ruses – but one must be wary because these stories were already clichéd in Harald's time. Harald, we are led to believe, used the old 'incendiary bird' trick to set fire to the roofs of a besieged town, a ploy credited to a Dane in Saxo, to Saint Olga in the *Russian Primary Chronicle*, and even to Guthrum in his attack on Cirencester during his war with Alfred the Great. If it was such a cunning plan, why is that up to five *other* cunning planners get the credit for it elsewhere? Similar doubts arise concerning Harald's infiltration of a church by means of a mock funeral, springing from his coffin, sword in hand, to the understandable surprise of the congregation. The same story, or rather the same plot occurs twice in Saxo, and in three other authors. It is notable that these incidents do not occur in the extant verses of Harald's personal skalds – his poets describe him as tough and brave, but not cunning.

A more trustworthy account, chiefly for its businesslike recitation of facts, was found in 1881, in a Byzantine manuscript that turned up in the archives of a Moscow church. Written in the 1070s by someone who claimed to have served with Harald himself, the *Advice to an Emperor* confirmed that a Harald (in Greek, *Araltes*), brother of Olaf (*Julavos*) had come to Byzantium with 500 men, fought on the empire's behalf in Sicily and Bulgaria, served faithfully and was eventually granted the honorary rank of *spatharokandates* ('troop leader' – hardly the generalship implied by his saga). In time, this Harald asked leave to return to his homeland. When this was refused, says the anonymous account, he stole away.[10]

The *Advice to an Emperor* is not clear on why he should have done so, although the saga evidence presents several possibilities. Harald was still in his mid-twenties, at the height of his powers, and, if we are to believe the insinuations of some authors, now cut a figure dashing enough to catch the eye of the Empress Zoe. Her husband, Michael IV, made Harald an official of the court, and within a few months he had supposedly risen to be leader of the palace guard. But Harald's promotion brought him closer to the intrigues that surrounded the throne. Michael IV announced his intention to put down an uprising in Bulgaria, despite his advanced years and an agonizing case of gangrenous gout.[11] Thanks partly to his Varangian cohorts, but chiefly to internal struggles among the rebels, he was able to return to Constantinople in triumph.

But the Bulgarian campaign was the last hurrah for the dying Michael IV. Abdicating and retiring to a monastery, he left the empire in the hands of his nephew Michael *Calaphates* – Michael the Caulker, whose father had worked in the Constantinople shipyards. Enthroned as Michael V, the new emperor began by paying lip service to Zoe, and to his uncles, all plainly intending to use him as a puppet ruler. But the new emperor soon flexed his imperial muscles, abhorring the long courtly rituals that formed part of his daily routine – as a commoner, he must have felt immensely out of his depth amid the rarefied protocols of Constantinople. He dismissed many of the associates of the former Emperor, including the Varangian Guard itself. For reasons unclear, this led to Harald's imprisonment. The most romantic explanation, supplied by Snorri Sturluson, whose ancestor Halldor was Harald's cellmate, was that Harald had fallen out with Zoe. One is a fairytale excuse involving his refusal to send her a lock of his hair.[12] Another, more dramatic, involves Harald's decision to marry Maria, a lady-in-waiting to Zoe. Zoe reputedly flew into a jealous rage, refusing his request and throwing him in jail.[13]

It is, however, likely that Harald's fall from grace was associated with more worldly, and historically verifiable, matters. The secret of his true identity (if it ever was a secret in the first place) was finally out, as was the news that his enemy King Canute was dead in England, and that Canute's sons were fighting over his domains. Meanwhile, St Olaf's son Magnus the Good had seized Norway (or at least, his 'supporters' had done so in the name of the boy, who was still only 11 years old), and Canute's son Harthacanute had enough problems elsewhere to grudgingly acknowledge his right to the territory. In other words, Norway was back in the hands of a kinsman of Harald's, and Harald regarded Magnus's birthright as one that deserved to be 'shared' with him. Accordingly, it was time for him to return to his native land. It may well be that it was only at this point that it became clear how much gold and treasure Harald had embezzled during his sojourn in the south. He had regularly sent large amounts of valuables, some legitimately acquired, some pilfered, back up the rivers of the Rus to his putative father-in-law Jaroslav the Wise.[14]

Whatever the real reason for his imprisonment, it became a subject of Viking legend, thanks perhaps to Halldor's apparent habit of ceaselessly retelling it in his dotage. Harald and his fellow prisoners had to contend with a snake in their cell, a tale that grew gradually taller, until other sources had him fighting a dragon, and even a lion. Reportedly, they were also rescued by the intercession of the spirit of St Olaf, who appeared to a Byzantine noblewoman and instructed her to rescue the prisoners – perhaps this is the Maria mentioned in some sources. It is more likely, however, that Harald's release was occasioned by his sometime tormentor, the Empress Zoe. Banished to a convent by her rebellious foster-son Zoe fought back in April 1042, inciting the populace to a riot. Several buildings were damaged during the unrest, and one of them may have been Harald's prison. Harald and his closest Varangians joined the mob, while other Vikings remained loyal to the new emperor, leading to a battle of Viking upon Viking in the streets of Constantinople. With the tide turning in favour of the rebels, Harald's men dragged Michael Calaphates from his hiding place. Their instructions were to symbolically render him unfit to rule. In the brutal traditions of Byzantium, this required mutilation, and the sagas report that it was Harald himself who blinded the former emperor with a hot iron. Unfortunately, in doing so the sagas also manage to get the emperor's name wrong, somewhat compromising their value.[15]

However, *someone* certainly did blind the former emperor, and in the aftermath, the elderly Zoe took a third husband, who was enthroned as Constantine IX. But the Golden City had lost much of its lustre for Harald, and nobody was safe at the palace. Constantine himself was soon at odds with his aged wife, and Zoe's sister Theodora already had a faction building around her. Meanwhile, Harald's former superior, George Maniakes, had fled to Italy, and was threatening to march on Constantinople with an army of his own. Friend and foe were no longer clearly delineated, and it seemed likely that further service to Constantinople would be a thankless task with diminishing returns. It was time for Harald to leave, but his permission was refused.[16]

Once again, the sources are unclear. They paint a picture of Harald fleeing the city in his galley, successfully making it past the chain that blocked the Bosphorus strait at the entrance to the Black Sea. An accompanying Viking vessel was not so lucky, and had to be abandoned at the barrier. Harald was supposedly accompanied by the mysterious Maria, although he later set her ashore and left her behind – was she a hostage to secure his safe exit from Byzantium, or a true lover who had a sudden change of heart? It is far more likely that Harald's real reason for such a dramatic exit was his wealth; Byzantine customs would have exerted a heavy levy on his treasure, and any gold in his possession was not supposed to leave the city at all.

Harald escaped successfully from Byzantium, and sailed back up the eastern river roads to the domain of Jaroslav the Wise. Some writers romanticize his return as the princely wooing of a blushing bride, but even the sagas cannot hide the pragmatic elements of his marriage to Princess Ellisif. Jaroslav had demanded proof of wealth, and Harald had successfully earned, plundered and embezzled an amount so large that, in the words of Snorri 'no one in the northern lands had seen its equal in the possession of one man.'[17] Even in the surviving poetry Harald himself wrote about his wife-to-be, he referred to her as a 'gold-ringed goddess'.[18]

Jaroslav permitted the exiled prince to marry his daughter in the winter of 1045. The following spring, Harald sailed up the last of the river-roads to the Gulf of Finland, and then back to Scandinavia itself. He was, as his later actions made clear, determined to win a kingdom at any cost, although not overly concerned about which kingdom it was.

St Olaf's son Magnus now ruled Norway. The sons of Canute had given up on Norway while they fought over England, and now both of them were dead. Magnus did, however, already have a new enemy in Svein Estridsen,[19] Canute's nephew. Magnus had attempted to buy him off in 1042 by acknowledging him as the ruler of Denmark, but Svein almost immediately mounted a challenge on Norway itself. He was swiftly beaten back and hiding out in Sweden where his path crossed with the returning Harald. Somehow, these two dangerous and untrustworthy men reached an agreement that they should unite against a common foe. If Magnus was going to claim to be the ruler of Norway and Denmark, Harald and Svein would prove him wrong in a time-honoured fashion – they went *a-viking*.

For all their claims of nobility and kingship, Harald and Svein were still raiders at heart. Their policy of demonstrating Magnus's unsuitability to rule comprised a series of Viking raids on the coasts of Denmark itself, proof if proof was ever required that the Vikings excluded no one when choosing their victims. With a force of warriors from all over Scandinavia, the Harald-Svein fleet terrorized a kingdom that Magnus claimed to control.

But Harald was a mercenary Viking with mercenary ambitions, and his alliance with Svein was opportunistic. His saga reports a series of intrigues that led him to question his former alliance, though they are all likely to have been later attempts to put a human face on a harsh reality – Harald realized he stood a better chance of getting what he wanted if he switched sides.

In one saga account, Magnus's advisor, confidante and, perhaps, regent was Astrid, the widow of St Olaf and sister of the Swedish king. Astrid's involvement brought heavy support from the Swedes, and a sense of continuity. Unfortunately for her but handily for the saga-writing gossip, she was not Magnus's natural mother – that honour went to Alfhild, a former chambermaid. Alfhild, it is said, wasted no time in reminding Astrid who the king's mother actually was, while Astrid for her part was quick to remind Alfhild that she was the queen, and that Alfhild had been nothing but a serving wench until Olaf had bedded her. With such feuding behind the scenes, someone at Magnus's court sent word to Harald the Ruthless, in the name of King Magnus, that it was unseemly for two relatives to be quarrelling. He offered Harald half his kingdom, a joint kingship, if Harald agreed they pool their resources, and put his Byzantine gold to use in strengthening Scandinavia.

This, of course, was what Harald was after all along, but his saga biographers would not dare suggest that he accepted. Instead, they pre-empted him from going back on his word by suggesting that news somehow reached Svein of the secret negotiations. *Heimskringla* reports a tense dinner conversation between him and Harald, in which small talk turned all too quickly to umbrage. Purportedly, the men were discussing their most valuable possessions, which for Harald was his 'magical' banner Landwaster, a flag of some unknown material (probably Byzantine silk) said to guarantee victory to whoever bore it in front of his army. Svein, it is said, scoffed that he would believe such a claim when he saw Harald win three battles against his kinsman King Magnus. It was the word 'kinsman' that caused the argument – Harald thought that Svein had made too great a point of reminding him that he was fighting a member of his own family. In the heat of the moment, he even implied that the world would be a better place if he and Magnus were not enemies at all. Svein countered by musing about Harald's habit of only keeping those parts of promises that suited him best. Harald had the last word, crowing that Svein had *kept* more promises to Magnus than Harald had broken.[20]

That night, Harald returned to his ship at anchor, telling his men that he was suspicious about Svein's intentions. Sure enough, Harald wisely slept elsewhere that evening, while a would-be assassin clambered on to his ship and buried an axe where he would otherwise have been.[21] The treaty with Svein was at an end, conveniently through Svein's actions, not Harald's betrayal, thereby saving honour in the eyes of his biographers, and Harald sailed for a conference with his estranged nephew.

Magnus granted him half the kingdom of Norway, and subordinate status – in all matters of protocol, Magnus was to be considered the superior. Harald agreed, and discovered all too soon why his nephew was so keen to make a deal. When the time came for them to examine their finances, Magnus revealed that he was bankrupt.

The co-rulers embarked on a consolidation of the kingdom along the northern coasts of Norway – better described as the extraction of protection money in order to establish their rulership. Svein hid out on the coasts of Sweden, sailing to Denmark when he was sure he would be unopposed, and demanding similar tribute from the local inhabitants. Denmark was still his, whatever the rulers of Norway might say. Meanwhile, Harald and Magnus were not the happiest of allies. They had already almost come to blows over a parking spot – Harald's men having berthed their ship in a harbour slot designated for the superior king. Knowing well enough that he could not afford to give a single inch to Harald, Magnus drew up his own ships ready for battle. Harald backed down, commenting that Magnus was being petty, and noting that 'it is an old custom for the wiser one to yield'. Even in defeat, he still managed to have the final say.[22] Had Magnus lived, it is likely that he and Harald would have exchanged more than unkind words. However, Magnus died while on campaign in Denmark in 1047, leaving Harald as the sole ruler of Norway, and the overlordship of Denmark still open to question.

The Viking Age was drawing to a close. The initial conditions for the Viking invasions had waned – Scandinavian settlers had colonized Iceland and points beyond, while the coastal defences of medieval Europe were now significantly stronger. After almost 250 years of raiding and counter-raids, the 1040s find the people left behind in Scandinavia much as the original Vikings had left them – farmers and fishermen, preyed upon by belligerent crews of raiders.

The participants, however, would not have seen it that way. Svein, now 'collecting tribute' rather than raiding, had convinced many of the Danes that he was the one with the power to do them and others harm and hence protect them. One such supporter, in an apocryphal but evocative tale, was Thorkel Geysa, a landowner on the Danish coast who refused to believe that Harald the Ruthless would return. Thorkel joked that Harald's fleet, if it existed, was so feeble that he imagined his own daughter Dótta could fashion anchors out of cheese sufficient to hold it fast.[23]

Such unwise words put Thorkel's farm right at the top of Harald's hit list. As *King Harald's Saga* puts it:

> It is reported that the watchman who first caught sight of King Harald's fleet said to Thorkel Geysa's daughters, 'I thought you said that Harald would never come to Denmark.'
>
> 'That was yesterday,' replied Dótta.[24]

The daughters of Thorkel Geysa were carried off in chains, and only returned to their father after the payment of a heavy ransom. And so the raiding went on, in a seemingly endless round of pillage and counter-pillage that taxed the poetic skills of the most verbose skald. Eventually, in 1049, Harald sent home his 'farmer army' of conscripts, retaining only his professional soldiers and pirates for a terrible assault on Hedeby, at the heart of the Danish trade system. With Hedeby burning behind him, his treasure-laden fleet was pursued by an angry Svein. *Heimskringla* recounts Harald's desperate attempt to delay his vengeful pursuers as they gained on him, throwing first plunder, and then prisoners into the sea behind him as a distraction.

Harald's campaigns in this period were aimed at consolidating the deal he had made with Magnus. Their agreement, much as Harald had tried to bend the rules, was that they would be co-rulers of the region until one of them died, at which point the other would be the sole inheritor. This suited Harald very well with Magnus gone, but some of Magnus's subordinates were less willing to accept it. Paramount among the objectors were the troublesome inhabitants of Trondheim. While they were allies of Magnus, there was no love lost between them and Harald – although Harald only professed his belief in Christ when it suited him, the earls of Trondheim were unrepentant pagans, and refused to recognize his authority.

This, anyway, is how the pious Snorri would have us understand it – the nominal Christian, relative of the saint, builder of churches is preferable in the long-term to the devout pagan, at least in hindsight. However, while religion often featured in the conflicts in Norway, it was not necessarily the reason, but an excuse. Unrest in Harald's Norway had less to do with religion than it did with the unwelcome redistribution of wealth.

Einar Paunch-shaker was someone strongly in favour of redistributing wealth in his own favour. Once an enemy of the rulers of Trondheim, he was now married into their dynasty. For years, Einar had collected taxes in Trondheim as Magnus's representative, but kept the money for himself – better this, Magnus must have reasoned, than the conflict that would otherwise ensue between the 'king' of Norway and the fractious earldom. While Harald made a show of finishing the building of Trondheim's church to St Olaf, begun by Magnus but left unfinished at his death, Einar mounted a publicity stunt of his own, sailing into town with a flotilla of nine ships and several hundred men, daring Harald to find some cause to call him to heel. Harald, however, merely observed the force arriving from his balcony, and said:

> Einar of the flailing sword
> Will drive me from this country
> Unless I first persuade him
> To kiss my thin-lipped axe.[25]

The round of feud and counter-feud, posturing and slander was about to begin again, but Harald was not known for his patience. Einar was a typical man of Trondheim, highly reluctant to accept the authority of whoever called himself the king of Norway, and ready to prove it with a show of force, if necessary. In most cases, this attitude manifested itself at local assemblies, where Einar loudly boasted of his adherence to the letter of all laws. In matters where Harald's own decisions were subject to ratification by an assembly of local farmers, Einar would often argue a case for rejecting Harald's rulings. The message he sent to southern Norway was clear – in Trondheim, it was he, not Harald who was in charge.

The uneasy peace between him and Harald continued for

some time, until an occasion when a thief came to trial at the local assembly. Since the thief was one of his own men, Einar was presented with a difficult situation – he could act like Harald, and do whatever he liked, or he could behave as he had always boasted he did, and leave the sentencing to the assembly. Einar overstepped his position by liberating the accused man. Before long, he was summoned to give an account of himself before Harald, and arrived with a heavily armed company. Einar, it seems, was expecting more bluster and posturing, but Harald's patience had run out. Without waiting for an explanation or warning, Harald's men cut Einar and his son Eindridi down where they stood. Doubly leaderless, the Trondheim opposition soon melted back to their farms, Einar's widow Bergljót, lamented that her relative Hakon was not present to bully the men of Trondheim into an act of revenge: 'Eindridi's killers would not be rowing down the river now if Hakon had been here on the bank.'[26]

The slaying of Einar may have removed a potential opponent, but it created considerable ill feeling towards Harald in the region. It also initiated a feud, which threatened to run out of control. Already, Bergljót had sent messengers to Hakon Ivarsson, detailing Harald's crimes against her family, while Harald was assembling an army in southern Norway.

But Harald had also made political matches in keeping with his new interests. Ellisif, the bride he had laboured for ten years to win from Jaroslav the Wise, was replaced in his affections by Thora, the daughter of Thorberg Arnarson. Ellisif remained Harald's official wife in Christian eyes, but it was Thora who shared his bed.[27] While Ellisif might have been a trophy wife, and represented a useful eastern alliance, Thora brought alliances closer to home. Her uncle Finn Arnarson was powerful enough in the Trondheim region to intercede on Harald's behalf, brokering a deal in which Harald would compensate

Hakon for his crimes. It was the political scandal of its day – a king with a reputation for ignoring the law when it suited him, suddenly forced to attend, or at least appear to attend to the ruling and judgements of a council of farmers. However, Finn was able to secure a deal 'out of court' as it were, by approaching Hakon in private and making him an offer. Finn pointed out that Hakon's situation was going to cost him dearly. If he came out against Harald openly, it would be seen as a revolt – he would either lose and thereby lose his life, or win and be coloured ever more as a traitor.

Harald, however, was not done with the Arnarson family. He also found himself an accidental ally of Finn's brother Kalf, one of the men who had so brutally cut down St Olaf. On a raiding party in Denmark, Harald saw to it that Kalf was put ashore ahead of the rest of the company, facing insurmountable odds and with reinforcements suspiciously late in arriving. Kalf was killed in the ensuing battle, and Finn immediately suspected that Harald had planned it. For his part, Harald was remarkably reluctant to deny the charges, instead boasting in a poem of his consolidation of power and removal of potential threats:

> Now I have caused the deaths
> Of thirteen of my enemies;
> I kill without compunction
> And remember all my killings.
> Treason must be scotched
> By fair means or foul
> Before it overwhelms me;
> Oak-trees grow from acorns.[28]

With the removal of another threat from within his own country, Harald was finally able to turn back to the last great impediment to his overlordship of Scandinavia – the continued presence of Svein Estridsen in Denmark. Harald moved a large part of his military operation to the south of Norway, and at the northern end of the same Vik bay that may have given its name to the Vikings themselves, he founded a new town near modern-day Oslo. The site was carefully chosen for its military advantages; it had good access to surrounding farmland, and was an excellent harbour for assembling warships. It was, moreover, close enough to Denmark to forestall swift raids.

After many years of intermittent warfare, Harald and Svein finally clashed in a major sea battle at Nissa in 1062, in which dozens of longships were lashed together in a marine brawl, and which ended with 70 Danish ships emptied of their crews. Skirmishes went on for a couple more years, but Nissa had taken a lot out of the combatants – not just in terms of their willingness to keep fighting, but also because of the expense. It is possible that Harald's reserves of cash from his Byzantine days were running low, and he was experiencing some difficulty in collecting taxes, particularly from the Trondheim region that had constantly resisted his rule. Ten years was long enough to fight over Denmark, and Harald was prepared to sue for peace. At a meeting with Svein, the two men conceded that each was the true ruler of his kingdom, and departed in a state of truce.

There was, however, already trouble brewing elsewhere, dating back to the agreements with his nephew that had brought Harald back to Scandinavia in the first place. The co-ruler arrangement with Harald was not the only double-or-nothing bet that the late King Magnus had made during his life. He had made a similar promise to Harthacanute, king of England, that whoever of them outlived the other would inherit the domains of both. But Harthacanute had died in 1042, five years before Magnus. In the strictest terms of their agreement, Magnus had been the rightful king of England for five years before his own death, and in the strictest terms of the *other* agreement, Magnus's lands were Harald's by right. With Harald established as Magnus's rightful heir, he had thus inherited a tenuous claim to the throne of England itself. This fact was not lost on the English earl Godwine, who attempted to persuade King Edward the Confessor to send a fleet of ships to the aid of Svein Estridsen, who, like Harthacanute, was a grandson of Svein Forkbeard.

In the first week of January 1066, the English king Edward the Confessor died in his early fifties. His last surviving nephew had predeceased him a couple of years earlier, and he had no children of his own. With the passing of Edward, there was no obvious candidate for the throne of England – the original Saxon line was all but at an end. The only available adult candidates were the descendants of Vikings.

Edward's half-Danish brother-in-law Harold, son of the scheming earl Godwine, was proclaimed as the new king of England. Meanwhile, Edward's Norman cousin, William the Bastard, not only claimed that he had been promised the throne by the ailing Edward, but that Harold Godwinson (called Godwinson hereafter to avoid confusion with Harald the Ruthless) had sworn, on holy relics no less, to do all in his power to ensure that promise would be made good. Not only was Godwinson a usurper in William's eyes, he had broken an oath made before God.[29] For some reason, Godwinson's younger brother Tostig, Earl of Northumbria, thought that *he* should have the throne of England.[30] It was Godwinson's claim that the dying Edward had promised the kingdom to *him*. It was Tostig's complaint, very much in the Viking spirit, that regardless of Godwinson's family seniority, the elders of England should choose the 'king whom they deem most fitting'.[31]

Tostig certainly involved himself in enough drama elsewhere. Siward, his predecessor as the ruler of Northumbria, had kept the Scots busy by supporting the exiled Malcolm against the usurper Macbeth – a tale told better elsewhere.[32] Malcolm repaid his English supporters by raiding along their borders, but Tostig made a careful treaty between Scotland and England. However, when Godwinson became king in Edward's place, he showed little friendliness towards his brother. In fact, when Northumbria rose in revolt in 1065, Godwinson was prepared to listen to the rebels' demands, and to exile his troublesome sibling from England altogether. With nothing left to lose, Tostig went looking abroad for help against Godwinson, turning first to the Scots, then to his cousin Svein Estridsen in Denmark.

According to Harald's saga, Svein, in a remarkably civil and un-Viking reply, turned Tostig down. Although Tostig appealed to Svein's ancestry, the conquests of Forkbeard, and the empire of Canute the Great, Svein meekly announced that he knew his limitations. He refused to accept flattering parallels drawn between himself and his uncle Canute, and announced that he lacked the finances, endurance and right to embark upon the invasion of England on Tostig's behalf. Tostig taunted him with hints of who his second choice of ally would be. 'I shall,' he said, 'find a chieftain who is less faint-hearted than you to engage in a great enterprise.'[33] Tostig next called on Harald the Ruthless. He, his sagas claim, could not see much potential in persuading Norwegians to sail across the North Sea on behalf of an allegedly disinherited Englishman, particularly one who was half-Dane. 'The English,' said Harald, 'are not altogether reliable.'[34]

But Tostig would not let up. *Heimskringla* reports a heated debate between him and Harald, with Harald reluctant to discuss the invasion of Britain, and Tostig cunningly drawing parallels between England and Denmark. Denmark, argued Tostig, had eluded Harald for a decade because the local people's hearts and minds belonged to Svein Estridsen. Yet if he wanted England, the presence of Tostig would ensure that the local people supported Harald. His army would be welcomed as liberators, and England would be his for the taking. None of this was actually true, and it is likely that both Harald and Tostig were planning to double-cross each other. However, Tostig won Harald round to the idea of an English invasion. The word went out from Oslo and Trondheim, that Harald was preparing the raid to end all raids.

The invasion fleet assembled in the waters off Trondheim, plagued by bad omens – warriors in Harald's company reported dreams of carrion birds perched on all the prows of the ships, and of an unearthly woman riding a man-eating wolf into battle at the head of the English army. Harald himself dreamed of his brother St Olaf, who warned him that there was a difference between an honourable death while fighting for one's birthright, and falling in battle while attempting to steal someone else's.[35] Such portents are mere touches of extra drama in the sagas, added by later chroniclers – had Harald become the next king of England, it is likely that old soldiers' memories would have dredged up far more positive predictions. But the reports of the bad omens do suggest a sense of guilt, as if many of the Norsemen knew that they had only excuses for war, not legitimate reasons. The invasion of England was merely one more Viking raid, on the scale of the earlier Great Heathen Host.

Perhaps Harald had some presentiment of disaster. He left his son Magnus behind, not as regent or viceroy, but as a king with equal powers. He took his first wife Ellisif and their two daughters with him, dropping them off at the Orkneys en route. When he reached the coast of Scotland he took his fleet south, landing in the Cleveland area and finding no resistance – the usurper Godwinson was busy in the south, making preparations to repel another invasion, this time threatened from Normandy. He was also occupied with a succession of pirate raids on England's south coasts, which turned out to be led by Tostig – had Harald and his unlikely ally agreed that Tostig would cause a diversion while Harald softened up Tostig's old earldom in Northumbria?[36]

Tostig arrived in the north of England, meeting Harald at the mouth of the River Tyne on 8 September. If Harald had been expecting Tostig to bring a significant number of fighting men with him, he would have been annoyed to discover his 'ally' arriving with only a dozen ships, and most of those were likely to have been Orkney vessels that would have joined Harald anyway. Nevertheless, the combined party laid siege to Scarborough, burning part of the town before its capitulation. Their fleet sailed south along the coast of Northumbria, looting where there was resistance, and taking hostages where there was not. Tostig knew Northumbria well, and knew the likely dispositions of troops in the region.

Harald's ultimate target was York, the seat of power of Erik Bloodaxe a century earlier. If the fleet met with no worthy resistance on the coasts, they would find their enemies in York. The fleet sailed up the River Humber, and the soldiers disembarked ready to face a foe on land. Had the local earls, Edwin and Morkere, had more faith in Godwinson, they might have retreated behind the walls of York and waited for reinforcements. They had sent word to the south of the Viking invasion, but did not expect any help, and resolved to meet the Vikings head-on.

The two sides finally met on 20 September, two miles south of York, at a place identified by modern historians as Gate Fulford.[37] The armies faced each other on the road itself, their flanks cut off by the River Ouse on one side, and impassable swamp on the other. Harald kept his men on the left of the Viking line, prominently displaying his banner, Landwaster. Tostig was kept highly visible on the right side, presumably to lure the English into a charge against the traitor, instead of more sensibly holding their ground. If it was a deliberate ploy, it worked, with the English concentrating their attack on Tostig, allowing Harald to direct Landwaster straight at a weakened front line. The Northumbrians were routed, and York lay undefended.

Harald was clearly settling in for the long haul. York was left relatively unharmed. Harald took hostages from the people of York, but also left some of his own – the arrangement has all the signs of an alliance or treaty, and not a victory. This, perhaps, is where Tostig's true value began to show; had Harald been the leader of an army of Viking conquest, he might have expected no help, but as the supporter of an English claimant to the throne, he had better treatment. York became the centre of the resistance to Godwinson. People of Northumbria were even invited to swell the ranks of Harald's army, turning it from an army of conquest into an army of restoration.

If anything defeated Harald's designs on England, it was an ancient relic of forgotten conquerors. Almost a thousand years earlier, legions such as XX Valeria Victrix and II Augusta had kept their troops busy with immense public works. Since Roman times, England had been crossed by a network of good roads, as straight as possible, slicing through hills and across dales, and built to last. Wide enough to permit 16 horsemen riding abreast, they had lasted for many centuries as the arteries of England, carrying merchants and farmers safely without the hindrances of marshy ground or impenetrable woodland. The network embraced the core of old Britannia –

only petering out to the west, where it ran into the territories of Wales and Cornwall. Thanks to the old Roman roads, it was still possible to quickly march a force of military men from London, the Romans' Londinium, all the way to the old Roman city of Eboracum – York. Even as Harald and Tostig celebrated their conquest of Northumbria, Godwinson was on his way north. The Viking invaders had grossly overestimated the time it would take for the English army to extricate itself from the south. On 24 September, as they finalized the surrender of York, Godwinson's relief force was less than a day's march away, in Tadcaster.

It is impossible to know the exact date when Godwinson heard of Harald's arrival. He had between one and two weeks to put a plan into action, and, perhaps conveniently, already had an army preparing to resist invasion, albeit from another direction. Nevertheless, for him to move several thousand men 200 miles north in such a short time was an incredible feat. Many of them may have been mounted on horseback, which would have made the journey somewhat easier for them, if not on the horses. Others may have been picked up en route, as Godwinson's force passed through towns on its northward journey, but it is likely that a significant proportion of Godwinson's army had all but jogged 20 miles a day, some for as long as a week.

On 25 September, much to everyone's surprise, Godwinson's army arrived in York, where the townsfolk were swift to deny that they had made any deals with the invader – the sources imply that although they had agreed to swap hostages, the exchange had not yet taken place. Godwinson did not stop at York, but kept his troops moving, until they ran into the astonished Vikings on the banks of the River Derwent, at Stamford Bridge.[38]

The impression left by both the more reliable the *Anglo-*

Saxon Chronicles, and the dubious King Harald's Saga is that Harald was put very much on the defensive. He also received yet another portent of his demise, when he was thrown from his horse while reviewing his troops. Godwinson himself approached the enemy lines, calling out to Tostig that there was still time for him to switch sides, and promising him 'a third of his kingdom' (presumably his reinstatement as lord of Northumbria) if he abandoned the Viking cause. Tostig, however, refused – Harald for his part was annoyed because he only learned of Godwinson's identity after the man had retreated back out of arrow range.[39]

When the battle itself began, Harald fought out in the front of his men, overexposed, and was hit in the throat by an arrow.[40] In a moment of unfortunate inaccuracy, Manuscript 'D' of the Anglo-Saxon Chronicles says at this point '. . . so was killed Harald Fairhair,' confusing this Harald with one who had died some 130 years earlier.[41] The battle went on for a considerable time without him, with the Vikings rallying first to Tostig until he was also killed, and then to Eystein Orri. Eystein was the son of Thorberg Arnarson and the betrothed of Harald's daughter Maria. King Harald's Saga makes much of the brave reinforcement provided by Eystein and his men, alluding to their terrible exhaustion after having dashed over from the beached Viking fleet – forgetting, perhaps that the men they were fighting had been on a week-long forced march. In the end, the Vikings were routed.

With Harald and Tostig dead, both the Vikings and the English rebels had lost the leaders that galvanized their campaign. Within the Viking army, the death toll was particularly severe among the 'nobility' – many leaders of war-bands lay dead on the field at Stamford Bridge. The new leader of the Vikings was Harald's son Olaf (later King Olaf III the Peaceful), who was granted permission to leave in his ships. Such was the speed of his departure, that he left the body of Harald the Ruthless behind. It would be another year before it was returned to Norway, where it was interred in Trondheim.

The Viking Age in England had fittingly come to an end, in Northumbria, the place that had seen its beginnings. Godwinson turned his exhausted men around and began a second forced march, back to the south. On 14 October, he would die in the Battle of Hastings, where William the Bastard, the great-great-grandson of the Viking leader Hrolf, would be re-branded as 'the Conqueror' and become the new ruler of England.

10

CHILDREN OF THOR

ONE THOUSAND YEARS LATER

The years after Stamford Bridge saw the players in the Viking drama slowly recede into history, leaving their 'Viking' heritage behind. Magnus and Olaf 'the Peaceful', the sons of Harald the Ruthless, ruled Norway between them, and renewed hostilities between their lands and the Danish holdings of Svein Estridsen. For his part, Svein married Thora, the widow of Harald the Ruthless. While Olaf the Peaceful remained in Scandinavia, a coin bearing his face somehow made it all the way across the Atlantic to Godard Point, Maine, either through shipwreck, or trade between Arctic Inuit and Greenlanders, or perhaps even one final, unrecorded visit to Vinland.

Svein Estridsen and, after his death, his son Canute (later St Canute) plotted to send a massive Danish fleet against England. Canute was assassinated before he could act on it, and the threat to England from Scandinavia faded permanently. If

Vikings counted on any support from Northumbria, they could forget it after 1080. William the Conqueror laid waste to northern England, to ensure that it never rose up in support of any rebels against him.

Edgar the Atheling, the grandson of Edmund Ironside and the true heir to the English throne, made a half-hearted attempt at claiming the throne of England, before becoming a patsy of the new regime, fighting in Normandy on behalf of the Normans, and accompanying William the Conqueror's son on a crusade to Jerusalem. Eastern Europe was the destination of many other exiles. Tostig's sons stayed on in Norway with King Olaf's blessing, and their descendants fell into obscurity there. Godwinson's daughter Gytha remained in Russia, as the wife of the prince of Kiev, Vladimir II. Kiev continued to send Varangian mercenaries to Constantinople, but in the years after 1066 the Byzantine army was swelled by many Englishmen fleeing the new Norman order to seek their fortune elsewhere. The 'Viking' nature of the Varangians was permanently diluted, and the Varangian guard henceforth gained a far more Anglo-Saxon character.[1] Others were rumoured to have permanently settled on the coast of the Black Sea with the Emperor's blessing, at an unknown location that may have been the Crimea, which they called *Nova Anglia* – New England.

In Scandinavia, the rulers of the areas we now call Norway, Denmark and Sweden continued to jockey for position. As Christianity took firmer hold, they found new causes to unite them. Throughout the thirteenth and fourteenth centuries, they continued to war and raid in foreign lands, but in eastern Europe, and in the name of the Lord. The Northern Crusades turned swathes of the southern Baltic kingdoms into vassal states of the Swedes and Danes. As the family trees branched and interwove, a time came in the fifteenth century when a

single monarch presented a reasonable claim to all the thrones
of the region; Sweden, Denmark and Norway were joined for a
century or so in the medieval Kalmar Union, before Sweden
broke away again. Denmark and Norway continued to function as a single entity, before Norway seceded after the
Napoleonic wars to form a union with Sweden. The union
was eventually dissolved in 1905, supposedly because the
Norwegians were unhappy with being ruled by a foreign
power. As an indicator of just how confusing and contradictory this was, when the newly independent Norwegians
decided to find a new king, their choice settled on a *Danish*
prince, who ascended to the Norwegian throne as Hakon VII.

Norwegian influences continued among the people of the
Celtic fringe. Viking expeditions continued in the Irish Sea,
some led by the grandson of Harald the Ruthless, King
Magnus Barelegs, who gained his name after he showed a
predilection for wearing a kilt. Viking influence in Ireland had,
however, been curtailed by the Battle of Clontarf in 1014,
although modern historians dispute its importance – the Vikings had already been going native by that point.[2] Their
mixed-race offspring remained separate enough to gain their
own identity – *Ostmen*, a name derived from their dwelling
predominantly in the east of Ireland, but local intermarriage
and Christianity wore away Viking elements. Although the
Vikings have been blamed for destroying countless treasures of
monastic Ireland, their function as traders and the founders of
towns did much to bring it into contact with other parts of
Europe.

As late as 1171, Orkney islanders with names as un-Scottish
as Svein Asleifarson made seasonal raids westward towards
the Hebrides and Ireland, and preyed upon English shipping.
The twelfth-century leader Somerled, who counted Scots and
Vikings among his ancestors, kept Argyllshire and Caithness

free from Scottish sovereignty, preferring to pay his allegiance to the king of Norway. According to popular myth, Land-waster, the fabled banner of Harald the Ruthless, somehow made it into Scottish hands as the 'fairy flag' of Clan MacLeod, carried in battle as late as the sixteenth century, but now kept in Dunvegan Castle on the Isle of Skye.

But the Viking spirit was waning, and the families of the isles were steadily losing their connections to their distant home-land. The nascent Scottish kingdom gradually retook the Norse-dominated areas chief by chief, until 1263, when the Norwegian King Hakon IV felt obliged to lead a fleet to remind his Hebridean subjects who he was. After his death in the Orkneys, his son sold the Isle of Man and the Hebrides to the Scots. The Orkneys followed in 1472, in lieu of a dowry for Margaret of Denmark, the wife of the Scottish King James III. The highlands and islands of Scotland finally became possessions of that kingdom, and would remain so, although Norse words persist in Shetland and Orcadian dialect. Despite being the *northernmost* region of Scotland, the region known as *Sutherland* retains a name based on its position relative to Norway and the isles, not Britain itself.

The Vikings were similarly edged out in other parts of the world. The ill-fated voyages to Vinland were not repeated, although vessels continued to make occasional trips to arctic Canada to collect timber for the Greenland colony. By the beginning of the twelfth century, the Earth's climate had taken a turn for the colder.[3] The first places to feel the effects were the Viking colonies on Iceland and Greenland's western coast, where farmers noticed that the winters were becoming sig-nificantly harsher. Drift ice, once merely a seasonal hazard, became increasingly prevalent off the north coast of Iceland. In Greenland, it began to clog the northern fjords for much of the year, and made the voyage east to Europe ever more perilous.

The old straight route to Europe, pioneered by Leif the Lucky, was no longer possible. Navigators were forced to swing farther to the south to avoid icebergs, and the trip became even less appealing than it already was.

Greenland and Iceland were officially made dominions of Norway in 1261, an acknowledgement of the stranglehold on communications held in olden times by the port of Trondheim, and in later years by the flourishing harbour at Bergen. The king of Norway promised to send one ship a year to Greenland, but even that annual lifeline became irregular as Norwegian trade was undermined and surpassed by the German Hanse in the later Middle Ages. The Germans had no family ties with the remote Viking colonies of the north Atlantic, and Greenland in particular suffered from the lack of communication. By the fourteenth century, the length of time between ships had reached dangerous proportions – once, nine years elapsed with no communication between Greenland and the outside world, causing some to speculate that the colonists had turned their back on Europe, and on Christ. In fact, although no bishop could be persuaded to go there, Greenland remained resolutely Christian, its inhabitants holding fast to every single aspect of the faith from their glory days in the eleventh century.[4]

As the ice grew worse, and they clung suicidally to a way of life that only really worked in temperate Europe, the former raiders found themselves subject to incursions by unwelcome visitors. Perhaps crossing new bridges formed by new ice, perhaps following seals as they headed south, the Skraelings came to Greenland. It is unlikely that the people who came to Greenland were the same tribe of 'wretches' who had fought with the Vikings in Vinland. Instead, these new arrivals were Inuit from the Arctic regions, fully adapted to life in an unforgiving climate. Around 1200, the Inuit occupied an area of fjords and islands termed the Northern Hunting Grounds by the European settlers. It is thought that there was some trade between the Inuit and the Greenlanders – iron ship rivets have been found deep in the Canadian arctic, where any metal object was highly prized.[5] Such trade also led to conflict, as the 1379 records of the Icelanders demonstrate – 'The Skraelings attacked the Greenlanders, killed eighteen of them and carried off two boys, who they made their slaves.'[6]

Some have assumed a gradual thinning out of the Greenland colony, until the last few stragglers left, perhaps on a forgotten voyage back to Iceland that never made it. Some have assumed a friendly assimilation, with the Greenlanders adopted into the Inuit way of life, melting into the arctic wastes with their newfound allies. However, there has yet to be any genetic proof of extensive medieval intermarriage between the Green-landers and the Inuit. In fact, Inuit legends often sound more like the more violent of the Viking sagas. One tells of an Inuit hunter coming across a Greenlander collecting shells, and immediately killing him with a spear. This act of murder was followed by Greenlander retaliation, and still greater Inuit revenge, in a series of escalating atrocities. Another recounts the activities of two outlaws who kidnap and assault a Green-lander girl, and their successful repulse of a punitive raid by the girl's kinsmen.[7] In the later Inuit accounts, we hear of a Norse leader, Ûngortoq (thought to be an Inuit corruption of Ingvar), fleeing from his burning house, and casting his infant son into the icy waters rather than leave him to the pursuing Inuit.[8]

By the late fifteenth century, when parties of Inuit arrived in the Eastern settlement, they found it devoid of human habita-tion. Gardar, across Eriksfjord from the settlement of Erik the Red, where the people of Greenland had once proudly built a cathedral, was now empty. The Inuit called it *Igaliko*, 'the deserted cooking place,' a name it bears to this day. But, setting aside for a moment the unreliability of mere anecdotal evidence, if the Inuit *found* it deserted, then where did the Greenlanders go?

For a generation after 1420, Iceland and the Faeroes were subject to a series of attacks by English pirates. The chief aim of such attacks was, it seems, the kidnap of young and able-bodied boys and girls, something which became a source of some embarrassment to the English crown. Pope Nicholas V even brokered a return of some of these unfortunates to their native land. It is highly likely, if Iceland was subject to major raids by English marauders, that Greenland could have been too, and with no ships to carry the news back to Europe, the Greenlanders had no protection.

This would certainly explain another Inuit story, related to a Christian missionary many centuries later. According to this version of events, Inuit heading south ran into the Norse Greenlanders on the western coast, and lived peacefully alongside them for some time. However, the settlement was attacked by three ships, which the Greenlanders only forced away with great loss of life. Many more ships returned the following year, stealing the Greenlanders' livestock and possessions, and causing a large number of the Greenlanders to sail away permanently – presumably in search of help from Iceland – leaving the remainder in the care of the Inuit. When the raiders returned in even greater numbers, the Inuit fled. When they returned, the last of the Greenland settlements was a smoking ruin – Herjolfness on the southern tip, is still known today to the Inuit as *Ikigait* – 'the place destroyed by fire'. The only survivors were five women and a few of their children left for safe-keeping with the Inuit, and co-opted into the tribe as wives of local men.[9]

But not even these were truly the last of the Vikings in Greenland. As late as 1540, an Icelander sailing in a German vessel found himself blown off course from his native land, and made landfall at the southern tip of Greenland. When he went ashore, he found a dilapidated town devoid of inhabitants. Lying face down on the ground was a dead body – a man clad in sealskin clothes, left where he had fallen because there was nobody to bury him. This Norse hermit, an antique metal knife lying by his side, must have been the last descendant of the Vikings in the New World.[10]

During the late Middle Ages, Iceland was similarly cut off from its roots, with a sharp fall in the number of vessels plying the increasingly dangerous waters, particularly after the eclipse of Trondheim as the port of contact with the north Atlantic. The Icelanders were not completely isolated from the world like their counterparts in Greenland – far from it, since although their home had a reputation as an unpleasant place to live, the cold, dry gales were perfect for drying catches to make stockfish, a staple food of the late Middle Ages.

On several occasions, Iceland was seriously considered as another extraneous arm of the Scandinavian world that could be lopped off in much the same way as Shetland and the Orkneys. Still reeling from the dissolution of the Kalmar union, the Danish king scrabbled for means to bring new money into his treasury. Danish levies were imposed on traffic in the Baltic, and there was a plan to use Iceland as the collateral for a permanent loan of 100,000 florins from England's King Henry VIII.[11] Although nothing came of this offer, Iceland was offered to England a second time in the 1780s, as a straight swap for Crab Island in the Caribbean. For a burgeoning maritime power, the acquisition of a territory in the north Atlantic was a sound strategic move, and presented a possible alternative to distant Australia as a suitable place to banish convicts. However, the plan came to nothing due to a sudden improvement in relations with Denmark. A later proposal, that Iceland be ceded to Britain if Britain backed Denmark's bid to hang on to the Schleswig-Holstein region in the 1860s, also came to nothing. Iceland maintained its reputation as Europe's remotest point, until the nineteenth century, when its rich repository of sagas and stories rekindled interest in medieval Scandinavia and created the image of Vikings that persists to this day.

Once North America was more than merely a memory of legendary Vinland, Scandinavian settlers established the short-lived colony of New Sweden there in 1638, and the fortress of Elfsborg on the Delaware river in the 1640s. Sweden's power in the New World, however, was already on the wane, and by 1655 the Swedish possessions were handed over to the Dutch. This, however, did not eradicate the Scandinavian presence – the oldest church in America is the Old Swedes Church in Wilmington (formerly Fort Kristina), Delaware.[12]

When Scandinavian settlers arrived in the United States in the nineteenth century, advertisements for colonists emphasized the new lands to the west, and that they might be reached by rail – by the 1870s, San Francisco was suggested as the ultimate destination. The Allan Mail Line, which had several routes from Norway, Sweden and Denmark to England, also made regular crossings to New York and Quebec. From those destinations, Scandinavian colonists were likely to enter the United States through the Great Lakes, to Chicago, and thence along the railway further west. But many of them did not make it too far, preferring to settle among the lakes and forests in America's north, Wisconsin, Michigan and Minnesota, lands which often bore an uncanny resemblance to the ones they had left.[13]

Old stories about Vinland soon gained new credence, and the race was on to prove that the Vinland sagas were factual reports. The surge in interest in the Vikings in the English-speaking world saw a statue of Leif Eriksson unveiled in Boston in 1887, and culminated in 1893 with the voyage of the *Viking*, a full-sized vessel inspired by the design of the Gokstad ship, that successfully made the voyage from Bergen to Newfoundland in an impressive 28 days. Arriving in America as the Norwegian entry in an exposition that was supposed to celebrate the 400th anniversary of Columbus's 'discovery' of America, the *Viking* instilled considerably national pride, both at home and among Americans of Scandinavian ancestry. The period also saw a disappointing number of hoaxes and bogus claims. The coin of Olaf the Peaceful, found in Maine, was a verifiable archaeological find. Others were of more doubtful origin.

Olof Ohman joined many of his countrymen as an immigrant settler in Minnesota. He had been farming his land for eight years or so when he uncovered a slab of stone in one of his fields in 1898, etched with what appeared to be runes – an illiterate scrawl from which could be discerned occasional words identifiable with modern Norwegian, Danish, Swedish and English ones. With the same year seeing the publication of the second edition of Samuel Laing's landmark translation of *Heimskringla*, the American public were ready to hear more about Vikings, particularly if it related directly to them.

The discovery of the so-called Kensington Stone was largely ignored, until it was championed some 20 years later by Hjalmar Rued Holand, a writer in Wisconsin, who argued that it was a sign of a much deeper penetration into Vinland than had been previously thought. If the inscription on the stone was true, the Vikings had not turned back at Cape Cod at all, but ventured along the Great Lakes to Minnesota itself. What were the odds? The inscription, if a translator was feeling very flexible, could be interpreted as reading:

. . . 8 Goths [Swedes] and 22 Northmen on an exploring
journey from Vinland westward. We had our camp by two
rocky islets one day's journey north of this stone. We were out
fishing one day. When we came home, we found ten men red
with blood and dead. AVM [*A Virgine Maria?*] save us from
evil. Have ten men by the sea to look after our ships, fourteen
days' journey from this island. 1362.[14]

Scandinavian scholars immediately dismissed the Kensington
Stone as a forgery, but away from the groves of academia,
others found Holand's arguments very persuasive. There were,
of course, plenty of reasons for the Minnesotans to want to
believe in an earlier visit by their ancestors. The 1893 voyage
of the *Viking* had swelled them with ancestral pride, and there
was always some mileage to be gained by claiming America to
have been discovered by Protestant Norsemen instead of
Catholics led by Christopher Columbus. It was not until the
1950s that the hoax was exposed, the mysterious rune-carver
established not as a beleaguered explorer from the fourteenth
century, but a modern Minnesotan hoaxer with a well-
thumbed dictionary of runes.

In 1940, Reider Sherwin published *The Viking and the Red
Man*, a misguided attempt to prove that the Old Norse
language had made a considerable contribution to the vocabulary of Algonquin Indian. If this were true, it would mean
that the Vikings had played a significantly greater part in the
history of North America than was previously believed. Unfortunately for Sherwin, his thesis held little water – his book
was largely a comparative dictionary of Scandinavian and
Native American languages, and demonstrated little grasp of
historical linguistics. Many of his supposed cognates are mere
coincidences or laughably different, while others can be ex-
plained by simple onomatopoeia.

In 1957 an Italian bookseller began hawking yet another artefact around antiquarian booksellers in Europe. It was a battered book, *The Tartar Relation*, purportedly from some-time around 1440, containing a fragment of a report by a Franciscan monk who had visited the court of the Mongols in the 1240s. Friar Carpini's 21-page account of China was interesting enough in itself, and constituted a rare find, but what interested Scandinavian scholars was the map that accompanied it. It showed the known world of Carpini's time, including Japan, Tartary, what was known of Africa, and, with increasingly more accurate detail, Europe. Most crucially of all, far to the west of Europe, past Iceland and Greenland, was the unmistakable outline of Newfoundland and Labrador, marked *Vinilanda Insula* – the isle of Vinland. If the map were genuine, it represented conclusive proof, not only that the Vikings had visited America, but also that the discovery had been appreciated and accepted in Europe itself. Such a find would destroy much of the historical achievement of Colum-bus and his successors.

Some historians were sceptical from the outset. The worm-holes on the map did not match those on the rest of the book, nor did the ink used to draw it. If the map was not associated with the manuscript that accompanied it, then its date could not be established, and that rendered its inclusion of a 'Vinland' almost worthless. It was, however, regarded as an interesting enough find to be worthy of exhibiting at Yale University, its eventual owner. The manuscript was displayed for a decade, until mod-ern forensics advanced to the stage where it could be examined not just for its content, but also for its material. Sadly for its creator, whoever he may have been, the Vinland Map was pronounced a forgery, with a high ink content of titanium dioxide, not found in inks before the early twentieth century.

*   *   *

Despite such muddying of the academic waters, the twentieth century did see a Vinland finding of undeniable importance, in the small Newfoundland village of L'Anse aux Meadows. Helge Ingstad, a Norwegian Arctic biologist, spent 1959 scouring the American coast north of New England, in search of any island redoubts that could conceivably fit the descriptions left in the Vinland sagas. In 1960, he heard of the Anse aux Meadows site – a series of humps and hollows known to the locals as the 'Indian Camp'. It had indeed once been a campsite for Indian hunters, but at some point in the distant past, a different kind of settler had briefly occupied the windswept ground. These mystery visitors had stacked turf sods in order to create temporary shelters, presumably roofed over with tarpaulins from their ships.

At the time of its construction, around AD 1000, the time of Leif Eriksson's voyage, the Anse aux Meadows site had been a beachfront – the intervening millennium has let a hundred metres of boggy ground silt up in between it and the sea. It was not an obvious place to site a settlement, but would have been ideally suited for the beaching of ships and their maintenance. In a separate enclosure were found relics of a small smith's workshop, presumably set aside from the living quarters to avoid a risk of accident – and wisely so, since the building had caught fire at least once during its brief use.

In terms of tangible objects, there is not all that much at the Anse aux Meadows site. There is, however, definite evidence of human habitation, very clear residue from metal smithing, cracked flagstones in what appears to have been a sauna building, and a pin designed to hold a Norse cloak. Whoever had lived there had not been Native American, and their habitation had been brief. Ingstad believed that he had finally located the site of Leif Eriksson's camp, and with it, proof of a Viking visitation.

There was, understandably, some doubt in the academic community that such a fantastic site should be found by a man who was not even a professional (Helge's wife Anne Stine Ingstad was the archaeologist of the team, Helge more the publicist), but extensive surveys have backed up the majority of the Ingstads' claims. A later excavation by Bengt Schönbäck determined that the Ingstads had been overzealous in believing that some natural depressions in the ground were 'boat-sheds', but that their findings were otherwise sound. In fact, the Schönbäck excavation uncovered even more material of Viking origin – mainly wooden fragments of furniture and household items. It was established to the satisfaction of Schönbäck that the Ingstads were essentially correct in their findings. Europeans of Norse origin had lived at L'Anse aux Meadows for a few years, before presumably departing whence they had come.

In June 2000, on the estimated 1,000th anniversary of Leif's supposed arrival, crowds flocked to the tiny L'Anse aux Meadows settlement for a double millennial celebration. The replica Viking vessel *Islendingur* led a small flotilla of Norse vessels back to the place the Vikings had left so long before, accompanied by captain Gunnar Eggertsson, a modern descendant of Leif the Lucky. The celebrations were even attended by representatives of the local Native Americans, happy to remind visitors that while the celebration was of the Vikings, the Vinland settlement had been chased away by the Indians, who had 'discovered' America considerably earlier than anyone else.

The modern replica houses built near the original L'Anse aux Meadows site are slightly misleading. They are not the turf 'booths' of saga and archaeological record, but buildings with stone foundations and turfed roofs and despite their supposed educational function, they give a far more permanent and lasting impression of the Vinland voyages than is perhaps warranted; they have probably already been occupied for longer than the originals. This willingness of the people of the twenty-first century to adapt Viking culture to their own ends is typical. When the Norse men and women first came to America, there were perhaps no more than 150 of them with their plans for a colony. A thousand years later, 15,000 people, a hundred times the headcount of the original settlers, turned out at L'Anse aux Meadows to welcome the *Islendingur* and its accompanying ships. The empire of the Vikings has faded, but their influence lives on – they are fictional creations today, the creatures of movies and comics, and figures of fun or lurid horror. Our impression of them is created largely through literature – the tales, tall and otherwise, spun by their isolated Icelandic descendants, and the retellings of the sagas by Victorian authors.

Modern research into DNA has established a heavy Viking presence in many places outside Scandinavia. Unsurprisingly, the prevalence of Y-chromosomes with a Danish or Norse origin runs in close correlation to the Norse place names to be found on an English map. The further north one goes in Britain, the more likelihood there is of Viking ancestry, and once into the Scottish isles, Norwegian genes are dominant. Such racial relics are less obvious in other places; the Rus, for example were bands of single men who most often took local wives and concubines, thus swiftly diluting the Scandinavian genes in their descendants.

The Vikings do not, *should not*, exist any more. The last vestige of the Viking spirit can be found in criminals and chancers, and hopefully, that is where it will stay. They are a part of our nature that we would like to deny – robbers, thieves and pirates, that we like to believe are expelled by modern times.

If anything can be learned from more recent studies of history, it is the role that climate and ecology can play in population movements. In the Viking Age and the centuries that preceded it, northern Europe's unpredictable climate periodically forced barbarian tribes to go in search of new resources. In our supposedly enlightened age, the search for such resources has been sublimated, corporatized, sanitized perhaps, but it has not receded. You did not, I hope, steal this book from someone else. The clothes on your back were not snatched from Irish monks, and you did not appropriate your money by smashing up priceless holy relics, but there is still a perilously thin line that separates you from the hungry and the cold, and from the need to secure food and warmth. Few of us are more than a few months away from bankruptcy. We hand over new forms of *manngjöld*, hoping to shield ourselves against misfortune by paying tax and insurance. Our faith in our governments and welfare systems keeps us from having to consider what we would do if they were not there.

While the Vikings are inhabitants of the past, the forces that created them are not. Ours is still a world with famines, floods and incidents of overpopulation. Our battles over resources are fought by proxy in distant lands, but they are still fought. You do not lead a band of men to take from those less able to protect themselves, but somewhere far away, others do on your behalf. It takes only the tiniest turn of fate, the slightest lapse of law, to make Vikings of us all.

APPENDIX

RULERS DURING THE VIKING AGE

Kings of Norway

Harald Fairhair	?–930s (SW Norway)
Erik Bloodaxe	?–c.948 (SW Norway)
Hakon the Good	c.940–c.960 (S Norway)
Harald II Greycloak	c.960–c.968 (S Norway)
Olaf 'Crowbone' Tryggvason	995–999
Olaf II the Stout (St Olaf)	1015–28
Svein Alfivason (regent for Denmark)	1030–34
Magnus the Good (see Denmark)	1035–46
Harald III the Ruthless	1045–66
Magnus II	1066–69
Olaf III the Peaceful	1067–93
Hakon Magnusson	1093–95
Magnus III Barelegs	1093–1103

Kings of Denmark

Gorm the Old	c.936–58
Harald Bluetooth	958–87

Svein Forkbeard	987–1014
Harald II	1014–18?
Canute the Great (K. of England)	1019–35
Harthacanute (K. of England)	1035–42
Magnus the Good (K. of Norway)	1042–46
Svein Estridsen	1046–c.1075
Harald III	c.1074–80
Canute the Holy	1080–86
Olaf Hunger	1086–95
Erik the Evergood	1095–1103

Kings of Sweden

Erik the Victorious	980–95
Olaf Skötkonung	995–c.1018
Onund Jacob	c.1018–c.1050
Emund the Old	1050–60
Stenkil Ragnvaldsson	1060–66
Halsten	1066–70

Law-Speakers of Iceland

Hrafn Haengsson	c.930–49
Thorarin Oleifsson	c.950–69
Thorkel Moon Thorsteinsson	970–84
Thorgeir Thorkelsson	985–1001
Grim Svertingsson	1002–3
Skrafti Thoroddsson	1004–30
Stein Thorgestsson	1031–3
Thorkel Tjorvason	1034–53
Gellir Bolverksson	1054–62
Gunnar the Wise Thorgrimsson	1063–5
Kolbein Flosason	1066–71

(post survives until 1271, when Iceland is annexed to Norway)

Princes of the Rus

Rurik	c.862–79 (legendary)
Oleg	c.879–913 (legendary)
Igor (Ingvar)	c.913–45

Svyatoslav I	945–72
Jaropolk	972–c.980
Vladimir the Great (Valdemar)	c.980–1015
Jaroslav the Wise	1019–54
Svyatopolk II	1093–1113

Rulers of Normandy

Hrolf the Walker	911–c.925
William Longsword	c.925–42
Richard the Fearless	942–96
Richard the Good	996–1026
Richard III	1026–7
Robert the Devil/Magnificent	1027–35
William the Bastard	1035–87
(King of England, 'the Conqueror' 1066)	

Kings of Wessex and the English

Aethelred I, King of Wessex	866–71
Alfred the Great (Wessex)	871–99
Edward the Elder (Wessex)	899–924
Athelstan (England)	924–39
Edmund I	939–46
Eadred	946–55
Eadwig	955–59
Edgar	959–75
Edward the Martyr	975–79
Aethelred II Unraed ('Unready')	979–1016
Svein Forkbeard	1013–14 (5 weeks)
Canute the Great	1016–35
Harold I	1037–40
Harthacanute	1040–42
Edward the Confessor	1042–66
Harold II Godwinson	1066
William I 'the Conqueror'	1066–87

Kings of Norway & Denmark

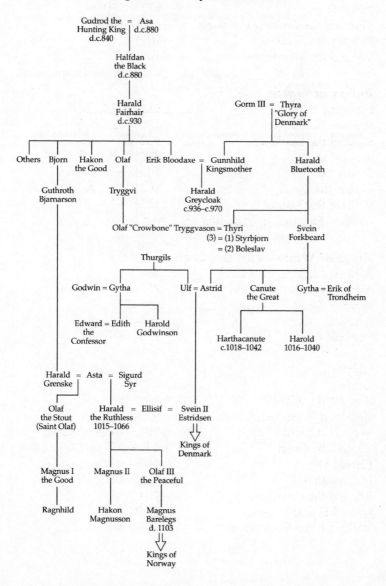

Rulers of Sweden

Erik the Victorious = Sigrid the Haughty = Svein Forkbeard
c.930–c.994 (K)   c.950–c.1013   King of Denmark

Olof   Daughter = Ake   Astrid = (1) Robert the Devil (Normandy)
Skötkonung (K)   = (2) Ulf
c.950–1022

Ingegard = Jaroslav   Onund   Astrid = Olaf the   Edmund   Svein Estridsen
c.1001–1050 the Wise Jacob (K)   Stout   the Old   King of Denmark
                                                         c.1050–1060 (K) c.1020–1074

                                                                          Kings of Denmark

Ellisif = (1) Harald the Ruthless (K. of Norway)   Ingvar the   Harald
          (2) Svein Estridsen (K. of Denmark)   Wide-farer   d.1041
                                                        1016–1041

Rulers of Trondheim

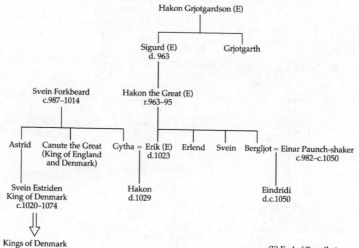

(E) Earl of Trondheim

Rulers of Russia and Byzantium

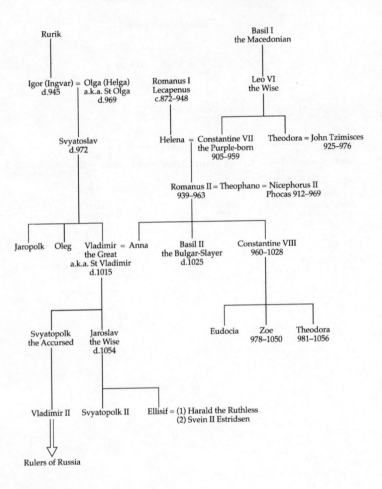

Dukes of Normandy and Earls of Orkney

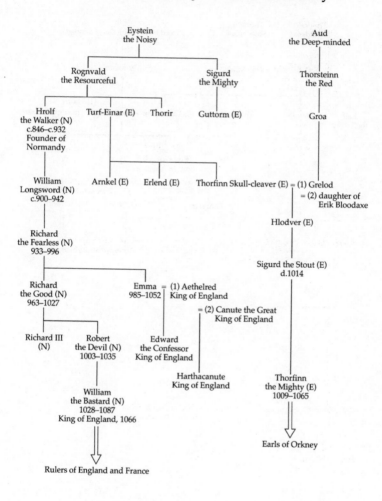

Rulers of Greenland

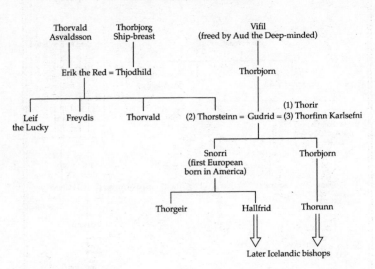

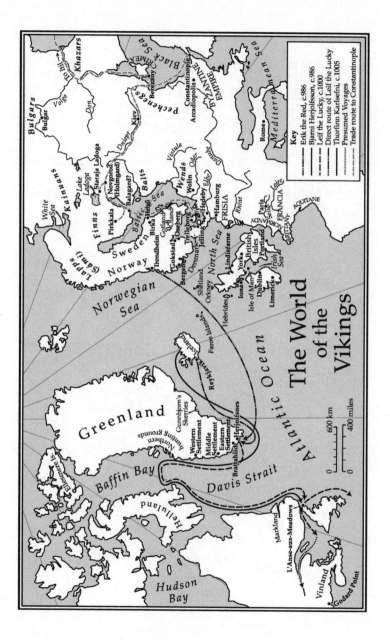

The World of the Vikings

Key
——— Erik the Red, c.986
—·—·— Bjarni Herjolfsson, c.986
– – – Leif the Lucky, c.1000
——— Direct route of Leif the Lucky
——— Thorfinn Karlsefni, c.1005
········ Presumed Voyages
·········· Trade route to Constantinople

England, Ireland and the Danelaw

N

Key
- - - Danelaw
- Extent of Danelaw, 902

Shetland

Orkney

Hebrides

Sutherland

Caithness

Picts

Iona

KINGDOM OF THE SCOTS

North Sea

STRATHCLYDE

Tweed

Lindisfarne

0 — 160 km
0 — 100 miles

Northern Uí Néill

Lough Neagh

Armagh

CONNACHT

MEATH

Lough Ree

Lough Owel

Dál Cais

Shannon

Boyne

Dublin

Ossory

Liffey

LEINSTER

Limerick

MUNSTER

Waterford

Wexford

Cork

Irish Sea

Isle of Man

Tyne

NORTHUMBRIA

Tees

Ouse

KINGDOM OF YORK

York

Humber

Trent

Lincoln

Nottingham

FIVE BOROUGHS

Derby

Stamford

Repton

Leicester

GWYNEDD

ENGLISH MERCIA

Welsh

DANISH MERCIA

Ouse

Thetford

EAST ANGLIA

Cambridge

Ashingdon

Maldon

Thames

Edington

London

Atlantic Ocean

Athelney

WESSEX

Wareham

Hastings

Portland

English Channel

FURTHER READING

Abels, R. *Alfred the Great: War, Kingship and Culture in Anglo-Saxon England*, Harlow: Longman, 1998.

Abu-Chakra, F. *Vikings Through Arab Eyes: 'Ibn Fadlan'* A.D. *922*, Helsinki: Ammatour, 2004.

Adam of Bremen. *History of the Archibishops of Hamburg-Bremen* [trans. Francis Tschan], New York: Columbia University Press, 2002.

Alliott, S. *Alcuin of York*, York: William Sessions, 1974.

Anon. 'Viking Famines Echoed in Japan,' in *New Scientist*, vol 131, issue 1779, 27 July 1991. p.21.

———— *The Saga of the Jómsvíkings* [trans. Lee Hollander], Austin: University of Texas Press, 1955.

Austin, D. and Leslie Alcock, eds, *From the Baltic to the Black Sea: Studies in Medieval Archaeology*, London: Routledge, 1997.

Barlow, F. *The Godwins: The Rise and Fall of a Noble Dynasty*, Harlow: Pearson, 2002.

Bell-Fialkoff, A., ed., *The Role of Migration in the History of the*

Eurasian Steppe: Sedentary Civilization vs 'Barbarian' and Nomad, New York: St. Martin's Press, 2000.

Blackburn, B. and Leofranc Holford-Strevens, *The Oxford Companion to the Year*, Oxford: Oxford University Press, 1999.

Blöndal, S. 'The Last Exploits of Harald Sigurdsson in Greek Service,' in *Classica et Medievalia*, I, 2, 1939, pp.1–26.

Brønsted, J. *The Vikings* [trans. Kalle Skov], Harmondsworth: Penguin, 1965.

Christiansen, E. *The Northern Crusades*, Harmondsworth: Penguin, 1997.

Davidson, H. *Gods and Myths of Northern Europe*, Harmondsworth: Penguin, 1964.

———— *The Viking Road to Byzantium*, London: Allen & Unwin, 1976.

DeVries, K. *The Norwegian Invasion of England in 1066*, Woodbridge: The Boydell Press, 1999.

DuBois, T. *Nordic Religions in the Viking Age*, Philadelphia: Pennsylvania University Press, 1999.

Duczko, W. *Viking Rus: Studies on the Presence of Scandinavians in Eastern Europe*, Leiden: E.J. Brill, 2004.

Encyclopaedia Britannica, DVD-ROM edition, 2002.

Faulkes, A., ed., *Stories from the Sagas of the Kings*, London: Viking Society for Northern Research/UCL, 1980.

Fleming, F. *Barrow's Boys: A Stirring Story of Daring, Fortitude and Outright Lunacy*, London: Granta, 2001.

Fletcher, R. *Bloodfeud: Murder and Revenge in Anglo-Saxon England*, Harmondsworth: Penguin, 2002.

Gilbert, T. 'Death and Destruction,' in *New Scientist*, vol. 178, issue 2397, 31 May 2003, p.32.

Godden, M. and Michael Lapidge, eds., *The Cambridge Companion to Old English Literature*, Cambridge: Cambridge University Press, 1991.

Gribbin, J. and Mary Gribbin, 'Climate and History: The Westvikings' Saga' in *New Scientist*, vol. 125, issue 1700, 20 January 1990.

Griffith, P. *The Viking Art of War*, London: Greenhill Books, 1995.

Halldórsson, Ó. *Danish Kings and the Jomsvikings in the Greatest Saga of Óláfr Tryggvason*, London: Viking Society for Northern Research.

Haywood, J. *Dark Age Naval Power: A Reassessment of Frankish and Anglo-Saxon Seafaring Activity*, London: Routledge, 1991.

——— *Historical Atlas of the Vikings*, Harmondsworth: Penguin, 1995.

Herbert, K. *Peace-Weavers and Shield-Maidens: Women in Early English Society*, Frithgarth: Anglo-Saxon Books, 1997.

Hoppäl, M. and Juha Pentikäinen, eds., *Uralic Mythology and Folklore*, Helsinki: Finnish Literature Society, 1989.

Hreinsson, V., ed., *The Complete Sagas of Icelanders*, Reykjavík: Leifur Eiríksson Publishing, 1997 [5 volumes].

Huurre, M. *9000 Vuotta Suomen Esihistoria*, Helsinki: Otava, 2004.

Ibn Battúta, *Travels in Asia and Africa*, London: Routledge and Kegan Paul, 1929 [1984 repr.].

Ioannisyan, O. 'Archaeological evidence for the development and urbanization of Kiev from the 8th to the 14th centuries', in Austin, D. and Leslie Alcock, eds., *From the Baltic to the Black Sea: Studies in Medieval Archaeology*, London: Routledge, 1997, pp.285–312.

Jolly, K. *Popular Religion in Late Saxon England: Elf Charms in Context*, Chapel Hill: University of North Carolina Press, 1996.

Jones, G. *A History of the Vikings*, Oxford: Oxford University Press, 1984 [2nd ed.].

Jones, P. and Nigel Pennick, *A History of Pagan Europe*, London: Routledge, 1995.

Jutikkala, E and Kauko Pirinen, *A History of Finland*, Helsinki: Werner Söderström, 2003.

Kennedy, H. *The Court of the Caliphs: The Rise and Fall of Islam's Greatest Dynasty*, London: Weidenfeld & Nicolson, 2004.

Keppie, L. *The Making of the Roman Army: From Republic to Empire*, London: Batsford.

King, C. *The Black Sea: A History*, Oxford: Oxford University Press, 2004.

Kuparinen, E. *An African Alternative: Nordic Migration to South Africa 1815–1915*, Helsinki & Turku: Finnish Historical Society & Institute of Migration, 1991.

Larsson, M. *Vikingar I Österled, en samlingsutgåva av Ett Ödesdigert Vikingatåg: Ingvar den vittfarnes resa 1036–1041; Väringar: Nordbor hos kejsaren I Miklagård; Rusernas Rike: Nordborna och Russlands födelse*, Stockholm: Atlantis, 1997.

Magnusson, M. *Vikings!* London: Bodley Head/BBC, 1980.

———— and Hermann Pálsson, trans. *The Vinland Sagas: The Norse Discovery of America*, Harmondsworth: Penguin, 1965.

Malmer, B. 'What does coinage tell us about Scandinavian society in the late Viking Age?', in Austin, D. and Leslie Alcock, eds., *From the Baltic to the Black Sea: Studies in Medieval Archaeology*, London: Routledge, 1997, pp.157–67.

Marcus, G. *The Conquest of the North Atlantic*, Woodbridge: The Boydell Press, 1980.

Marsden, J. *The Fury of the Northmen: Saints, Shrines and Sea-Raiders in the Viking Age*, London: Kyle Cathie, p.1993.

McEvedy, C. and Richard Jones, *Atlas of World Population History*, Harmondsworth: Penguin, 1978.

Melvinger, A. *Les premières incursions des Vikings en Occident d'après les sources arabes*, Uppsala: University of Uppsala, 1955.

Meyer, W. 'Climate and Migration,' in Bell-Fialkoff, ed., *The Role of Migration in the History of the Eurasian Steppe: Sedentary Civilization vs 'Barbarian' and Nomad*, pp.287–94.

Mills, A. *Dictionary of London Place Names*, Oxford: Oxford University Press, 2001.

Mithen, S. *After the Ice: A Global Human History 20,000–5000 BC*, London: Phoenix, 2003.

Mundal, E. 'The perception of the Saamis and their religion in old Norse sources', in Pentikäinen, J., ed., *Shamanism and Northern Ecology*. Berlin: Mouton de Gruyer, pp.97–134.

Myres, J. *The English Settlements*, Oxford: Oxford University Press, 1989.

Nesheim, A. 'Eastern and Western Elements in Culture', in Hoff, et al. *Lapps and Norsemen in Olden Times*, Oslo: Institute for Comparative Research in Human History, 1967. pp.104–163.

Newton, S. *The Origins of Beowulf and the Pre-Viking Kingdom of East Anglia*, Cambridge: D.S. Brewer, 1993.

Niiteme, W., Jussi Saukkonen et al., eds., *Old Friends – Strong Ties: Finland and the United States of America*, Turku and Vaasa: Institute of Migration, 1976.

Norwich, J. *Byzantium: The Apogee*, Harmondsworth: Penguin, 1993.

O'Donoghue, H. *Old Norse-Icelandic Literature: An Introduction*, Oxford: Blackwell, 2004.

Ogier, J. 'Eddic Constellations', paper presented at the International Medieval Congress, Western Michigan University, Kalamazoo, 3 May 2002.

Ogilvie, A. 'Letters: Viking's Tale,' in *New Scientist*, vol. 125, issue 1707, 10 March 1990. [Critique of Gribbin and Gribbin, qv.]

Orchard, A. *Dictionary of Norse Myth and Legend*, London: Cassell, 1997.

Ostrogorsky, G. *History of the Byzantine State* [trans. Joan Hussey], Oxford: Basil Blackwell, 1980.

Page, R. *Chronicles of the Vikings: Records, Memorials and Myths*, London: The British Museum Press, 1995.

Popovic, A. *The Revolt of African Slaves in Iraq in the 3rd/9th Centuries*, Princeton: Markus Wiener Publishers, 1999.

Price, N. *The Viking Way: Religion and War in Late Iron Age Scandinavia*, Uppsala: Uppsala University, 2002.

Richards, J. *Blood of the Vikings*, London: Hodder & Stoughton, 2001.

Rink, H. *Tales and Traditions of the Eskimo*, Edinburgh: Blackwood and Sons, 1875 [1997 repr. Dover].

Rugg, D. 'German Migrations East,' in Bell-Fialkoff, ed., *The Role of Migration in the History of the Eurasian Steppe: Sedentary Civilization vs 'Barbarian' and Nomad*, pp.117–32.

Saunders, J. *A History of Medieval Islam*, London: Routledge, 1965.

Sawyer, P. *Kings and Vikings: Scandinavia and Europe 700–1100*, London: Routledge, 1982.

Saxo Grammaticus. *The History of the Danes: Books I–IX* [ed./ trans. Hilda Davidson and Peter Fisher], Woodbridge: D.S. Brewer, 1996.

Sherwin, R. *The Viking and the Red Man: The Old Norse Origin of the Algonquin Language*, New York: Funk and Wagnalls, 1940.

Shippey, T. *The Road to Middle Earth*, London: Harper Collins, 1982.

Simeon of Durham. *A History of the Kings of England*, trans. J. Stevenson, 1858, Dyfed: Llanerch Enterprises, 1987.

Simonsen, P. 'Relations Between the Lapps and Scandinavians in Early Times – An Archaeological Survey,' in Hoff, et al. *Lapps and Norsemen in Olden Times*, Oslo: Institute for Comparative Research in Human History, 1967, pp.65–77.

Smyth, A. *Scandinavian Kings in the British Isles 850–880*, Oxford: Oxford University Press, 1977.

Sommarström, S. 'Ethnoastronomical Perspectives on Saami Religion', in Ahlbäch, T., ed., *Saami Religion*, Turku: Donner Institute for Research in Religious and Cultural History, 1987, pp.211–250.

Stafford, P. *Queen Emma & Queen Edith: Queenship and Women's Power in Eleventh-Century England*, Oxford: Blackwell, 1997.

Sturluson, S. *Heimskringla: History of the Kings of Norway* [trans. Lee Hollander], Austin: University of Texas Press, 1964.

———— *King Harald's Saga: Harald Hardradi of Norway* [trans. Magnus Magnusson and Hermann Pálsson], Harmondsworth: Penguin, 1966.

———— *The Poetic Edda* [trans. Lee Hollander], Austin: University of Texas Press, 1962.

Swanton, M., ed. *The Anglo-Saxon Chronicles*, London: Phoenix Press, 2000.

Theodoricus Monachus, *The Ancient History of the Norwegian Kings* [trans. David and Ian McDougall], London: Viking Society for Northern Research/UCL, 1998.

Treadgold, W. *Byzantium and Its Army 284–1081*, Stanford, CT: Stanford University Press, 1995.

Turville-Petrie, G. *Haraldr the Hard-ruler and his Poets*, Dorothea Coke Memorial Lecture in Northern Studies, 1 December 1996, London: University College, 1968.

Volkoff V. *Vladimir the Russian Viking*, London: Honeyglen Publishing, 1984.

Wahlgren, E. *The Kensington Stone: A Mystery Solved*, Madison: University of Wisconsin Press, 1958.

Wawn, A. *The Vikings and the Victorians: Inventing the Old North in 19th Century Britain*, Cambridge: D.S. Brewer, 2000.

Weir, A. *Britain's Royal Families: The Complete Genealogy*, London: Pimlico, 1996.

Wikander, S. *Araber Vikingar Väringar*, Lund: Svenska Humanistiska Förbundet, 1978.

Williams, A. *Aethelred the Unready: The Ill-Counselled King*, London: Hambledon and London, 2003.

REFERENCES

Introduction – Britannia Deserta
1 Myres, *The English Settlements*, pp.119–20.
2 Keppie, *The Making of the Roman Army: From Republic to Empire*, p.211.
3 Haywood, *Dark Age Naval Power*, pp.5–6.
4 Ibid., pp.9–10.
5 Ibid., p.35.
6 Gribbin and Gribbin, 'Climate and History: The Westvikings' Saga.' This geologically brief time in the sun came to an end in the sixteenth century, with the onset of a mini-ice age and a *drop* in temperature of two degrees, one of the results of which was the abandonment of the Greenland colony. See Chapter 10.
7 Myres, *The English Settlements*, p.16.
8 *Encyclopaedia Britannica*, 'Arthur' notes that Arthur first appears in the writings of Nennius, who appears to have confused and conflated earlier accounts that explicitly refer to Ambrosius.
9 Julian, *Works of*, Loeb Classical Library, 1, XXXIV, pp.89–91.
10 Brønsted, *The Vikings*, pp.36–7.
11 Wawn, *The Vikings and the Victorians*, p.3.
12 McEvedy and Jones, *Atlas of World Population History*, p.52, adds that of that number: '. . . perhaps half lived long enough to tell their

children how they sailed with Ragnar Lothbrok, Rollo, or Sveyn Forkbeard.'

13 Jones, *History of the Vikings*, p.261 and 267.

14 Griffith, *The Viking Art of War*, p.48.

15 Kennedy, *The Court of the Caliphs*, p.173.

16 Ibn Battúta, *Travels*, p.292 and 371n.

17 These incidents are respectively from *Gisli Sursson's Saga*, CSI II, p.31; *Grettir's Saga*, CSI II, p.66 and *Valla-Ljot's Saga*, CSI IV, p.133.

18 Haywood, *Historical Atlas of the Vikings*, p.45, notes that women played a much larger role in the settlement of Iceland and Greenland, as these were relatively peaceful ventures.

19 McEvedy and Jones, *Atlas of World Population History*, p.52.

Chapter I – Songs of the Valkyries

1 In summer 2003, I swam in the evening Baltic with a Dane and a Swede, listening as they argued over which of the lights above us was Thor's Hammer – one was convinced it was the *bright* one, Venus, the other the *red* one, Mars; a nearby Finn then unhelpfully suggested it might be the *other* one, Sirius. See Ogier, 'Eddic Constellations' for an excellent appraisal of the work undertaken so far in the field. The most promising answer currently lies in the possibility of finding cognate constellations among the Sámi. See Sommarström, 'Ethnoastronomical Perspectives on Saami Religion.'

2 *Heimskringla*, p.6.

3 Jones, *History of the Vikings*, p.323; Sawyer, *Kings and Vikings*, p.131.

4 *Encyclopaedia Britannica*, 'Sampo'.

5 Davidson, *Gods and Myths of Northern Europe*, p.97.

6 Jones, *History of the Vikings*, pp.36–8. There is much more on these lines, and I have ignored several controversies within modern Viking studies, most notably the precise identity of the Geats, and whether or not they may have instead been the Jutes, a people of Jutland, north Denmark.

7 Saxo Grammaticus, *History of the Danes*, II, p.2.

8 Price, *The Viking Way*, pp.106–7.

9 Or so claims Orchard, *Dictionary of Norse Myth and Legend*, p.188.

10 Griffith, *Viking Art of War*, p.135. *Saga of Grettir the Strong*, CSI II, p.76. Duelling was eventually banned to prevent thugs from stealing whatever they wanted and using trial-by-combat as their get-out clause.

11 Price, *The Viking Way*, pp.338–9.

12 *Heimskringla*, p.12. It has been pointed out to me that the wealth found in the tombs of young Vikings may have been regarded as a type of compensation for dying *too* young, rather than a celebration

of dying at the right time. Although this may be the case, it is not the spin put on it by the skalds. Edward James, personal communication.

13 This possibility is all the more obvious in those places where Christmas is still called Yule in local languages – e.g. Sweden (*Jul*) and Finland (*Joulu*).

14 A cursed sword, however, would only bring tragedy, as in the case of Legbiter, in the *Saga of the People of Laxardal*, CSI V, p.41; or Greysides, in *Gisli Sursson's Saga*, CSI II, p.2.

15 Davidson, *Gods and Myths of Northern Europe*, p.49.

16 Nesheim, 'Eastern and Western Elements in Culture,' p.108.

17 Davidson, *Gods and Myths of Northern Europe*, p.56. As with the Viking Age itself, we must also bear in mind that Strabo was referring explicitly to a *comitatus* or war-band – a sector of barbarian 'society' more likely to have a war-god as its patron.

18 Ibid., pp.174–6.

19 Ibid., p.169.

20 The Jotunheim range was officially named as late as the twentieth century, after being called Jotunfjell (Giants' Fells) since 1822. It is, however, mentioned in the sagas under that appellation. The prevalence of goat-herding in the region helps explain many of the Thor-stories about goat husbandry and his quarrels with 'giants'.

21 Davidson, *Gods and Myths of Northern Europe*, p.76.

22 Ibid., p.83.

23 Price, *The Viking Way*, p.57.

24 For example, even though such parallels have been discussed in some scholarly circles since 1877, it was not until 1999 that DuBois published *Nordic Religions in the Viking Age*, a landmark work on the previously under-researched areas of connection between the Vikings and the Finnish/Sámi peoples to their immediate east.

25 Mundal, 'The Perception of the Saamis,' p.112.

26 *Heimskringla*, p.173.

27 Compare this to the gods of Finland, who are often physically weaker than the heroes.

28 Davidson, *Gods and Myths of Northern Europe*, p.189.

29 Ibid., p.184.

30 See also Davidson, *Gods and Myths of Northern Europe*, p.166, for the tale of another guardian with a similar name, Mimir, this time shielding wisdom itself from unwelcome thieves.

31 Saxo Grammaticus, *History of the Danes*, p.75.

Chapter 2 – Fury of the Northmen

1 Swanton, the *Anglo-Saxon Chronicles*, p.57n regards the original manuscript's 'Jan' as a transcription error for 'Jun'. Haywood's *Encyclopaedia of the Viking Age* prefers 7 June as the date of the sack of Lindisfarne, p.122.

2 This omen was reported sometime later by Alcuin, a native of Yorkshire who feared that the Viking raids were the punishments of an angry God. Brønsted, *The Vikings*, p.32.

3 Simeon of Durham, *A History of the Kings of England*, p.43. Danger of further raids eventually caused Lindisfarne to be abandoned, and the last monks moved to Durham in 875.

4 Melvinger, *Les Premières Incursions des Vikings en Occident d'après les sources arabes*, p.90. Bregowine: 'de crebris infestationibus improborum hominum in provinciis Anglorum seu Galliae regionis,' and Dicuil 'causa latronum Nortmannorum.' *Galliae* could be a reference to Wales, rather than France.

5 Ibid., p.91.

6 Swanton, The *Anglo-Saxon Chronicles*, pp.54–55n.

7 O'Donoghue, *Old Norse-Icelandic Literature*, p.8. The apparent disparity between the written forms is because most extant works in Anglo-Saxon are in the Late West-Saxon dialect, and not in the northern variants that were closer to Norse.

8 Alliott, *Alcuin of York*, p.19.

9 Brønsted, *The Vikings*, p.141.

10 Magnusson, *Vikings!*, p.38.

11 *Complete Sagas of Icelanders*, vol. V, p.398.

12 *Erik the Red's Saga*, CSI I, p.2; for the etymology, see Magnusson, *Vikings!*, p.189. Technically, *knorr* applies to any ship in Old Norse, but the term has come to be used by modern marine archaeologists to refer specifically to the merchant class of vessel. Other translations for this most charming of terms include CSI's 'Shipbreast', and 'prow-tits', from an adviser who would doubtless prefer to remain anonymous.

13 Haywood, *Encyclopaedia of the Viking Age*, p.132.

14 *Tale of Hromund the Lame*, CSI V, p.351.

15 *Saga of Grettir the Strong*, CSI II, p.76.

16 *Saga of the People of Laxardal*, CSI V, p.47.

17 *Olkofri's Saga*, CSI V, p.237. See also Price, *The Viking Way*, p.395.

18 Brønsted, *The Vikings*, pp.143–6.

19 *Heimskringla*, p.49; Magnusson, *Vikings!*, p.52.

20 Jones, *History of the Vikings*, p.99.

21 *Encyclopaedia Britannica*, 'Denmark'.

22 Jones, *History of the Vikings*, p.109.

23 Haywood, *Encyclopaedia of the Viking Age*, p.193. Note that books on the Vikings published before the 1990s tend to assume that the Trelleborg forts were constructed by Svein Forkbeard to train his British invasion force, but that recent dendrochronological analysis of the timbers has now proved otherwise.

Chapter 3 – Great Heathen Hosts

1 *Saga of the People of Laxardal*, CSI II, p.2.
2 Richards, *Blood of the Vikings*, p.72.
3 Ibid., p.88.
4 Magnusson, *Vikings!*, p.159.
5 Ibid., p.160.
6 Haywood, *Encyclopaedia of the Viking Age*, p.194. It would be entertaining to believe that this devilish woman would find God and become Aud the Deep-Minded in old age – the dates do almost match but it seems unlikely.
7 Haywood, *Encyclopaedia of the Viking Age*, p.194. The story is suspiciously similar to that of the retaking of the Theban acropolis by the Sacred Band under Pelopidas in 379 BC.
8 Jones, *History of the Vikings*, p.207. I have heavily simplified events here, as whole books have been written about the confused Olafs and Ivars of rival accounts.
9 Supposedly they were the sons of Ragnar Lothbrok, who may have been the same Ragnar who attacked Paris in 845. But the stories of Ragnar Lothbrok are so confusing that entire books have written about them. See Smyth, *Scandinavian Kings in the British Isles 850–880*.
10 Magnusson, *Vikings!*, p.130; Griffith, *The Viking Art of War*, pp35–36.
11 Abels, *Alfred the Great*, p.113.
12 Ibid., p.149.
13 Magnusson, *Vikings!*, p.143.
14 Abels, *Alfred the Great*, p.176.

Chapter 4 – Brother Shall Fight Brother

1 Jones, *History of the Vikings*, p.89n.
2 *Heimskringla*, p.61.
3 Ibid. However, some of the Icelanders' claims may have been rooted more in their dismay at their loss of independence to Norway in the thirteenth century when the sagas were composed, rather than actual origins in dissent against Harald.
4 Jones, *History of the Vikings*, p.91.
5 Magnusson, *Vikings!*, p.59.
6 For example, *Egil's Saga*, CSI I, p.38.
7 Ibid.
8 Jones, *History of the Vikings*, p.231.
9 *Heimskringla*, p.80.
10 *Orkneyinga Saga*, translated by Palsson and Edwards, p.28. The same story is told in *Heimskringla*, p.83.
11 *Orkneyinga Saga*, p.31.
12 Notably, Harald Bluetooth's wife was also called Gunnhild; see Adam of Bremen, p.56.

13 *Heimskringla*, pp.88–90.

14 Ibid., p.93.

15 For a detailed account of the historical sources for the reign of Hakon, see Jones, *History of the Vikings*, pp.191, 121–122n. Perhaps the most important is the *Bersöglivísur* or *Plain Speaking Verses* of the eleventh century Sighvat Thordarson, which echo (and may have in fact informed) *Heimskringla*'s claims of Hakon's good reputation.

16 Jones, *History of the Vikings*, p.119.

17 *Heimskringla*, p.110.

18 His funeral lay, *Hákonarmál*, survives, and praises its subject as a defender of the old ways; see Haywood, *Encyclopaedia of the Viking Age*, p.89.

Chapter 5 – The Road East

1 *Heimskringla*, p.250. Viking swords have been found as far east as Kiviniemi, in Karelia. See Huurre, *9000 Vuotta Suomen Esihistoria*, p.134, for likely distribution of communities during the Viking Age as shown by the locations of burials and cremations.

2 Jones, *History of the Vikings*, p.247n.

3 Jutikkala and Pirinen, *History of Finland*, p.35.

4 Jones, *History of the Vikings*, p.25. It was even discussed as such in the court of King Alfred the Great. People were helped in making this assumption by the earlier writings of Tacitus, who had claimed that the region was ruled by women.

5 Duczko, *Viking Rus*, p.66. To the Vikings, Ladoga was probably Lake Nevo, cognate with the river that led from it, the Neva, which would later be the site of a famous battle, and in turn lend its name to the prince Alexander Nevsky.

6 Ibid., p.69.

7 *Russian Primary Chronicle*, quoted in Brønsted, *The Vikings*, pp.67–68.

8 Duczko, *Viking Rus*, p.78 and 81. Volkoff, *Vladimir the Russian Viking*, p.40, goes further, equating the legendary Rurik with a historical Rorik who raided France and England, and eventually signed a treaty with Charlemagne's grandson, Lothaire I. Duczko, *Viking Rus*, p.235, also dismisses a nineteenth-century suggestion that Rurik was a composite character based on a group of Swedes who used the wings and beak of a falcon (Slav: *rarog* as their insignia.

9 For the cataracts and the rune stone, see Jones, *History of the Vikings*, pp.257–8; Davidson, *Viking Road to Byzantium*, p.85.

10 Jones, *History of the Vikings*, pp.249–50. These additional etymologies for Rus are from Davidson, *Viking Road to Byzantium*, p.59, and from Haywood, *Encyclopaedia of the Viking Age*, p.162. Duczko, *Viking Rus*, p.210, adds still another possible origin, noting that Rhosia may have been the 'Area of the *Rod*', an old term for

kinfolk. If this is true, then the Rus may simply have referred to their people as The Kin.

11 Norwich, *Byzantium: The Apogee*, p.66; Ostrogorsky, *History of the Byzantine State*, p.228; Duczko, *Viking Rus*, pp.83–5.

12 Magnusson, *Vikings!*, p.116 and Haywood, *Penguin Historical Atlas of the Vikings*, p.107, both believe that Oleg himself only 'negotiated' with Constantinople after threatening the city with his own army around 907, but Norwich, *Byzantium: The Apogee*, p.150 regards this story as 'almost certainly apocryphal'. However, in parts of Scandinavia, 11 June is the traditional day for the renegotiation of contracts – perhaps in some ironic way the fleet was indeed intended as a bargaining tool.

13 From the Arabic *sharq*, 'orient/sunrise' or possibly corrupted from 'silk'.

14 These are, of course, the Muslim profession of faith, along with passages CXII and IX:33 from the Quran. For the *dirham* inscriptions in full, see *Encyclopaedia Britannica*, 'Islamic Coins of the West and of Western and Central Asia.'

15 Davidson, *Viking Road to Byzantium*, p.52. Muslim *dirhams* form 35 per cent of the silver in Gotland graves. Of the remainder, 45 per cent are German and around 17 per cent are English, dating from the period after the tenth century. See Malmer, 'What does coinage tell us . . .?', p.157.

16 Griffith, *Viking Art of War*, p.48.

17 By accident or design, *bereza* is modern Russian for birch. Jones, *History of the Vikings*, p.258.

18 Abu-Chacra, *Vikings Through Arab Eyes*, p.8.

19 Jones, *History of the Vikings*, p.255.

20 Abu-Chacra, *Vikings Through Arab Eyes*, pp.35–36. There has been a long debate among scholars as to whether the Rus met by Ibn Fadlan were Vikings or Slavs. They appear to be both, with an allegiance to a king in Kiev (Igor) but offering religious observances at wooden poles, which is more in keeping with Slav traditions.

21 Ibid., p.38; also Duczko, *Viking Rus*, pp.137ff.

22 Jones, *History of the Vikings*, p.261. Duczko, *Viking Rus*, p.121, notes that *German* silver mines became productive in the 950s, and tempted European traders with cheaper silver closer to home that was easier to obtain.

23 Davidson, *Viking Road to Byzantium*, pp.280–1, even presents the intriguing argument that the tale of Beowulf's final battle with the fire-breathing dragon may be a confused reference to a battle between Scandinavians and dragon-headed ships that spit Greek fire.

24 The recipe for Greek fire remains unknown to this day, though it presumed to be a petroleum-based mixture.

25 Volkoff, *Vladimir the Russian Viking*, p.13.

26 Ibid., pp.17–19.

27 Ibid., pp.25–26.

28 Svyatoslav to Emperor John Tzimisces, 970, quoted in Norwich, *Byzantium: The Apogee*, p.211. Constantinople was an ultimate Russian objective thereafter, even as late as 1915, when it was promised to the last Czar in the secret Allied Istanbul Agreements.

29 See Volkoff, *Vladimir the Russian Viking*, pp.69–72.

30 Jones, *History of the Vikings*, p.247n. The idea of a double wave of Viking expansion in Russia would certainly help explain the differing nomenclatures. If it is correct, then the meanings of Rus and Varangian are not the same at all, but refer to different eras of arrival for Swedish settlers.

31 Some years earlier, Rogned had supposedly turned down the offer of Vladimir's hand in marriage, calling him a slave's son. She had insulted Vladimir even more by claiming that she would happily consider his brother Jaropolk. Volkoff, *Vladimir the Russian Viking*, pp.88–94.

32 Norwich, *Byzantium: The Apogee*, p.245.

33 Ibid., p.245.

Chapter 6 – Advent of the White Christ

1 So called because he had a grey cloak, and caused a brief fad for such clothing among his men. *Heimskringla*, p.137.

2 See Jones, *History of the Vikings*, p.124.

3 *Heimskringla*, p.142.

4 By this time, only two sons were surviving, Ragnfroth, who failed in an attempt to attack Trondheim, and another, Guthroth, who was only defeated much later, during the reign of Olaf Tryggvason.

5 Haywood, *Encyclopaedia of the Viking Age*, p.51. Payments began in 978, but were not regarded as tribute until 991, and not referred to as *danegeld* until retrospectively, after the Norman conquest. Although payment of *danegeld* officially ceased in 1016, kings would continue to levy *heregeld* until 1162.

6 Adam of Bremen, pp.75–6.

7 *Heimskringla*, p.147, uses the term 'viking' here, even though the captors are later revealed to be Estonian, not Scandinavian.

8 Ibid., p.171.

9 Swanton, The *Anglo-Saxon Chronicles*, p.125.

10 Ibid., p.126.

11 *Tale of Thorvald the Far-Travelled*, CSI V, p.358. For Forkbeard's mother, see Weir, *Britain's Royal Families*, p.25.

12 *Saga of Gunnlaug Serpent-Tongue*, CSI I, p.315.

13 Stafford, *Queen Emma & Queen Edith*, p.214. Upon her arrival in England, Emma took the local name Aelfgifu, but I have not used it here, since it only serves to confuse her with a later Aelfgifu, concubine of King Canute.

14 *Heimskringla*, p.185.

15 Ibid., p.204

16 *The Tale of Svadi and Arnor Crone's-Nose*, CSI V, p.355, recounts an incident where a Viking assembly votes to allow the old and infirm to starve to death in a time of famine, only to be told by dissenters that such behaviour is abominable. Christianity was already taking root.

17 Byock, *Viking Age Iceland*, p.299.

18 *Njal's Saga*, CSI III, p.123.

19 Ibid., CSI III, p.125.

20 Byock, *Viking Age Iceland*, p.300.

Chapter 7 – Beyond the Edge of the World

1 Some Roman coins have been discovered in Iceland, but it is thought that they were brought there by much later travellers, not Romans; Marcus, *Conquest of the North Atlantic*, p.24–7. It does not help that the chronicler Dicuil persisted in retroactively referring to Iceland as 'Thile' [*sic*], thereby leading later geographers to believe that Pytheas had visited it. Some authorities, e.g. Magnusson, *Vikings!*, p.182, suggest that some Romans may indeed have reached Iceland, if only to be wrecked on its shores.

2 Compare, for example, to the much later assumption that Australia belonged to Britain because a Briton had been the first to sail around it: Fleming, *Barrow's Boys*, p.277.

3 Compare to the similar double-crossing that accompanied the Freydis mission to Vinland, in *Greenlander Saga* 8, Magnsson and Palsson, *The Vinland Sagas*, pp.67–9.

4 O'Donoghue, *Old Norse-Icelandic Literature*, pp.55–7.

5 If Olaf the White can be matched with Amlaíb, King of Dublin, then Aud might even have been the daughter of Cerball mac Dúnlainge, and hence Irish herself. See Haywood, *Encyclopaedia of the Viking Age*, p.138.

6 Davidson, *The Viking Road to Byzantium*, p.102.

7 Ibid., p.298.

8 Ibid., p.300.

9 Marcus, *The Conquest of the North Atlantic*, p.55.

10 *Eirik's Saga*, 2, in Magnusson and Palsson, *The Vinland Sagas*, p.76.

11 *Eirik the Red's Saga*, CSI I, p.2.

12 *Íslendingabók* 6, in Magnusson, *Vikings!*, p.215.

13 Marcus, *Conquest of the North Atlantic*, p.57.

14 *Greenlander Saga*, 2, in Magnusson and Palsson, *The Vinland Sagas*, p.52.

15 Ibid., p.53.

16 Many authorities assume it was Labrador, but I have followed Haywood's *Historical Atlas of the Vikings*, p.99, chiefly for its consideration of climatic change. The land described in *Greenlander Saga* may

resemble modern Labrador, but Canadian forests extended considerably further to the north in the year 1000 than they do today.

17 *Greenlander Saga*, 4, in Magnusson and Palsson, *Vinland Sagas*, p.57.

18 *Greenlander Saga*, 4 and 6, in Magnusson and Palsson, *Vinland Sagas*, p.59 and 62.

19 Nesheim, however, in 'Eastern and Western Elements in Culture' p.156, suggests that *skrit* simply means 'on skis', and that it is (a) not pejorative at all, and (b) bears no cognate relationship with the Skraelings.

20 *Greenlander Saga*, 6, in Magnusson and Palsson, *Vinland Sagas*, pp.62–3, particularly the strange phrases that accompany Gudrid being 'comforted' by yet another man (confusingly also called Thorsteinn) before meeting Thorfinn.

21 *Greenlander Saga*, 7, in Magnusson and Palsson, *Vinland Sagas*, pp.65–6.

22 *Erik's Saga*, 9, in Magnusson and Palsson, *Vinland Sagas*, pp.96–7.

23 *Greenlander Saga*, 7, in Magnusson and Palsson, *Vinland Sagas*, p.66.

24 Freydis supposedly charged a group of attacking Skraelings while pregnant at this point. A variant manuscript of *Erik's Saga* mixes occurrences of the name Freydis and Gudrid. See *Erik's Saga*, 11, in Magnusson and Palsson, *Vinland Sagas*, pp.100–1.

Chapter 8 – London Bridge is Falling Down

1 Adam of Bremen, p.80; see also Jones, *History of the Vikings*, p.137.

2 Swanton, The *Anglo-Saxon Chronicles*, p.131.

3 Ibid., p.133.

4 Swanton, The *Anglo-Saxon Chronicles*, p.135n.

5 Williams, *Aethelred the Unready*, p.54 disputes the date of Gunnhild's death, and suggests it may have been considerably later. Since she probably didn't exist, this doesn't really make much difference!

6 Williams, *Aethelred the Unready*, p.52.

7 Swanton, The *Anglo-Saxon Chronicles*, p.135.

8 Magnusson, *Vikings!*, p.276–7. The entry from Pepys' diary is from 10 April 1661.

9 Swanton, The *Anglo-Saxon Chronicles*, p.139.

10 Barlow, *The Godwins*, p.26.

11 Jones, *History of the Vikings*, p.365.

12 Weir, *Britain's Royal Families*, p.23. Thorkell the Tall is the 'Thurcytel Thorgils Havi' in Weir's account, who may have married Aethelred's daughter Edith. Edith's sister Wulfhilda had been the wife of Ulfkell Snilling.

13 Swanton, The *Anglo-Saxon Chronicles*, p.141. Aelfheah, later Saint Aelfheah, was also known as Godwine, perhaps suggesting a con-

nection with the Godwin family who were so prominent in Aethel-red's England.

14 Ibid., p.144.
15 Since no source refers to Sigrid the Haughty as the 'Queen of England', we must assume that she was dead by this time.
16 Williams, *Aethelred the Unready*, p.132.
17 Stafford, *Queen Emma and Queen Edith*, p.12. A Norman Latin poem of the eleventh century suggested that Emma was like Semiramis, an Asiatic queen raped by Zeus in animal form.
18 Mills, *London Place Names*, p.199.
19 *Heimskringla*, p.264.
20 Ibid., p.400.
21 Jones, *History of the Vikings*, p.382.

Chapter 9 – The Thunderbolt of the North

1 DeVries, *Norwegian Invasion*, p.49, quoting Adam of Bremen.
2 *Heimskringla*, p.501.
3 Ibid., p.514.
4 Davidson, *Viking Road to Byzantium*, quoting *Skjaldedigtning*, p.209.
5 Davidson, *Viking Road to Byzantium*, p.210, outlines several alternate sources to confirm Harald's location in these years.
6 Davidson, *Viking Road to Byzantium*, p.191.
7 The inscription on the Piraeus lion (now in Venice) is illegible, and Davidson, *Viking Road to Byzantium*, discounts speculation that it contains reference to its carver as 'Harald the Tall', p.190.
8 Davidson, *Viking Road to Byzantium*, p.211; DeVries, *The Norwegian Invasion of England in 1066*, p.29; but compare to Turville-Petrie, *Haraldr the Hard-ruler and his Poets*, p.13, who regards his glorious career advancement with significantly more critical eyes.
9 Jones, *History of the Vikings*, p.405.
10 Ibid., p.208.
11 Norwich, *Byzantium: The Apogee*, p.288; for Harald's involvement see Davidson, *Viking Road to Byzantium*, p.220.
12 Davidson, *Viking Road to Byzantium*, p.223.
13 *Heimskringla*, p.587.
14 DeVries, *The Norwegian Invasion of England in 1066*, p.35, includes yet more possible explanations, one from William of Malmesbury, who claimed that Harald had raped a noblewoman (could this be the Maria of the sagas?), and Saxo Grammaticus, who gives the reason for his imprisonment as homicide.
15 *Heimskringla*, p.588.
16 Davidson, *Viking Road to Byzantium*, p.227, DeVries, *Norwegian Invasion of England in 1066*, p.37.
17 *Heimskringla*, p.590.

18 Magnusson and Palsson translate the term as 'golden lady in Russia' in *King Harald's Saga*, p.63; Hollander, *Heimskringla* has the more exacting 'gold-ring-Gerth from Garthar' – Gerth being a goddess's name, and Garda referring to Gardariki or Holmgard, both terms for Jaroslav's domain.

19 Also known as Svein Ulfsson. As his mother's pedigree was of greater value to Svein in Norway, Svein used her name in the place of the traditional patronymic.

20 *Heimskringla*, pp.593–4; DeVries, *Norwegian Invasion*, p.45, sees this as an attempt by Snorri to retroactively justify Harald's changing sides, but the incident is presented without editorial comment, and after Snorri has already revealed the initiation of secret negotiations. While Harald may have used the incident to justify such behaviour, Snorri does not allow him to get away with it.

21 This is, of course, Harald's version of events. Svein himself would describe an equally self-interested account of wrongs done against him to Adam of Bremen, whose history of Scandinavia becomes decidedly less reliable on some occasions in which he leans on his kingly informant.

22 *Heimskringla*, p.598.

23 Ibid., p.601.

24 *King Harald's Saga*, Magnusson and Palsson, p.80; compare to the translation in Hollander, *Heimskringla*, p.602. The former implies that Harald raped the girls before returning them, the latter is more ambiguous.

25 *King Harald's Saga*, Magnusson and Palsson, p.92. Once again, I have elected to go with the freer translation of this version; more exacting scholars may prefer Hollander, *Heimskringla*, p.611.

26 Ibid., Magnusson and Palsson, p.93.

27 The match may have been born of politics or passion, or perhaps from dynastic concerns – Ellisif gave Harald only daughters, while Thora provided him with two sons.

28 Ibid., Magnusson and Palsson, p.102.

29 Weir, *Britain's Royal Families*, p.38.

30 Tostig's argument was so persuasive that several contemporary accounts mistakenly believed that he was Godwin's oldest son. To confuse matters further, Godwin's first-born was actually another Svein, who infamously claimed to be the bastard son of King Canute. Luckily, that Svein was already dead by the time of the succession crisis, otherwise it would have been even more hard-fought.

31 *Heimskringla*, p.643.

32 I mean, of course, by William Shakespeare although those in search of more historical sources can look to DeVries, *Norwegian Invasion*, pp.173–4.

33 *Heimskringla*, p.644.

34 Ibid.

35 *Heimskringla*, pp.646–7.

36 DeVries, *Norwegian Invasion*, p.242ff., mounts a series of convincing arguments concerning Tostig's double-dealings with the Normans. He may have even been hoping to play Harald the Ruthless against William the Bastard, and emerge as the ultimate victor. But such discussions belong to a study of English history, and we must concern ourselves specifically with the Vikings.

37 DeVries, *Norwegian Invasion*, p.255. The town has grown to such an extent that there are now streets and houses all over the original site of the battle.

38 DeVries, *Norwegian Invasion*, p.269–70. The exact site of the final showdown is unknown today, as the river has changed course, but Battle Flats, where many skeletons were unearthed during the Victorian age, would appear to be a rather obvious contender.

39 *Heimskringla*, p.653.

40 Ibid., p.655. There are elements here of the Balder legend (or that of Achilles), since Harald's long coat of mail, incongruously named 'Emma', was said to be impervious.

41 Swanton, The *Anglo-Saxon Chronicles*, p.199.

Chapter 10 – Children of Thor

1 The last battle between the English and the Normans was fought in Albania, where Anglo-Saxon Varangians took great pleasure in attacking invaders from Norman Italy in the name of the Byzantine Emperor. They were, however, defeated.

2 Haywood, *Encyclopaedia of the Viking Age*, p.45.

3 Ultimately, the falling sea levels would cut off several of the greatest Viking ports – the waters around Hedeby were too shallow for deep-draft ships by 1071, and the famous entrepot was replaced by nearby Schleswig. Haywood, *Encyclopaedia of the Viking Age*, p.95.

4 Marcus, *Conquest of the North Atlantic*, p.155.

5 Haywood, *Historical Atlas of the Vikings*, p.97.

6 Jones, *History of the Vikings*, p.309.

7 Rink, *Tales and Traditions of the Eskimo*, p.323.

8 Ibid., p.313.

9 Marcus, *Conquest of the North Atlantic*, p.162.

10 Ibid.

11 Wawn, *Vikings and the Victorians*, p.16.

12 Niitema et al., *Old Friends Strong Ties*, pp.14–18.

13 Ibid., p.72.

14 Wahlgren, *The Kensington Stone*, p.3.

INDEX